S P A M
K I N G S

SPAM
KINGS

The real story behind the high-rolling hucksters
pushing porn, pills, and @*#?% enlargements

BRIAN McWILLIAMS

O'REILLY®

BEIJING · CAMBRIDGE · FARNHAM · KÖLN · PARIS · SEBASTOPOL · TAIPEI · TOKYO

Spam Kings
by Brian McWilliams

Published by O'Reilly Media, Inc., 1005 Gravenstein Highway North, Sebastopol, CA 95472.

O'Reilly books may be purchased for educational, business, or sales promotional use. Online editions are also available for most titles (*safari.oreilly.com*). For more information, contact our corporate/institutional sales department: (800) 998-9938 or *corporate@oreilly.com*.

Editor:	Allen Noren
Production Editor:	Matt Hutchinson
Cover Designer:	Ellie Volckhausen
Interior Designer:	David Futato

Printing History:

October 2004:	First Edition.

ISBN: 0-596-00732-9
[C]

To my family

contents

introduction

Most businesses jump at the opportunity for free publicity. But none of the email marketers, or spammers, profiled in this book were eager to see their stories in print. In fact, some have even threatened lawsuits over its publication.

No wonder that *Spam Kings* is the first book to publicly unmask the people behind the junk email problem. As Jennifer Archie, a leading anti-spam attorney, recently told me, a spammer's main protection is anonymity.

"Once you've exposed a spamming John Doe, he doesn't have a legal defense. So he'll guard his anonymity with everything he has," says Archie.

By deftly using anonymity, spammers have tapped into a vast market. Since most spam-related sales transactions are furtive, reliable statistics are hard to come by. But a study published by the U.S.-based Direct Marketing Association estimated that consumers spent over $32 billion in 2003 on products and services advertised by email.

In the process, some say spam has nearly ruined email. Over 60 percent of all email traffic in the first half of 2004 was spam, according to email filtering firm Brightmail. (Only three years ago, the volume of unsolicited commercial email was just 8 percent of all message traffic.) In 2004, an estimated five *trillion* spam messages will clog Internet users' in-boxes. AOL alone blocks over one billion spam messages every day. According to Ferris Research, junk email costs society $10 billion in lost productivity, filtering software, and other expenses.

Once a problem that vexed only Internet geeks, spam has now earned the ire of consumers, business leaders, lawmakers, regulators, and the mass media. For many, hearing "You've got mail" is no longer a happy sound.

The people behind the junk email problem are often unsavory characters running shady, if not outright illegal, businesses. So why descend into their world and find out what makes them tick? Why should we, as a society, need the gory details of how these high-tech hucksters make a buck?

As citizens, Internet-dependent businesses, and policy makers strategize for the next phase of the battle to save cyberspace, it's my hope that *Spam Kings* can provide an enlightening and entertaining response to the edict "know thy enemy."

Email was built on an architecture of openness and trust. But when spammers discovered the medium, they saw an opportunity that could be exploited. Like air pollution, overfishing, and roadside litter, spam represents the destruction of a public resource by private interests.

Internet users reacted to this overgrazing of their common land like angry villagers with pitchforks. They tried to run the junk emailers out of their virtual communities by publishing spam black-lists and closing off their networks to the abusers. In response, spammers learned a variety of stealthy tactics to disguise their acts and hide their identities.

Spam Kings chronicles five crucial years in the cat-and-mouse game between a dozen or so high-profile spammers and the people determined to drive them off the Internet. With perhaps thousands of spammers currently in operation and many, many people dedicated to fighting them, it's nearly impossible to tell the whole story of the junk email conundrum.

But study the rise and fall of one spammer, Davis Wolfgang Hawke, and you will learn nearly all you need to know about the intractability of the junk email problem.

Hawke is the central figure of *Spam Kings*, but not because he's the biggest spammer of all time. Hawke certainly had his successes. At the age of twenty-five, he became a millionaire by spamming penis-enlargement pills. In the process, he also became the target of numerous lawsuits designed to drive him out of business. A high-IQ chess player and honors student, Hawke chose spamming after his career as a brainy neo-Nazi leader imploded. Hawke put his pursuit of easy wealth ahead of everything else: his education, his family, his girlfriend, and even his own freedom.

Hawke's hubris leads him into a series of confrontations with spam opponents, the most important of whom is Susan Gunn. Gunn, a forty-something, mild-mannered computer novice, was dragged into the fight when her America Online account overflowed with spam. In time, her alias "Shiksaa" would strike fear into the heart of spammers everywhere.

Like many junk emailers, Hawke has the misfortune of crossing paths with Shiksaa, who becomes a volunteer for the anti-spam organization named Spamhaus. Throughout the book, she helps to unmask scores of spammers, and even land some in jail.

Spam Kings is the chronicle of Hawke's and Shiksaa's parallel paths through the spam underworld. Along the way, readers meet a bizarre cast of characters, including:

Sanford Wallace

One of the original spam kings, Wallace insists that spam is a First Amendment right. He buries the Internet with the stuff in the mid-90s. You'll learn what happens when lawyers from a dozen Internet service providers try to convince Wallace that there's nothing constitutional about spam.

Jason Vale

A champion arm-wrestler and cancer survivor, Vale gets into big legal trouble with America Online and the Food and Drug Administration for sending out spams promoting Laetrile as a cure for cancer. Vale blamed his legal problems on anti-spammers in general and Shiksaa in particular. But in the end, it is his own disregard for the law that landed him in jail.

Rodona Garst

She is a middle-class, white-collar worker living in the suburbs. So why is she running stock pump-and-dump scams by email? That's what an anti-spammer wants to find out when he hacks into Garst's computer and posted the embarrassing contents on the Internet.

Thomas Cowles

He's a lanky computer genius in Ohio who develops an assortment of technical tricks to "anonymize" his spams for everything from mortgages to pornography. But as it turns out, a short, middle-aged woman in his hometown tracks him down, outs him on her web site, and ultimately helps law enforcement put him behind bars.

Terri DiSisto

Not everyone is in junk email for the money. DiSisto spams the Internet in search of young men willing to sell homemade videos of themselves being tickled. But when Internet users decide to dig into DiSisto's past, they discover something shocking.

Alan Moore

Unlike most spammers, Moore doesn't hide behind fake names (although he prefers that his diet-pill customers call him "Dr Fatburn"). Moore even publishes his home address in his junk emails. But it turns out that Dr. Fatburn also has a big business selling pirated software via spam, which puts him in the legal crosshairs of two of the biggest technology companies in the world.

Scott Richter

He's a serial entrepreneur who discovers spam relatively late in the game. From the start, he forges alliances with anti-spammers as he builds one of the Internet's biggest "opt-in" junk email operations. But after Richter double-crosses Shiksaa, his empire begins to crumble. Soon, he's staring down the barrel of twin lawsuits from Microsoft and New York State.

You will discover that the line between spammers and anti-spammers is not always clear. The uneasy alliances between the two sides are shown here—along with the story of a handful of spam fighters who cross over to work for the "enemy."

This book is descriptive, not prescriptive. There is no Final Ultimate Solution to the Spam Problem (although you will find some buried treasure on how to keep your in-box free of junk email). *Spam Kings* may not show you the road toward solving the spam problem. But after reading this book, you will know precisely how we got where we are today.

Brian McWilliams
Durham, New Hampshire

chapter *one*

Birth of a Spam King

People are stupid, Davis Wolfgang Hawke thought as he stared at the nearly empty box of swastika pendants on his desk. It was April 22, 1999, two days after the one-hundredth anniversary of Adolph Hitler's birth. Dozens of orders for the red-and-black necklaces had been pouring into his Knights of Freedom (KOF) Nationalist Party web site every week since he built it nine months ago. The demand nearly outstripped what his supplier could provide, but Hawke wasn't celebrating his e-commerce success. As he stuffed the remaining pendants into padded envelopes and addressed them, Hawke gazed out the window of his mobile home at the hazy South Carolina sky and thought: *This is the ultimate hypocrisy. If even half of these people actually joined the party, I would have a major political movement. Instead, all they want is a pretty, shiny pendant.*

And if a snoopy reporter for the local paper hadn't recently blown his cover, Hawke might not have been spending all of the web site's income on rent, telephone, and electricity bills for the double-wide just off Highway 221 in Chesnee. But Hawke was forced to move into the trailer in March, after secretly operating KOF.net for six months from the dorm room his parents paid for at Wofford College in nearby Spartanburg. Hawke had always been an anomaly at the pricey Methodist school, with his penchant for dressing all in black, wearing his dark hair in a ponytail, and sporting a push-broom mustache. But the 20-year-old junior had managed to hold down a 3.8 grade point average as a double major in German and history without anyone knowing he was also the founder and chief executive director of the Knights of Freedom. His room in Shipp Hall had been festooned with Nazi flags, Hitler videos, and a collection of knives, but Hawke did no proselytizing on campus. In fact, he had little social contact with other students.

Although his ultimate goal was one day to be elected the nation's first white-power president, Hawke knew he had to lay some groundwork before his philosophy would become mainstream. That task would make him a target for leftists and the media. To shield himself, even with party comrades and web site visitors, Hawke used the pseudonym "Bo Decker" and listed a post office box in Walpole, Massachusetts as the Knights of Freedom mailing address.

Over a thousand people signed up for his monthly email newsletter, the *White Pride News Service*. Some 200 people joined as dues-paying members, paying five dollars a month for a membership card, a KOF armband, a videotape of speeches by Decker, and a subscription to the newsletter. Not bad for a movement that had been unheard of a year earlier. In fact, the Anti-Defamation League had recently said that KOF was the fastest-growing neo-Nazi group in the United States. Using the alias Bo Decker, Hawke had introduced the world to the Knights of Freedom in an August 1998 posting to several online discussion groups: "We must band together in unity to defend our Race. Either we stand together and battle for the right to racial existence or we will be wiped out by international Jewry and their nigger police."

As Hawke saw it, the Knights of Freedom had two major things going for it: its web site and his brains. The KOF.net site, dressed all in black like its owner, was the best white-power site on the Internet. Besides the merchandise section, there was a chat room, press release section, message board, and automated sign-up forms—all the bells and whistles. At one point, Hawke even posted a note on the site's home page offering to provide web design and hosting to other white-power groups. Hawke and his lieutenants also knew how to use the Internet for promotion. They worked newsgroups and discussion lists, talking up the Knights of Freedom and its web site. Hawke had put an automatic hit counter on the front page of KOF. net, and he got a kick out of checking the traffic statistics every day. It intrigued him that you could publish a message in a newsgroup or send out the newsletter emails and then a few hours later watch the bar graphs on the stats page suddenly shoot up.

As for Hawke's mind, it was quantitative, analytical. It made him a top student in high school and a formidable chess player, and it made his college studies a snap. He could think several moves ahead of his opponents.

However, in a moment of hubris, Hawke posted a large photograph of himself on the front page of KOF.net. It showed the lanky Hawke dressed in a Nazi uniform, with his arm outstretched in a "Heil Hitler" salute. When a Wofford student was out web surfing one evening in early February and happened to run across the site, Hawke was undone.

Soon a front-page exposé appeared in the Spartanburg Herald-Journal that fingered Hawke as the head of KOF. It said that he used the site for recruiting and to stoke racist fervor among party members, who addressed him as "Commander." According to the article, the Southern Poverty Law Center, an organization that monitors hate groups, had been tracking him since he was in high school in Westwood, Massachusetts.

But what hit Hawke like a punch to the gut was a matter-of-fact statement in the article attributed to Mark Potok, the head of the Southern Poverty Law Center. Potok told the paper that Hawke was a Jew who, to hide his heritage, had changed his name from Andrew Britt Greenbaum upon graduating from high school in 1996.

The article buried what would become Hawke's standard rebuttal to the charges: that his father, Hyman Andrew Greenbaum, was only one-quarter Jewish. And it omitted altogether that Hawke believed his true biological father was a German immigrant named Dekker with whom his mother had had an affair. Either way, Hawke knew he wouldn't have been considered Jewish even under Hitler's classification. As Hawke wrote in his application for a change of identity: "I have always responded to a different name and I wish to formalize my name prior to attending college in the fall as to avoid confusion."[1]

The article couldn't have come at a worse time. For the past few months, the Knights of Freedom had begun to attract attacks from other white-power groups. Some, jealous of Hawke's Internet skills, had taken to calling him the "Net Nazi" and were claiming that the KOF was a virtual movement with no real world presence. Others, suspicious of the KOF's quick rise into the limelight, posted mocking replies to his messages in online newsgroups. To Hawke's detractors, the falsehoods about his Jewish ancestry would provide delicious irony and damaging ammunition.

Indeed, the insults about him being a "Kosher Nazi" had already begun. Tom Metzger, head of the White Aryan Resistance—the same Tom Metzger whose name Hawke had placed in the hidden "MetaTag" code at KOF.net to bring in traffic from search engines—was quoted in the *Herald-Journal* article as saying, "If he is a Jew, he will have no stature left. People he is involved with will have nothing to do with him."

When the article appeared, part of Hawke was mortified that everything he had built was about to collapse. But he tried to stay cool-headed. He contemplated his damage-control options. He wouldn't say anything about the article to people in the Knights of Freedom unless they asked. And if they did, he'd remind them that the whole matter was a creation of the Jewish-controlled media or an effort by the Zionist Occupied Government, as he liked to refer to the controlling powers in the U.S., designed to undermine proud Aryan people. Bottom line, any publicity is good publicity, Hawke would tell his followers.

Fortunately for Hawke, people at Wofford were focused more on Hawke's message than on the revelations about him as a messenger. To his relief, he inspired fear, not laughter. Wofford professors abandoned their syllabi that day and instead devoted their classes to discussing the Knights of Freedom web site and the group's leader. Then, in the evening, around 300 Wofford students—nearly a third of the student body—gathered in the college's auditorium to hold a candlelight vigil to show their opposition to racism and bigotry.

While Wofford's dedication to principles of free speech prevented administrators from expelling Hawke, they were eager to relax the college rules and allow him to move off campus. In early March, he signed a lease for the cramped trailer in the woods, fifteen miles from the college. Hawke knew he was finished with Wofford; he'd complete the semester, but that would probably be the end of his college career. Bigger things awaited him. The publicity train started by the local paper was chugging along. The *Boston Globe* published a story about him in late February that put the Knights of Freedom on a national stage. Even *Rolling Stone* wanted to send a reporter to interview him.

There was a silver lining to Hawke's move off campus. A woman he had met in an online chat room offered to move to South Carolina and serve as party secretary. Her name was Patricia Lingenfelter. She was a beautiful Aryan, smart and tough—a green belt in karate—and ten years older than Hawke. Once he was out of the dorms, Hawke invited her to stay with him in Chesnee. To keep up appearances, he insisted that she still refer to him as "Commander" around other party comrades, but everyone knew Hawke and Patricia were lovers.

In late March, Hawke decided it was time to host an assembly of comrades in Chesnee. He wanted the First Party Congress to happen on the one hundredth anniversary of Hitler's birthday, but April 20 didn't coincide with Wofford's spring break. So he scheduled the meeting the week before the Fuhrer's 100th. While fewer than a dozen party members showed up, the atmosphere was charged by the presence of a camera crew from ABC News's *Hard Copy* program, which broadcast a snippet of Hawke's rousing speech, along with footage of party members marching around outside his trailer in their Nazi regalia.

Meanwhile, out in Colorado two kids at Columbine High School celebrated Hitler's birthday by going on a shooting rampage, killing twelve people, including themselves. Suddenly, TV news producers were grabbing for their Rolodexes, and Hawke's name, after his strong performance on *Hard Copy*, was coming out on top. A crew from the *Fox Files* television news program showed up at the trailer the next day to interview Hawke about the Knights of Freedom and his insights into the killings.

The media likes to buy and sell fear, Hawke thought as he and Patricia watched the Fox report on the TV in his trailer that evening on April 22. The program was trying to spin the Columbine massacre as a racially motivated hate crime, but Hawke wouldn't play along. At one point in the program, the Fox interviewer asked Hawke, who was wearing his Nazi uniform, if he ever hugged his father.

Hawke said no, and added that he didn't hug his mother either.

"Why not?"

"I never felt the need for physical contact of that sort," said Hawke.

"Did you feel the need for human affection?"

"Human affection is not something that I value at the moment, or then, or ever."

"Do you believe in love?"

"Sure, I believe in love, but I don't believe that I can ever have time for that. That's a human emotion," replied Hawke.

"Do you think that people would see that as sad or unfortunate, that here's a young man that says that he never felt any love for anyone growing up, or never hugged his mom or dad?"

"I don't really care what they have to say," Hawke answered.

When the program was over, Hawke switched off the TV. Patricia said she was going to head into town for a quick food run and to gas up the car. Hawke turned on the computer on his desk and was waiting for it to boot up when the phone rang. It was his mother. He hadn't spoken to her for several months.

"Are you happy now?" she yelled at him.

"What do you mean?" he replied.

Peggy Greenbaum said she had seen the *Fox Files* segment. "How do you know your web site didn't cause those boys to go crazy in Columbine? It makes me sick to think that you might have spurred them on," she said.

Hawke considered her question. To him, Dylan Klebold and Eric Harris were probably just disgruntled teens taking revenge against a school system that was force-feeding them the same old liberal nonsense day after day, year after year. But before he had a chance to explain this to his mother, she interrupted.

"I hope you're happy now," she hissed again, and hung up on him.

Hawke sat down at his desk. His parents had been paying his tuition and living expenses, but it was obvious he could no longer rely on them for anything. Yet he knew that if he was going to realize his dream of building the Knights of Freedom into a major political movement and creating an Aryan homeland out west, he'd need a lot of money. Hawke's personal savings—acquired through generous holiday gifts from his parents and other relatives—would carry him for a while. He was pretty certain that his grandparents on both sides of the family would someday will him a small fortune, maybe close to a million dollars. But in the meantime, there were bills to pay.

Hawke started up the web browser on his computer and typed in the address of the eBay auction site. He occasionally visited the site to check out auctions of Nazi paraphernalia—he'd picked up one of his SS uniforms that way. But this time he wasn't going to the site to shop. Instead, he surfed to the section of the site for creating a new account, and began rapidly filling out the form.

Hawke paused when he got to the section asking him to specify a username. After some thought he typed in "antiqueamerica"—a sturdy name that wouldn't provoke any suspicion. Then he launched himself machinelike into the repetitive task of setting up auctions for the knives, buckles, pendants, uniforms, and other Nazi gear he'd been selling at KOF.net.

When Patricia returned to the trailer an hour or so later, the change in Hawke wasn't visible. But he had begun his transformation from neo-Nazi organizer to Internet spammer.

The Education of an Anti-Spammer

Susan Gunn's first personal computer seemed preloaded with an endless supply of junk email. Almost from the moment she first signed on to America Online, even before she had given her newly minted email address to friends and relatives, Gunn began receiving electronic messages from total strangers who wanted to sell her all manner of products she didn't want, including pornography, body-part enlargement, and software that would enable her to enter the exciting and rewarding business of junk email.

Who are these people and how did they get my address? wondered Gunn, a resident of Stanton, California, a small, palm-tree-studded city built on land originally intended as a sewage farm for neighboring Anaheim. Gunn had bought the PC ostensibly to computerize some of her work as the property manager of a condominium complex owned by her father. But for Gunn, divorced and in her mid-forties, the computer was also a link from her sometimes too-quiet home office in the gated community to the brave new world known as the Internet.

It was late 1998. AOL had recently acquired its rivals Netscape and CompuServe and boasted around 15 million members. The dot-com bubble was still inflating rapidly, as new users such as Gunn swarmed online and began making purchases. But e-commerce wasn't only being conducted by high-profile dot-coms such as eBay, Amazon, and Yahoo!. Entrepreneurs of all types were trying to cash in on the information superhighway, including, apparently, the anonymous folks who had somehow gotten her email address, which they felt entitled them to barge through her virtual front door whenever they wanted.

At first Gunn blamed AOL for the messages. She assumed the online service had sold her name as soon as she signed up. But when she phoned the company to complain, a customer support representative assured her that was not the case. The rep said to forward any unwanted messages to a special email address, and AOL would investigate. For a few weeks, Gunn dutifully obliged, but the junk email kept on coming. In some cases the incoming spam stated that if she wanted to be removed from the sender's list, she needed to visit a special web page and type in her email address. But that had no effect. And whenever she hit the "reply" button and told the spammers to knock it off, her replies went unanswered or were returned as undeliverable. Either the return address on the original message didn't exist, or the mailbox on the other end was crammed to capacity.

Gunn's previous computer experience had consisted of plugging numbers into spreadsheets during a stint in an accounting firm. So she had no way of knowing that her mysterious spam problem was likely a consequence of having wandered into AOL's online chat rooms while they were being harvested by spammers. Using special "spambot" programs, junk emailers were able to pluck thousands of

AOL addresses out of the service's chat rooms in minutes. Similar harvesting programs were designed to automatically scour web pages and online bulletin boards looking for telltale "@" symbols and add the addresses to a database.

Then again, Gunn might have been the target of a dictionary attack, a technique used by junk emailers to guess their way into Internet users' in-boxes. Most spam mailing programs could blast out millions of messages to automatically generated addresses. By compiling various combinations of common names and numbers, followed by the domain of a big Internet service provider, such as "@aol.com," spam software could generate a small percentage of actual working addresses.

Little did Gunn know that by replying to junk emails that arrived in her in-box, she was actually making the problem worse by confirming to the senders that they had found a live body, thus becoming what is known to junk emailers as a "verified" email address. Because she had responded, it was likely that her address had been added to mailing lists marketed to other spammers. She even received a junk email advertising a CD-ROM claiming to contain 91 million verified email addresses (almost one third the population of the United States). Spammers, it seemed, had no use for target marketing.

Gunn wondered if there was some official agency charged with dealing with spam complaints, such as a Better Business Bureau for spammers. She asked about it in an AOL chat room where PC users could get real-time help for their computer problems from more sophisticated users. No one there had heard of such an agency, although someone provided her with an email address at the Federal Trade Commission to which she could forward copies of spam.

"Frankly, I just delete the stuff. It's not worth the trouble to report it," he told her.

But Gunn wasn't able to ignore her junk email problem. The type who went ballistic over people who litter, she would chase down and give a tongue lashing to anyone who tossed a crumpled up McDonalds bag on her property. To her, spamming was the same kind of anti-social, selfish act. In their efforts to reach a handful of interested customers, bulk emailers were blithely leaving their trash all over her part of the Internet. But the cowards, with their fake return addresses, left Gunn no way to run them down and share a few choice words.

One self-proclaimed computer expert on AOL suggested that Gunn get advice from an Internet bulletin board frequented by Internet system administrators and other sophisticated computer users united in their hatred of spam. The group was known as Nanae (pronounced NAH-nay), short for "news admin net-abuse email," and was one of the thousands of topics available from a free Internet discussion service called Usenet. Using a program called a newsreader, which was also built into the AOL software, Usenet participants around the world were able to read and contribute to online discussion newsgroups dedicated to everything from raising ferrets to practicing Far Eastern religions.

"But watch your step. There can be some real kooks in Nanae," he warned, noting that angry spammers sometimes dropped in on the newsgroup too.

By early 1999, the ratio of junk to legitimate email had made Gunn's AOL mailbox practically unusable. Fed up, she decided to pay Nanae a visit and seek advice. At the start, she treaded cautiously, reading but not joining the discussion. (One of the first messages she read warned that Nanae denizens did not suffer fools easily: "Wear your flame-proof underwear...never go Nanae-ing without 'em!") Unlike some hobby-related Usenet newsgroups she had frequented in the past, Nanae was very busy, often receiving hundreds of new postings every day. Some of the participants used their real names, but many posted under aliases such as "Dark Jedi," "Sapient Fridge," "Morely Dotes," and "Tsu Do Nimh." Most of the Nanae folk seemed to be men, although there were apparently a handful of women who frequented it as well. Few seemed to be fellow AOL users and instead posted their messages from obscure Internet service providers (ISPs) she had never heard of.

It wasn't clear to Gunn what exactly these people did for a living. From the technical jargon they slung around, she assumed most were either computer programmers or longtime Internet users. A few seemed to be fighting spam in an official capacity as system administrators: an anonymous user who went by the online alias Afterburner, for example, ended all of his postings with a signature line, or sig, that stated he handled spam complaints for Erols, a mid-sized ISP in the Washington, D.C. area. Later, she learned that Afterburner was one of the chosen few Nanae regulars who had received a Golden Mallet Award, a tongue-in-cheek honor given to longtime spam fighters for meritorious conduct. A special site known as the Pantheon listed the names of recipients and featured an illustration of a large gilded hammer smashing down on a map of the world.

Nanae had no official charter as far as Gunn could tell. The closest thing she could find to a mission statement was a message posted by Afterburner that summed up Nanae's purpose as "a cathartic release mechanism and a clearinghouse of info." Most of the postings contained businesslike reports of spam sightings or matter-of-fact complaints about ISPs that were slow to deal with spammers using their networks. But some messages were playful, such as one she spotted with the subject line "Confirmed Kill," which gleefully reported on an ISP that had responded to complaints by cutting off service to a junk emailer.

While Gunn easily picked up the Internet lingo used in AOL's chat rooms and instant messaging programs—overused shorthand such as *LOL* for "laughing out loud" or *BRB* for "be right back"—she was unprepared for the jargon in Nanae. The private slang of participants apparently wasn't developed for speed typing so much as to solidify spam fighters as a clique, or at least to add humor or spice to their postings. Several messages discussed the proper way to use a

LART—code for "loser attitude readjustment tool," which she learned was another name for an email notifying ISPs of customers who were spamming. A LART was also referred to as a "mallet," since it was sometimes used to clobber delinquent ISPs into action against spammers. (Hence the Golden Mallet awarded to top anti-spammers.)

The newsgroup was also full of talk about *UCE* (unsolicited commercial email) and of spammers who were violating the *TOS* (terms of service) or *AUP* (acceptable use policy) of an Internet service provider. (Almost all ISPs specifically forbade their customers from sending spam.) Other postings discussed the various ways to *munge* one's email address in Usenet postings—such as by adding the phrase "nospam" next to the "@" sign—to thwart harvesting efforts by spammers.

Especially puzzling were messages whose subject lines were prefixed with the letters *C&C*. One poked fun at Alaska Senator Frank Murkowski, whom the message referred to as a "Congress critter." In 1998 Murkowski had proposed legislation governing bulk email, and many Nanae participants were vehemently opposed to the bill, fearing that it might actually legitimize some forms of spam. Weeks later Gunn learned that C&C was Nanae shorthand for "coffee and cats" and was a warning to others that a humorous message followed that might produce sudden laughter and thus the spilling of coffee and upsetting of cats near the reader.

After following Nanae discussions over the course of a few days, Gunn stumbled onto a web site that contained answers to common questions about junk email. The spam FAQ (frequently asked questions), as Internet gurus called it, provided a gold mine of information on how to analyze spam messages to determine the true Internet address of the computer that sent them. There were also tips on how to track down the owners of web site addresses or domains by using a service known as whois, which provided phone numbers and other contact information for the individual who registered the domain.

Gunn also read up on how to file a complaint with an Internet service provider when one of its customers was sending spam.

But perhaps the most important anti-spam weapon she discovered was a specialized Internet search engine called Deja News. Gunn had been using AOL's search service, as well as a site called Google, to find material published on web pages. But Deja News was different; it gave users the ability to search a complete archive dating back to the 1980s of nearly every newsgroup in existence, including old Nanae discussions. For spam trackers, the newsgroup search engine enabled them to sift through old spam sightings and determine, for example, whether a spammer was a repeat offender, or whether an ISP had been warned in the past about chronic spammers. (Deja News was acquired by Google in 2001 and renamed Google Groups.)

But, as Gunn soon discovered, junk email opponents didn't confine themselves to filing complaints with ISPs. Some also resorted to more militant tactics.

Ho, Ho, Ho, the Nazis Didn't Show

In a matter of days, orders from Davis Hawke's eBay auctions started to roll in. He found that buyers, caught up in the excitement of the auction, were often willing to bid more than double the price he'd charge for the same item at the KOF site. And since eBay was brokering the deal, there was less of a chance of someone ripping him off with a bad check. The new, tax-free cash flow helped allay his fears about having to take a humiliating civilian job that summer, such as flipping burgers at McDonalds or mowing lawns for the ground crew at Wofford.

As classes finally ended in mid-May 1999, Hawke turned his attention to drafting what he called the Millennium Plan—a long-term strategy for turning the Knights of Freedom into a mainstream political party. The first step would be a new name, the American Nationalist Party (ANP), and a new web site, ANParty.com. To broaden the movement's appeal, Hawke decided he'd drop the Nazi graphics and replace them with American flags, bald eagles, and other patriotic symbols. He'd phase out using the Bo Decker moniker. To cap off the change, that summer ANP members would assemble at the group's to-be-built training camp on some property owned by a comrade in Virginia. They'd spend a weekend setting up a shooting range and an obstacle course. And there would be time for camaraderie with other proud Aryans. Then, by the end of the summer, the ANP would stage a massive rally in Washington, D.C., where he would give a speech in front of the White House.

In preparation for the event, Hawke had been on the phone with city police and the National Park Service about getting a demonstration permit. The bureaucrats seemed confused by the name of Hawke's group; he had to correct them several times when they referred to it as the American Nazi Party or the Nationalist Movement. The city, apparently still jumpy from a Ku Klux Klan march down Constitution Avenue in 1990 that resulted in injuries and arrests, wanted an accurate estimate of how many protestors would assemble and a detailed plan about where they would march and give speeches.

Since the *White Pride News Service* e-letter had over 1,600 subscribers, Hawke figured conservatively that 300 members would be at the rally. That was the estimate he gave D.C. police anyway, but Hawke secretly had his doubts. His top lieutenants—who comprised five people, including Patricia—were gung ho about the event. But Hawke wasn't sure about the rank and file. The party's member rolls had swollen quickly. But he had met only a handful of them face to face. Would these people take an active interest in promoting the interests of the White Race?

The previous November, Hawke had sent email to members announcing a January rally in Andrews, North Carolina, in support of serial bomber Eric Robert Rudolph. Rudolph, whom Hawke referred to in the email as an "Aryan Hero," was a suspect in the

1996 bombings of an abortion clinic and a gay nightclub and was thought to be hiding from federal authorities in the woods surrounding Andrews.

"It's time to stop talking and start acting!" Hawke had written, asking for an electronic show of hands from those who would attend. "We MUST make it known to the citizens of that town and to all the world that they are not alone in their struggle against world Jewry and federal tyranny, that an organization FINALLY exists which will not allow these crimes to continue!"

Hawke had been hoping for 200 volunteers to answer the call and make the midwinter trek to Andrews. But when only a few emailed him to say they could come to North Carolina, he quietly told them the rally for Rudolph had been called off.

One day in late May, Hawke was at his desk, musing about the logistics of the March on Washington. What if, despite all his careful planning and propaganda, only a couple dozen people showed up? What if the "Greenbaum development," as he referred to all the bashing he was taking from other neo-Nazis and the liberal media, had truly undermined his leadership?

Hawke pushed those doubts out of his mind. Instead, he tried to focus on a more manageable matter—a plan for boosting his income online. The eBay auctions had been labor-intensive, and Hawke was curious about running his own Internet shop, without eBay's constraints and commissions. He typed the address of a domain registration service into his web browser. Once there, he checked whether the name KnifeDepot.com was taken. Besides being something of a fetish for Hawke, knives were the items doing best in his eBay auctions. But the domain was already registered, as were KnifeMarket.com, KnifeShop.com, and nearly every other variation.

Then he tried Knifed.com. It was still available, so Hawke pounced, registering his first domain not connected to the white-power movement. To protect his image as the ANP's leader, Hawke listed Patricia as Knifed.com's owner. His plan was to develop it into an online megastore for all sorts of personal weaponry, including high-margin collectible items.

The American Knife Depot, as he named the site, was little more than a list of items and their prices, with a few pictures he had found in a clip art collection and some he had copied from other sites. Shoppers couldn't order online—they had to send a check to a post office box he had opened in Chesnee. But it was a start.

Next, it was just a matter of letting the world know the knife site was there. Drawing on a technique he had learned from promoting the Knights of Freedom site, Hawke seeded several online discussion groups with messages about the American Knife Depot. The messages—Hawke's first batch of spam—were terse and largely in uppercase, a far cry from the loquacious and colorful junk emails Hawke would broadcast by the millions a few years later. "WE'VE GOT THEM ALL AT THE AMERICAN KNIFE DEPOT! Lowest prices in the industry, quick shipping, top-quality - ABSOLUTELY GUARANTEED," shouted Hawke's nascent spams.

With Patricia's help, Hawke spent the early part of June getting the Knife Depot operational while managing his eBay auctions. Only a few orders came in from the Knifed.com web site, but Hawke's auctions were buzzing. His office in the trailer had become a shipping and receiving center, with his desk buried under cardboard boxes, bubble wrap, and rolls of packing tape.

Despite the distractions, in late June Hawke finally managed to nail down a date for the rally with the D.C. police—Saturday August 7. In just over a month, he would take the full measure of the movement he had built. The prospect both thrilled and terrified him. None of his white-power heroes—Metzger, Richard Butler, or Ben Klassen—had ever attempted such a daringly public display of Aryan pride and unity. Then again, Hawke reminded himself, none of them had harnessed the Internet the way he had. If all went well, the rally might even draw members of other groups, and provide a coalescing point for all American racialists.

In an email announcement, Hawke phrased the March on Washington as a challenge to ANP members: "I'm going to be there whether one person stands by my side or whether one thousand rally behind me. I'm going to be there whether I'm threatened, whether I'm shot at, whether I'm ridiculed, or whether I'm slandered. I'm going to be there—no matter what."

Hawke's police-approved plan was to assemble party members in James Monroe Park at three o'clock sharp. The comrades would greet each other with firm handshakes and salutes. There would be drummers or perhaps bagpipes to inspire the gathering. When the assembly reached a critical mass, with Hawke leading the charge they would march the six blocks or so down H Street to Lafayette Park, just across the street from the White House. They'd probably face heckling and even physical attacks along the route, but the police had promised to provide flanking protection the entire way.

At the park, the crowd would pause in front of the statue of President Andrew Jackson, and Hawke would give his speech, using a bullhorn to address the throng. Other party leaders and representatives of other groups would follow. Finally, participants would cross Pennsylvania Avenue and end the march with a picket directly in front of the White House. Hawke had obtained a three-hour demonstration permit, so they would need to disperse by six o'clock.

Word of the ANP's rally traveled quickly throughout the Internet, and not just among neo-Nazis. Several anti-fascist groups swung into action, putting their members on notice to be ready. Everyone from the NAACP and the American Jewish Committee to the Latino Civil Rights Center was abuzz with plans for counter-demonstrations advocating racial and religious tolerance.

A few days before the big weekend in August, Hawke and Patricia shipped some final orders for jewelry and knives. Hawke did a couple of phone interviews about the upcoming rally, including one with the *Washington Post*. Then he and Patricia packed a suitcase and made the six-hour drive to Fredericksburg, Virginia. There, they would stay at the home of "Doc" O'Dell, a party officer who had a farm about an hour from downtown Washington. The farm was to become the ANP training compound and would be the layover for demonstrators from out of state. With Patricia at the wheel, Hawke practiced reading his speech aloud several times.

Upon their arrival, Major O'Dell, despite being some thirty years Hawke's senior, dutifully pulled Hawke's old suitcase out of the trunk and carried it into the house. As O'Dell was setting the suitcase down in the entry hall, Hawke saw him check the name on the luggage tags—*Greenbaum*.[2] Hawke winced when he realized he had neglected to update the labels, but O'Dell didn't mention the matter.

Following Hawke's instructions, O'Dell had set up a camping area in the fields beside his house and had brought in food and drinks and even a rented Porta-Potty for the campers. Two large rental vans stood in the driveway, ready to taxi demonstrators into D.C. Many of the protestors would join them at a designated staging area at the edge of the city, from which the D.C. police would bus them downtown. But on the eve of the march, only three party members had arrived.

Just after two o'clock on the afternoon of August 7, over 2,000 D.C. police officers took their positions, in full riot gear, along Pennsylvania Avenue and around Monroe Park. Over 300 National Park Service police, with the support of Secret Service agents, also patrolled the area. Even D.C. Police Chief Charles Ramsey was on the scene, wearing a helmet and carrying a riot baton, seriously bothered by the million dollars the special police force was costing the city.

More than a thousand counterprotestors surrounded the twenty-block area that had been cordoned off by the police. The demonstrators were chanting and holding anti-Nazi, pro-love signs. Many of them wore bandanas around their necks in anticipation of tear gas. Scores of media people, who had staked out Monroe Park with their cameras, satellite uplink trucks, and boom microphones, were taking it all in.

When the appointed hour arrived and the ANP still hadn't made its appearance at the park, everyone began to grow restless. Had the neo-Nazis decided to move their rally to another location to avoid counterdemonstrators? Chief Ramsey stepped into the middle of H Street, surrounded by media. He told them his department was ready, but the ANP might not be, and he planned to give them all the time they needed to get to the park and hold their rally.

But at the parking lot designated as the pick-up spot, city busses idled empty when a lone American Nationalist Party member pulled up in a car just after three p.m. No sign of anyone except a few bored police officers sipping iced coffee outside their vehicles. Dressed in an SS uniform, the ANP member[3] walked up to the policemen and asked whether Davis Hawke and other party members had been transported to the park yet.

The officers looked the neo-Nazi up and down. Then one replied with a smirk, "No sign of your people, but there's plenty of company waiting for you at Monroe."

The policemen watched as the ANP member returned to the car. After a few minutes, the vehicle pulled out of the lot and quickly headed away.

When word that the march had been called off reached Lafayette Square, counterprotestors began to celebrate. In one section, a group of several hundred people joyously chanted, "Ho, ho, ho, the Nazis didn't show," while others banged plastic drums and blew whistles.

By that time, Hawke and Patricia had already been back in Chesnee for hours. They had climbed out the window of their first-floor bedroom in O'Dell's farmhouse at three in the morning, so Hawke wouldn't have to face the humiliation. They drove straight home, stopping only once for a fuel break. As the miles rolled past, Hawke had composed his letter of resignation. He tried to channel the anger and embarrassment he felt into eloquence. "Whether through laziness, cowardice, or lack of commitment, almost all of you have let down the Party and the white race itself," he chided the members who didn't show up for the march.

"The Party has failed to achieve the standards that I set forth one year ago, and as a man of honor I must therefore resign my position as Leader and Party Chairman," Hawke told them. He closed by saying he would disable the party's web site and his email account within a few days.

Hawke posted the letter at the ANP site and emailed it to his list that evening. By the time he went to bed, Hawke was already feeling better about the day's events. It had been an amazing twelve months since he first announced the Knights of Freedom on the Internet. He believed he might someday reemerge on the political stage. But until then, he would step out of the spotlight and turn his full attention to his Internet businesses. Freed from the constraints of being a public persona, Hawke could finally allow his online ingenuity to run wild.

Spamford Meets Hacker-X

From skimming old Nanae messages, Susan Gunn learned that anti-spammers were flush with power when she found the newsgroup in early 1999. They had rallied to force Sanford Wallace, the Internet's biggest spammer, into retirement just the year before. Wallace, who was head of Philadelphia-based Cyber Promotions, had emerged as a spam king in 1995 and boasted that his firm generated twenty-five million junk emails per day on behalf of clients ranging from pornography sites to spam-software vendors. By some estimates Cyber-Promo.com was responsible for 80 percent of the spam on the Net.

Unlike most spammers who chose to remain in the shadows, Wallace, a large man in his early twenties, regularly tangled with junk email opponents in Nanae discussions. Wallace argued that he was an entrepreneur and that spamming was his First Amendment right. Although he disliked being called a spammer—he preferred to say that he was in the bulk email business—Wallace eventually embraced the nickname given him by anti-spammers: Spamford. But while they may have admired his chutzpah, Nanae regulars abhorred Wallace's business practices, which included falsifying the return address on his spam messages, so that he wouldn't have to deal with complaints or bounces—the error messages returned by mail systems when they received an undeliverable message.

Anti-spammers cheered in late 1996 and early 1997 when Wallace was hit by successive lawsuits from a dozen ISPs. The litigation sought to establish some legal guidelines in what had previously been uncharted waters. AOL argued that it was not obligated to deliver email solicitations to its members from spammers such as Cyber-Promo. EarthLink alleged that Wallace had violated state and federal business laws by incessantly spamming its subscribers. Earth-Link's attorney, Pete Wellborn, a former college football star turned high-tech lawyer, said CyberPromo was guilty of electronically trespassing on EarthLink's mail servers with its spam.

When Wallace hired a team of lawyers and announced he would fight the lawsuits, an anonymous vigilante decided to take matters into his own hands. He hacked into the Cyber Promotions web site and rummaged through the server. The attacker, who came to be known simply as Hacker-X, gathered up a trove of information, including Wallace's customer list and the administrative password to the machine. Using a stolen account at a university, Hacker-X then posted the information in a March 19, 1997, message to alt. 2600, a newsgroup frequented by fans of the hacking magazine 2600. In confessing to the break-in, Hacker-X wrote that he was tired of the flood of junk email from Cyber Promotions.

"Nobody else was fighting back ... So I decided to kick them and their clients in the balls," wrote the unidentified intruder. "This won't end. Ever. Myself and others will continue to expose spam operations weaknesses. To those who think that spam is a good idea: think again."

Using the opening created by Hacker-X, over the course of several days in late March, other unidentified hackers repeatedly replaced the regular home page of Cyberpromo.com with ones of their own design. One version of the defaced page featured an image of a can of Hormel SPAM, a hyperlink to a page containing a list of customer accounts, and the words "CYBERPROMO ... NOT JUST BULK EMAIL ... it's SPAM."[4]

Wallace was furious. He issued a press release that offered a $15,000 reward and announced that he had alerted the Federal Bureau of Investigation (FBI) about the intrusion. But Wallace's response only seemed to add fuel to the conflict. On April 6, Hacker-X struck again. He posted another message to alt.2600, taunting Wallace ("that low-life, degenerate, festering pile of goo") and offering up more purloined information, including technical datafiles required to provide Internet service to scores of other sites connected to Cyber Promotions.

A few weeks later, the battle escalated. Someone on Nanae suggested anti-spammers join in a "Cinco de Mayo Cyberpromo Mailbomb Day," during which participants would coordinate a variety of attacks on Wallace's web site and email server beginning May 5. Similar calls to electronic arms were published in other newsgroups, including misc.consumers, an online bulletin board for discussing product reviews and other information about consumer issues.

When the so-called cyber-doomsday arrived, Cyberpromo.com—to the surprise of no one—suddenly became unreachable by web surfers. Two days later, Wallace issued another press release, stating that his company's network was under attack by anti-spam hackers who had also targeted an Internet router operated by Apex Global Information Systems (AGIS), the Michigan ISP used by Cyber Promotions. The announcement said Cyber Promotions was in the process of tracking the criminals, whom Wallace vowed to report to federal authorities.

Wallace never found the hackers. But in apparent retaliation for the attacks, he registered a new web site, NetScum.net. It contained an online directory with the names, email addresses—and in some cases home street addresses and phone numbers—of hundreds of spam fighters and other Internet users who had complained about Usenet postings and junk email or were otherwise deemed too strident in their requirements that other Internet users practice good online manners, or "netiquette."

The NetScum directory was actually a reincarnation of a site created by unidentified Internet users in 1996 and briefly hosted on a succession of obscure web pages. Among the entries in the new edition was one on Afterburner, the respected Erols abuse-desk manager whose true name was revealed at the site as Michael A. Hanks. (In one of his first acts at the ISP, Afterburner had convinced Erols to cancel Wallace's accounts there to protect the company's reputation.) In an attempt to discredit Afterburner, NetScum's anonymous editors had dug up and reposted messages from 1996 by Afterburner's girlfriend to a Usenet newsgroup named alt.sex.bondage. The postings discussed her kinky sexual activities with what she referred to as her "master" Afterburner and invited readers to visit her web site dedicated to "BDSM," or bondage/domination/sado-masochism. Although Afterburner laughed off his NetScum entry, he became an infrequent contributor to Nanae after the incident.

The computerized attacks on Cyber Promotions and its ISP continued unabated throughout the summer of 1997, leading some Nanae regulars to grow alarmed at the new trend toward electronic violence by anti-spam vigilantes. Bill Mattocks, the recipient of a Golden Mallet Award, argued that the spam wars must be fought ethically, with tactics that kept anti-spammers on the moral high ground. On August 8, 1997, Mattocks, the operator of a computer-consulting firm in Wisconsin, posted a four-page note to Nanae with the subject line, "HACKERS, WISE UP!" In the message he noted that anti-spam crusaders had successfully built a nonviolent grassroots movement opposed to junk email.

"We're gaining converts who are not technically proficient with computers, but they are on the Internet, and they hate spam, too. They are our allies. We must reach out to them and teach them to teach others," wrote Mattocks. He argued that the spam war was as much a public relations fight as anything and chided Nanae readers who had used the information from Hacker-X to attack Wallace.

"Shame on you," he wrote. "You are going to bring discredit on the rest of the anti-spammers. STOP IT!"

Mattocks's advice went largely ignored. The very next day, an unidentified person hacked into NetScum.net and replaced its usual home page with lewd messages about Wallace and Phil Lawlor, the chief executive officer of AGIS, Wallace's ISP. The site went offline shortly thereafter, returned in its original form a few months later, and then went dark again for good in the middle of October 1997, when AGIS cut off service to Cyber Promotions, citing the constant attacks from anti-spammers. Six months later, after failing to line up a new ISP, and finding himself hamstrung by legal settlements with ISPs that forbade him from ever again spamming their members, Wallace announced his retirement.

In an April 1998 note on Nanae, Wallace apologized for his past actions and said that newsgroup participants, in particular Mattocks and a popular anti-spammer named Jim Nitchals, had earned his respect. "It is now clear to me that most of you *are really here* to stop spam - not just for the thrill ride...BOTTOM LINE: You folks are WINNING the war against spam."

With Wallace vanquished, anti-spammers turned their attention to smaller foes, whom they jokingly referred to as chicken-boners. Unlike big operators such as Wallace who incorporated their businesses and maintained office space with hired employees and other trappings of legitimacy, chickenboners were imagined by spam fighters as living in mobile homes with a personal computer on the kitchen table, surrounded by beer cans and buckets of take-out fried chicken.

Veteran spam fighters tended to dismiss the skills of chicken-boners, but Gunn was taking no chances when she finally decided to join the ranks of anti-spammers in early 1999. Her first move was to create a new screen name under her master AOL account, which was based on a permutation of her real name, to protect her true identity. "Shiksa" was her first choice. A few years back, the mother of a Jewish man Gunn had been dating called her that when the woman thought Gunn was out of earshot. It was a derogatory Yiddish term used to describe non-Jewish females, but Gunn liked the name. When she tried to sign up for Shiksa at AOL, however, it was already taken. So she added an extra letter, and "Shiksaa," her new anti-spam persona, was born.

Hawke Mails the Web Manual

While most of South Carolina was bracing for the impending arrival of Hurricane Floyd on September 15, 1999, Davis Hawke was calmly surfing the Internet from Chesnee. The hurricane, packing 130 mile-per-hour winds at sea, was expected to make landfall on the Carolina coast that evening. Governor Hodges had ordered the mandatory evacuation of four coastal counties, causing a massive snarl of cars on I-26, the state's biggest highway. Over half a million people sought higher ground ahead of the forecasted damaging winds, heavy rain, and widespread flooding.

A category three storm like Floyd could easily level a flimsy structure like Hawke's rented mobile home. But he was staying put. Chesnee was two hundred miles from the shore, sheltered in the southern foothills of the Blue Ridge Mountains. As evening approached, wind gusts occasionally rattled the trailer's sheet-metal siding, and sporadic sprinkles of rain drummed on the metal roof. But the power and phone service remained on as Hawke logged onto InnovaNet, an ISP in nearby Clemson. Hawke had recently signed up for the service under a new pseudonym, James Kincaid.

Hawke had been spending a lot of time in the trailer since the disastrous rally in Washington, D.C. In recent days, as fall classes resumed at Wofford College, he'd managed to resist a strong seasonal force akin to what migratory birds must experience each autumn. For fifteen years he had found comfort in the cyclic back-to-school ritual. But this year Hawke stayed hunkered down in his trailer, working mostly on his eBay auctions.

Even if he hadn't renounced Wofford, there was no way Hawke could fund a return to the college. His mother had threatened to leave his father unless he completely cut Hawke off financially. So now Hawke was forced to live off his dwindling savings and the income generated by his remaining stock of Nazi knives, buckles, and other paraphernalia. Meanwhile, the college was sending him notices about paying last spring's tuition. And a bank in Spartanburg was on his case for a nearly $5,000 credit card bill. Hawke was a month shy of his twenty-first birthday, and already his credit was nearly shot.[1]

To help with the finances, Patricia was working as an assistant at a karate studio in a Spartanburg shopping plaza. That left Hawke alone in the trailer most afternoons. It was a bit like his high school days, when he would come home from school and read or go online for hours. His mother used to beg him to get outside for fresh air or to call a friend to play tennis. But aside from weekend chess tournaments, Britt, as his parents called him, rarely ventured out and instead spent much of his free time on the Internet. Sometimes he'd play chess with other Internet users, but mostly he was surfing the Web or hanging out in chat rooms. When his mother would came and checked in on him, Britt quickly pushed the Alt and Tab keys to bring up a chessboard screen.

Peggy Ambler Davis Greenbaum had no reason to be suspicious of her son. Throughout his childhood, Britt never needed disciplining. When he was an elementary and middle school student in rural Lakeville, Massachusetts, teachers singled him out, praising him for both his schoolwork and his chess. ("The next Bobby Fischer!" they'd exclaim.)

Teachers didn't realize that in their efforts to motivate other students to be like Britt, they had incited some to hate him. Kids detested his braininess, his pretty-boy looks, and his Jewish last name. A shy child, Britt was an easy target for teasing and, eventually, physical abuse, although he never reported it to his parents. Once in sixth grade when he was in his room changing, his mom noticed scratches and bruises all over his back. When she forced him to explain, he told her bullies had thrown him over a chair. The next day his mom marched Britt into the principal's office to complain. But the principal only made her more furious.

"Tell Britt to fight back," he advised, "and if he manages to beat up the kids, take him out to dinner to celebrate."

There were no celebratory dinners. Instead, Britt's parents moved the family to Westwood, a suburb of Boston they hoped would have fewer rednecks. The strategy worked. In the more affluent town his last name and scholarship were much less conspicuous. But as other Westwood High students were being drawn into sports or social events after school, Britt was rereading Hitler's *Mein Kampf* or wandering the Internet's back alleys, where he discovered white-supremacy web sites.

Now, after shuttering his own neo-Nazi web site and email accounts, Hawke had lost contact with his former comrades. The trailer was still loaded with Nazi gear, but it no longer had such a powerful effect on him. He still liked to carry around his SS dagger, but he never wore the uniforms anymore. Most of the Nazi items had just become eBay inventory. The stuff practically sold itself, and he completed around a dozen successful auctions every day. Yet Hawke quickly grew weary of the labor involved. He calculated that selling a swastika pin that netted him five dollars in profits easily consumed half an hour of his time, if you figured in exchanging emails with prospective buyers, packaging and shipping, and the occasional hassles over collecting payments. He could be making that kind of money working retail at the Spartanburg mall.

Fortunately, Hawke had stumbled upon an easier way. Around Labor Day, he received an email at his Yahoo! account advertising an Internet marketing kit. For ninety-nine dollars, Hawke could buy Stealth Mail Bomber—a software program for sending emails in bulk—along with a mailing list of one million addresses, and a manual about selling on the Internet.

As he read the ad, Hawke brightened. The most effortless way to do e-commerce, he realized, would be to sell digital rather than physical goods—products such as software or electronic newsletters and books that could be marketed and delivered over the Internet without any heavy lifting. Hawke visited the web site listed in the message and ordered the kit using his nearly maxed-out credit card. The next day, an email arrived with directions on how to copy the kit from an Internet site.

After downloading and unpacking the files, Hawke skimmed the manual. As he expected, it was thin on content—just a twenty-page Microsoft Word document full of e-business platitudes the author had probably cut and pasted from a web site or cribbed from a booklet off a supermarket rack. (As Hawke had hoped, there was no copyright notice or even the author's name anywhere in the document.) Stealth Mail Bomber, on the other hand, appeared packed with features, although it was a bit confusing. And the address list intrigued him. As he scrolled through the seemingly bottomless file, Hawke did some quick calculations. If he could sell the manual to just 1 percent of the people for, say, twenty dollars, he'd make $200,000 on his hundred-dollar investment.

Television news reports that evening said Hurricane Floyd was whipping Hilton Head Island and other coastal towns with several inches of rain per hour and winds over sixty miles per hour. Something about the approaching storm spurred Hawke to move ahead quickly with his new venture. He surfed to the Network Solutions web site and registered a new domain, WebManual2000.com. When prompted for his name, Hawke listed James Kincaid, although he provided his real Spartanburg post office box as the mailing address as well as his own phone number. He also made arrangements online with Interspeed Network, a California ISP, to host the WebManual2000 site on its servers.

The next day, Floyd swerved up the coast to North Carolina, sparing South Carolina major damage. The sun was shining in Chesnee as Hawke began designing the WebManual2000.com site using Netscape Composer, a program for writing hypertext mark-up language (HTML), the code used to display web pages. In his haste he didn't realize he had neglected to update the author setting on Composer's preferences menu since creating the Knights of Freedom site. As a result, buried in the code of the new site was one of Hawke's former aliases: Walther Krueger, a German officer decorated in World War II. Hawke intentionally borrowed one feature from KOF.net: a special order form with which shoppers could input their name, email address, phone number, and credit card information. When they clicked a button, the information would be sent from WebManual2000.com to a new email account he set up for the business: *attainwealth@yahoo.com*.

A few days later, WebManual2000.com was almost ready for business. Then came the most important part: composing an email ad for the manual. He decided to sell the Web Manual for $19.99, taking a no-hype approach that borrowed much of its language from the original message he had received for the kit:

> *I know what you're thinking, another cheap sales pitch, another scam. There are hundreds of "get rich quick" schemes on the Internet and you're probably convinced this is just another fraud. But if you've gotten this far, please read on. The information that I'm selling is not going to make you rich overnight, and you won't be passing Bill Gates in a Porsche next week. But you WILL learn the most important money-making skills in the world today: Internet marketing and sales…*

On the following Saturday night, Hawke finally had all the pieces in place. With Patricia watching over his shoulder, he fired up Stealth Mail Bomber. He configured the program to use "Learn How to Make $1,000,000 In Six Months—GUARANTEED!" as his message subject line. Then he signed on to the Internet and, with a smile at Patricia, clicked the program's start button. They went to bed while the program slowly churned through his mailing list.

Hawke awoke early the next morning, eager to learn the results of his mailing. He was annoyed to find that his computer had somehow disconnected from the Internet during the night. According to the status window on Stealth Mail Bomber, the program had successfully sent out just over 108,000 copies of the Web Manual ad before going offline.

Hawke quickly reconnected to the Internet and logged in to the Yahoo! email account to check his orders. A message in red letters at the top of the in-box page cried out that his account was over quota and no longer able to accept new messages. It was jammed full of hundreds of notices from mail systems at AOL and other ISPs, informing him that addresses in his mailing list did not exist or were otherwise unreachable. Hawke scrolled through the in-box, hoping for some actual orders, but he could find none. He began deleting the bounced messages to make way for legitimate email.

After trimming his mailing list to avoid remailing the first hundred thousand addresses, Hawke started up Stealth Mail Bomber again and began a new run. As the program chugged along, firing out round after round of email ads, he realized that he'd eventually need a better-targeted list, ideally one consisting of eBay sellers or other Internet users who actually had an interest in doing business online. But he figured he had nothing to lose by sending the Web Manual ad to the rest of his list. After all, he told himself, sending email was essentially free.

Late the next afternoon, as Hawke was combing through a new batch of undelivered messages in his Yahoo! in-box, the phone rang.[2] Patricia answered it.

"Someone wants to speak with James Kincaid," she whispered with her hand cupped over the phone's mouthpiece.

Hawke frowned, got up from his desk, and warily took the phone from her.

"Hello?"

"Mr. Kincaid? This is Roger over at InnovaNet," drawled the voice at the other end.

"Okay … What can I do for you Roger?"

"It has come to our attention that your account has been used to send out bulk unsolicited emails."

Hawke paused. "I don't know anything about any bulk emails," he said innocently.

"Well, Mr. Kincaid, we have determined that your account was used to send out the emails. We have a policy against that," said Roger.

Hawke wasn't sure what to say.

"Have you read our acceptable use policy? It's on our home page," asked Roger.

"Ah, no, I don't believe I have."

"Well, I need to inform you that if this happens again we will terminate your account."

"Okay," Hawke replied slowly.

"All right then, Mr. Kincaid. If you have any questions, please don't hesitate to call. You have a nice day."

Hawke hung up the phone. He did not like being made to feel guilty, and he was puzzled by the call. Stealth Mail Bomber's instructions specifically promised that the program contained special cloaking code that would make it undetectable by the user's ISP. So how did InnovaNet know he was sending out the ads? Were they tapping his line somehow? He could have asked Roger, but that would have been an admission of guilt. Hawke decided it was time to begin shopping around for a new ISP.

Shiksaa, the Spammer Tracker

Though she was a quick study, Shiksaa's first attempts at anti-spamming were fraught with rookie mistakes. On one occasion she angrily LARTed (filed an abuse report about) a company that had sent her spam and was later forced sheepishly to confess to Nanae that she had voluntarily signed up to receive mailings from the firm. Another time a Nanae veteran chewed her out for posting a 700-line message containing the entire contents of a FAQ on spam, rather than just providing a hyperlink to the document. Her tendency to become verbally combative when insulted or threatened also put her at odds with some newsgroup participants. When one of Nanae's resident *trolls*—a term used to describe newsgroup users who posted messages aimed at annoying other participants—argued once that anti-spammers were akin to the Ku Klux Klan, Shiksaa launched into a vehement counter-attack.

"Your mistake is that you assume anyone cares what you think," Shiksaa snapped back. "When you stop talking out of your derrière and want to help stamp out spam, come on back," she wrote.[3] The man responded by addressing her as "whorebot" and deriding her behavior as "typical of juniors enlisted into vigilante causes." The conversation (or *thread* in Usenet-speak) ended after several Nanae regulars rallied to Shiksaa's defense.

Though it didn't stanch the flow of junk email into her AOL account, Shiksaa found herself spending a couple of hours each day reading and commenting on Nanae. She enjoyed bantering with the newsgroup's regulars, who had a twisted and sometimes scathing sense of humor that she found exhilarating. At one point she even signed up for membership in the group's official anti-spam club, The Lumber Cartel. It was formed in 1997 as a humorous response to assertions by some bulk emailers that wood-products companies were funding anti-spammers in order to preserve paper-based direct-mail promotions.

The Cartel's web site featured images of clear-cut forests and logging trucks piled high with timber. At the site, prospective members could type their names into a form, click a button, and out would pop a certificate bearing the new member's name, membership number, and the following words:

> The certificate bearer swears to uphold and defend the Constitution and principles of NANAE and to carry a Big Mallet. It is by accepting this certificate that the bearer swears in their belief of individual freedom from UCE (spam), to crater web sites, LART luzers, nuke accounts and otherwise "deal with" spammers. While doing so with morality, ethics, personal responsibility, and the NANAE way - that is to be left alone.

To further whip up the paranoia of spammers, Cartel members made a point of littering their Nanae postings with thinly veiled references to payoffs received from lumber companies, along with denials that the anti-spam group existed. Many signed their messages with the phrase "there is no Lumber Cartel" or simply used the acronym TINLC. In early June 1999, Shiksaa configured her newsgroup reader so that it automatically added a signature line to her Nanae postings: "I am not a member of a nonexistent group of anti-spammers but if I were, I would be honored to be #782." She abandoned the sig a few days later after deciding it looked tacky.

Despite her lack of experience and technical sophistication, Shiksaa proved to be a precocious spammer tracker. One early incident in particular earned the respect and admiration of veteran junk-email opponents. It occurred in early June of 1999, when she received email advertising PCs that could be purchased with monthly payments. ("YOU NEED A NEW COMPUTER!" shouted the spam's subject line.)

Studying the message's headers—the technical data that revealed the email's path across the Internet to AOL's mail server—

Shiksaa determined that the sender had forged the return address so that the email appeared to originate from a site catering to kids. In the body of the message, there was a web site address for ordering the computer systems online. But to shield himself further, the spammer had obfuscated the URL; unlike normal web addresses that contain ordinary alphanumeric characters, it had been translated by the spammer instead into hexadecimal data easily decipherable only by a computer.

Shiksaa cut and pasted the encoded URL into a form at a special anti-spam web site she had read about on Nanae called SamSpade.org. It converted the obfuscated address back into regular characters, which enabled her to determine that the spammer's site was hosted on a computer operated by a small ISP in California.

On a whim, Shiksaa then tried a simple investigative technique she had read about on Nanae. In her web browser's address bar, she trimmed off some of the characters to the right of the final forward slash in the site's address and then hit the Enter key. Rather than displaying an ordinary web page designed by the site's operator, the new address provided a peek behind the curtain, revealing instead a list of files stored on the web server. When she clicked on one of the files, her browser displayed what appeared to be hundreds of orders.

Shiksaa gasped in disbelief. Besides street and email addresses, the file included customers' credit card numbers and telephone numbers, all totally unsecured and accessible to anyone who stumbled upon it with their web browsers. Whoever had created the site obviously placed a higher priority on concealing his own identity than on protecting his customers' personal information. (Most legitimate shopping sites never store credit card numbers on their web servers, and when they do, the numbers are locked away from prying eyes using encryption.)

Shiksaa quickly scanned some of the other exposed files on the server. There were several large ones containing email addresses, likely the spammer's mailing lists. One file contained a log that appeared to include the spammer's true AOL email address. She typed the address into Deja News, the newsgroup search engine, and found several spam complaints linking the address to an Oregon man named Glenn Conley. Besides sending spam touting cheap computers, Conley had apparently also been LARTed for numerous junk emails touting pornography and get-rich-quick schemes.

Shiksaa posted a message to Nanae announcing her discovery and asking for advice on what to do next. The experts told her to copy all of the files from the server and dispatch them immediately to AOL's legal department as well as to the ISP hosting the site. She obliged and promptly got an automated acknowledgement from AOL. But weeks went by, and the spammer's site, including the growing list of customer orders, was still online. When Shiksaa mentioned this to Nanae regulars, they told her to get used to it. Most abuse reports, they said, end up in what they called the bit bucket—the electronic garbage can.

But as it turned out, Shiksaa's notification to AOL may have done some good. Seven months later, in February 2000, AOL helped federal authorities indict Conley for using spam to commit securities fraud. From October 1999 through January 2000, Conley and a partner had used stolen credit card numbers to open accounts at twenty ISPs. Then they purchased thousands of shares of penny stocks in companies with little or no revenue. Next they proceeded to pump up the stocks' value by sending millions of spams to AOL users, touting the stocks' prospects. (Conley composed some of the messages to make them appear like communication between two friends, using subject lines such as "Hey Bob...This STOCK is gonna BLOW UP!") Gullible investors reacted to the messages by purchasing the stocks, which drove up the stocks' prices. That's when Conley and his partner dumped their shares, but not before making a cool million dollars. Conley was eventually sentenced to twenty-seven months in prison for his role in the scam.

With Shiksaa's rising profile in Nanae, and her daily slew of LARTs, it wasn't long before spammers took notice of the new "anti" in town. One morning in early July of 1999, Shiksaa was sitting at her computer when AOL's instant message service popped up a window from a stranger.[4]

"Hi, anti spammer, are you ready to die?" asked the person, who used the nickname Lime Pro.

Shiksaa froze when she read the words. At long last, she was virtually face to face with one of the low-life scum who had become her obsession for the past several months. Shiksaa couldn't recall where she had seen Lime Pro's nickname, but she guessed he was one of the dozens of people she had recently reported for spamming. After making sure that her computer was keeping a log file of the AOL chat session, she cautiously engaged Lime Pro in conversation.

"Are you ready to lose your account?" she replied.

He instantly began slinging insults at her ("How much of a dumb ass are you") and said he was in the process of hacking her IM account. Fighting against adrenalin, Shiksaa tried to remain calm. *Could he really do that?* She had heard reports of AOL hackers exploiting flaws in the service's software to take control of other users' accounts. And sure enough, when she tried to click the Messenger program's "Notify" button, which was designed to alert AOL about abusive users, nothing happened.

Shiksaa knew that she could just sign off the service and avoid the confrontation. But she couldn't resist asking Lime Pro a question first.

"Why do you spam?"

Now it was Lime Pro's turn to be dumbfounded. He stumbled over his words a bit and then finally explained that he was earning $800 per week sending junk email, and that he owned a new Corvette and was co-owner of a restaurant in Pennsylvania. All of this, he added, despite the fact that he was only seventeen.

When Shiksaa typed "LOL" and told him she sincerely doubted it, Lime Pro went silent. Moments later, it was he who signed off the service.

Shiksaa waited for several minutes for Lime Pro to return. Unsuccessful, she emailed a copy of her log file to AOL's online abuse team. Then she posted a lighthearted description of the encounter on Nanae, with the subject line "[C&C] First death threat from spambag." One anti-spammer who read it said she shouldn't worry about the threats from Lime Pro, whom he said was probably "a zit-faced, scrawny 17-year old puke living in the back of mommy and daddy's trailer." But some folks in the newsgroup were troubled by Shiksaa's report. "Not taking a threat seriously can be deadly," warned one woman, who recommended that Shiksaa report the incident to her local police.

Shiksaa ignored the woman's advice. She considered Lime Pro mostly harmless, and besides, she had been very careful about not saying anything to anyone online that would reveal her true identity. Still, when she went to bed that night, she checked her dresser to make sure the .357 Magnum handgun she had owned since 1975 was still there.

About a week later, in hopes of getting out from beneath the avalanche of spam burying her AOL account each day, Shiksaa signed up for a new email address with Microsoft's free Hotmail service using her married name, Susan Wilson. Her plan was to use the address, carefully munged (camouflaged) of course, in her future Usenet postings. As she had done in the past, she would give out only her first name in any messages. In her newsreader's setup menu, she replaced her AOL address with her new Hotmail account. But when she tried out the new account for the first time by posting a message to the alt.test group, for some reason her newsreader automatically signed the message with her full name, which is what she had used to sign up for Hotmail. On the Internet, the alias Shiksaa and Susan Wilson were now indelibly linked. It was the type of care-less mistake that Shiksaa's enemies would someday exploit.

Shiksaa Plays Peacemaker

Eight copies of Hawke's Web Manual ad somehow landed in the America Online in-box of Karl Gray, an AOL user in London. Like most ISPs in the United Kingdom at the time, AOL's service was metered, which meant that Gray paid a per-minute charge while online. Downloading and dealing with spam therefore wasn't just a nuisance; it cost him money. While most AOL users might have deleted the Web Manual ads in disgust, Gray posted a copy of the spam to a newsgroup named alt.stop.spamming, along with the words, "Any one want to help me wage war?"

Morely Dotes, the online alias of a Nanae regular named Richard Tietjens, spotted Gray's posting during his regular morning sweep through anti-spam newsgroups. Dotes looked up the domain registration record for WebManual2000.com and posted the infor-mation as a reply to Gray's message. Dotes also noted in his message that the ad's headers indicated it had been transmitted from an Inno-vaNet user operating a spam program with "direct-to-MX" capabili-ties. Such technology routed the ads directly to recipients' email servers, leaving no trace at InnovaNet's mail server.

"It is obvious from the fact that Kincaid used direct-to-MX spamware that he knows what he is doing is wrong," wrote Dotes.

Had Shiksaa been a regular reader of alt.stop.spamming, those words might have inspired her to pounce on the case and run searches on Kincaid's phone number and email address. Eventually, she would have her first online encounter with Hawke. But on that day in September 1999, Shiksaa still stuck mostly to news.admin.net-abuse.email, and she was embroiled in an ugly conflict with Andrew Brunner, the 27-year-old developer of a new program for sending bulk email.

Brunner's Avalanche software was among scores listed at The Spamware Site, which was maintained by a frequent Nanae contributor from England who went by the alias Sapient Fridge. Since most ISPs refused to host sites selling bulk emailing software, business could become quite difficult for any companies named to the Spamware roster. Brunner, a slim, clean-cut, and ordinarily soft-spoken man, was livid when he learned in August 1999 that his Pennsylvania-based firm, CyberCreek, was listed. He complained to spam fighters that they were interfering with his legal right to communicate with prospective customers, and he hurled legal threats at Sapient Fridge, insisting that he remove CyberCreek or risk being sued for defamation.

But the antis held their ground. They acknowledged Brunner's claim that Avalanche could theoretically be used for distributing electronic newsletters and other non-spam purposes. They noted, however, that the program also included a number of features with no legitimate purpose, such as the ability to create fake headers aimed at covering the digital footprints of the software's users and a technical trick that enabled Avalanche to force its messages into email servers intentionally locked down against spam.

In a show of support, Shiksaa posted a mirror image of Sapient Fridge's Spamware list on her new personal home page. (The home page was a freebie that came with the new EarthLink ISP service she had signed up for a few weeks previously to test as a possible AOL replacement.) A couple of other antis, including Morely Dotes, followed with mirrors of their own. Meanwhile, Steve Linford, the operator of UXN, a London-based ISP, added CyberCreek to Spamhaus, his list of spam support services. Clearly, Brunner's lawsuit bluff had failed.

Then, in late August, an anonymous person sent an email to all of the companies on the spamware list. The message was a call to action for spammers to fight fire with fire by filing complaints with the ISPs hosting the sites operated by Sapient Fridge, Linford,

Shiksaa, and others. The sender of the message, who called himself Jolly Roger, also encouraged spammers to launch attacks against the sites, with the aim of knocking them offline with a flood of malicious traffic.

"Remember, if you don't do this then you are giving up," he wrote. "Imagine how good it would feel to get some revenge. Won't it be ironic when we shut their asses down?"

Although the spamware vendors never rallied to Jolly Roger's call to cyber war, Shiksaa watched with dismay as Nanae boiled with new disdain for Brunner. To taunt him, anti-spammers began referring to Brunner as "Spamdrew" and to his company as "Cyber-Crook," and they mercilessly mocked him for his tendency toward misspellings such as "law suite." Yet earlier that summer, some of the same people were memorializing the one-year anniversary of the death of Jim Nitchals, whom they described as the Dr. Martin Luther King, Jr. of the anti-spam movement. Just before dying of a brain hemorrhage in June of 1998, Nitchals had helped lead peace talks aimed at persuading Sanford Wallace to give up his spamming ways. (Ultimately, however, it took lawsuits to get Wallace to stop.)

Feeling emboldened by her recent conversations with spammers such as Lime Pro, Shiksaa decided to approach Brunner privately as an emissary from Nanae. One morning a few days before Labor Day weekend, she looked up CyberCreek's phone number on its web site and called Brunner.

Brunner answered his cell phone on the first ring. He sounded surprised that she had called, and he remained suspicious, even after she earnestly announced her intention of ending the flame war. (In fact, Brunner's high-pitched, scratchy voice made it hard for Shiksaa not to picture the gawky kid Alfalfa from the *Little Rascals* TV show.) But after they chatted a bit, including about the need for both sides to respect the other, Brunner clearly was disarmed. He confessed that he preferred not to sell software to spammers but that he was only trying to earn a living. At one point, he suggested he could modify Avalanche to disable the spamware features such as cloaking.

"If I do it, can you talk to those guys and get them to take me off their lists?" he asked.

"I can't make any promises, Andy," she replied, "but I don't see why they wouldn't do it."

Shiksaa reported her conversation with Brunner on Nanae the following day, noting that she had made some progress in bringing him back from the dark side.

"I told him that he would be treated with respect if he would cut the shit and name calling," she wrote. "I would hope that everyone could get beyond the past and work for the common goal. Let's stop the flame war and work to stop the spam."

But rather than applauding Shiksaa's diplomatic efforts, many spam fighters criticized her for trying to strike a deal with Brunner.

"You seem terribly naïve. Con men do not reform and you are just making yourself the fall guy for another con," wrote one Nanae regular, who added, "You seem to have an affinity for believing stories made up to appease you."

Another chimed in: "It seems Susan is sort of new to this and is trying to reason with these individuals. It doesn't work."

Even Alan Murphy, a long-time spam fighter who had helped Shiksaa on a number of spam investigations, was skeptical of her attempts to get Brunner to revise Avalanche.

"I honestly don't understand what you think Andrew intended to do with it beside promote spam. It was designed to abuse," wrote Murphy.

Stung by the criticism and condescension, Shiksaa fired off a post to Nanae saying that she believed that treating Brunner with respect was the best tactic for bringing him around.

"Shoot me for trying," she wrote.

Fearing Shiksaa was dangerously close to resigning from the corps of spam fighters, Murphy posted a public plea asking the group to back off in its criticism: "I'm very impressed by Susan's ability to get people on the phone . . . She doesn't deserve the heat she got, and I know that she felt it."

Shiksaa had little time to brood over the debate surrounding her peacekeeping mission. Two days later the operators of the Realtime Blackhole List (RBL) added CyberCreek to their powerful and controversial spam blacklist. Run by Mail Abuse Prevention System (MAPS), a nonprofit consortium founded in 1997, the RBL included the network addresses of major spam operations as well as companies that provided them services. By configuring their mail servers—and in extreme cases, their network routers—to reject any traffic to or from addresses on the RBL, ISPs effectively were able to isolate spammers from communicating with parts of the Internet.

When he found out his company had been placed on the RBL, Brunner snapped. Jettisoning the conciliatory tone he had taken with Shiksaa, Brunner went into full verbal-combat mode. He configured his newsreader to add a new signature line at the bottom of all of his Usenet postings, "DEATH TO ALL NET-NAZIS!!!" His new sig also included the name, address, and home phone number of MAPS cofounder Paul Vixie, a California-based consultant and network engineer, as well as contact details for a handful of other leading anti-spammers. On September 9, 1999, Brunner posted a message to Nanae, calling Vixie a "fascist piece of anti-American, anti-business dirt" and warning that "When I am done with you, you won't be able to wipe the dingle berries off Bill Gates' ass."

Brunner's display of vitriol wasn't aimed at Shiksaa, but it bothered her deeply. There she was, putting Andy forward to her Nanae brethren as a businessman who could be reasoned with. Instead, he revealed himself to be a cretin, justifying the warnings of those who had called her naïve. It cultivated in Shiksaa a strong desire to retaliate.

After contemplating some options, she launched Microsoft FrontPage Express, the HTML editor that came with her computer.

In a couple of hours, she had whipped together a web page entitled "The Brunners of Chickenbone Creek."

Using some photos she found online, Shiksaa assembled a simple collage on a bright red background. Beneath the photo of a Winnebago trailer she placed the caption "Home," while she captioned a photo of an AirStream trailer with the words "Summer home." Below an image of a young girl holding a bucket of fried chicken, Shiksaa added "The Future Mrs. Spamdrew Brunner." She also found a photo of a can of Hormel SPAM in which the product's name had been changed to SCAM. She gave it a caption that read "Staple of the Brunner household...err...trailerhold."

To complete the page, Shiksaa added background music in the form of a midi file, which played a computer-generated version of the dueling banjos piece from the movie *Deliverance* whenever someone viewed the page. Then she uploaded the files to her Earthlink personal site and published a link to the page on Nanae.

The spam fighters were delighted with Shiksaa's little creation. Several quickly posted glowing reviews. "A classic...truly inspired...You have earned a special place (TINSP) in the hall of NANAE-ites with that little gem," wrote one.

After checking out Shiksaa's Brunner parody page, a Nanae participant named Rick navigated to her new personal home page, where she had published a small photo of herself.

"Would it be ok if I had a mild crush on you?" he wrote.

Before Shiksaa could respond, a user from England named Ian chimed in, "Get off. She's mine!"

Brunner, on the other hand, was not amused in the slightest. He posted an ominous, if grammatically puzzling, public challenge to Shiksaa.

"Why don't you make it *easy* on me and give me your real address. When I find you I won't let go until you are either penniless. At the very least you won't be able to have a charge card. Enjoy the rest of your pathetic life," wrote Brunner.

Shiksaa knew it was just another one of Brunner's bluffs. He was a beaten, ineffectual man. Unless he drastically changed his business practices, CyberCreek.com would remain hopelessly black-holed from the rest of the Internet. At that point, there was really no reason to kick Brunner while he was down. But Shiksaa simply couldn't resist.

"I meant to tell you," she wrote in reply to Brunner's threatening note on Nanae. "You have a little whiny voice and you sound like you can't be older than 20. Has your voice finished changing yet? Get rid of that annoying adolescent acne?" Shiksaa signed the note, "Smooch, smooch, precious."

Rereading her message when it appeared on Nanae, Shiksaa realized it sounded catty and mean-spirited. But it wasn't really meant just for Brunner. She also intended it as a deterrent to spammers everywhere. *Don't mess with The Lady of LART.*

Hawke's Publishing Company in a Box

At the time, Davis Hawke didn't know the term LART, but he knew firsthand its potentially awesome power. Within days of Karl Gray filing complaints about receiving eight Web Manual spams, InnovaNet had shut down Hawke's dial-up account, and Interspeed had pulled the plug on hosting the WebManual2000.com domain—all before Hawke had a chance to make more than a handful of sales. He paced the floor between his office in the trailer and the kitchen. He was ready to move ahead with his life. He had shaved off his push-broom moustache. He'd taken the swastika flags off the walls and the Nazi death's head off his dresser. He'd tossed the remnants of a box of American Nationalist Party business cards into the garbage. He was keen to print up a fresh set bearing the name of his new online enterprise: Venture Alpha Corporation. It frustrated Hawke to know that people were still determined to get in the way of his plans.

Hawke was having a hard time clinging to the belief that great-ness was his historical destiny. It had been drilled into him as a boy, when his mother would quiz him at mealtimes on the Ambler family tree—her side of the family. Who did great, great, great Grand-mother Polly from Virginia marry? Why, U.S. Chief Justice John Marshall, of course! And who signed their marriage certificate? Then-Governor Thomas Jefferson! And who turned down a mar-riage proposal from soon-to-be-President Jefferson? Great, great, great, great grandmother Rebecca!

During these dinner-table genealogy lessons, Hawke's father just smiled and listened. They never devoted much conversation to the Greenbaum side of the family. So when Britt's fourth-grade teacher assigned students the project of drawing up a family tree, the young boy focused exclusively on the Ambler clan. When it was Britt's turn to present his project to the class, he unfurled his drawing, which he had labored over for hours with his mother, and began talking about his family's patrician roots.

The teacher took one look at the neatly drawn chart and ordered him back to his seat. "Shame on you, Britt Greenbaum," she scolded, certain he had fabricated it all.

Looking back now on his aborted show-and-tell, Hawke real-ized that one of the greatest skills chess had taught him was not to allow small setbacks to thwart his grand strategy. Although his mother was furious to learn of the teacher's reaction to his genealogy report, Hawke let the incident slide by. But eight years later, he qui-etly made the trip down to the Dedham courthouse to change his name. And neither parent opposed the move.

Hawke thumbed through the Greenville/Spartanburg Yellow Pages. He was looking for the section on Internet services. After a few phone calls, he arranged for a new dial-up account with a com-pany in Anderson called Carolina Online. He signed onto Carol.net and began piecing together his next Venture Alpha offering.

This time, he would market something called Million Dollar Publishing Company in a Box. He had got the idea a few weeks back from a piece of junk email that arrived in his Yahoo! in-box. The message, apparently sent by a company in western Massachusetts, advertised a CD-ROM with advice on how to start a home-based business selling "information through the mail." For ninety-nine dollars, the author was willing to part with full reprint rights to hundreds of reports on topics ranging from how to win a sweepstakes contest to how to become a TV or movie star.

Hawke recognized the offer for the scam it was. Like the Web Manual, the only people likely to buy the Publishing Company in a Box were other spammers. It wasn't quite a pyramid scheme, but it relied on some of the same twisted logic. Hawke chuckled at one especially clever part of the ad:

> I am sending this ad to 10,000 other people…and I will only allow 50 kits to be sold. It wouldn't make much sense if I sold this kit to 1,000 or 2,000 people…The market would be saturated with these same manuals…and I don't want to do that. To make sure that the people in this offer get the same results I have…ONLY 50 people can have it for $99.00!

The author even promised to return, uncashed, any checks he received after selling his quota of fifty kits. Hawke realized he would be ecstatic if he made $5,000 from his hundred-dollar investment. Then again, if hundreds of orders rolled in, who would know besides him? Hawke purchased the CD-ROM, determined this time to make some serious money before spam haters got in his way.

When the CD arrived in the mail, Hawke took it to a computer store in Spartanburg that charged five dollars per CD to burn two dozen copies for him. Since Interspeed had shut down his WebManual2000.com site for violating its terms of service, Hawke had to come up with a temporary work-around until he could find a new host for the domain. He uploaded a copy of the old site's files, slightly modified for his new venture, from his PC to a home page he had created at Angelfire.com.

A free, ad-supported home page provider catering to consumers, Boston-based Angelfire had two big drawbacks. It didn't allow members to advertise their home pages using spam or to run programs for processing online orders. To fill the latter gap, Hawke signed up at CartManager.net for a fourteen-day demonstration. The Utah-based electronic shopping cart service would enable him to seamlessly submit orders from his Angelfire site to his account at CartManager.

After creating a new email account for the project, *netwealth_99@yahoo.com*, Hawke worked on his ad copy. He used the original message almost verbatim, with necessary changes to the ordering information. Hawke also modified a section at the bottom of the ad that instructed recipients on how they could opt out of future mailings. In hopes of mollifying spam haters, Hawke whipped up this version instead:

> *We are STRICTLY OPPOSED to spam! You are receiving this email because you have either signed up for one of our services or you have authorized your email address to be given out by filling out an "opt-in" form when signing up for any type of free service. If you wish to be removed from this email list, please send a message to "attainwealth@yahoo.com" with the word "UNSUBSCRIBE" in the subject field. We apologize if you have received this email in error.*

As a further countermeasure against complaint-related interruptions, Hawke decided to switch mailing programs. He'd received a spam advertising a package called Extractor Pro, which, according to its web site, was designed to send ads onto the Internet through third-party mail servers known as open relays. These machines, usually operated by businesses, universities, and other organizations, had been configured (either out of courtesy or neglect) to allow unauthorized users to bounce their messages off the servers en route to their final destinations. As a result, recipients of the messages who examined the headers could trace their origin back to the open relays but usually not to the sender's ISP. Hawke purchased and downloaded a copy of Extractor Pro from the company's web site.

On October 20, 1999, Hawke was ready to broadcast his new ad for Publishing Company in a Box. He signed on to Carol.net and configured Extractor Pro to use the half-million fresh email addresses that came with the program.

Meanwhile, nearly five hundred miles away in Washington, D.C. , Heather Wilson, a republican from New Mexico, was introducing the Unsolicited Electronic Mail Act of 1999 to the U.S. House of Representatives. If enacted into law, the bill would require email marketers to use real return addresses on their messages, provide opt-out features, and abstain from forging their messages' headers. A failure to comply could open them up to private lawsuits from individuals or ISPs to the tune of five hundred dollars per infringing message.

But Hawke wasn't paying attention to national news, much less to pending federal legislation. After double-checking to make sure Extractor Pro had successfully connected to a set of relay servers, he took a deep breath and pushed the program's start button. Tomorrow, the 21st, he would turn twenty-one—his golden birthday. Who knew what it might bring?

chapT3r
tHree

Shiksaa Meets the Cyanide Idiot

Jason Vale was in big trouble. For nearly two hours he'd been trapped in a windowless conference room in the U.S. Attorney's office in Brooklyn. A government lawyer was grilling Vale, 29, about his Internet-based apricot seed business, which he operated from his home in Queens, New York. It was April 2000, and the Food and Drug Administration (FDA) had been after Vale's company, Christian Brothers Contracting Corporation, since 1997, when they sent inspectors to his home.

It was just a deposition, but Vale felt like he was already on trial. He really needed to use the bathroom, but his interrogator—a woman in her mid-twenties—wouldn't let up.

"How would you characterize your feeling, your religious beliefs in relation to the work that you do?" asked Allison Harnisch, a trial lawyer with the Department of Justice's Office of Consumer Litigation.[1]

Vale wasn't certain where she was going with the question, but he lurched into his standard answer about how Genesis 1:29 contained a prescription for life without cancer:

> Then God said, "I now give you every seed-bearing plant on the face of the entire earth and every tree that has fruit with seed in it. They will be yours for food."

There are way too many lawyers in this room, Vale thought. Besides Assistant U.S. Attorney Harnisch, there was Vale's lawyer, another attorney from the Department of Justice, and one from the FDA. Vale was just an online entrepreneur, filling orders in his basement for bags of apricot seeds; tablets of the extract from the seeds called Laetrile, or vitamin B_{17}; as well as an injected form of the compound. He used several computers to send out email advertisements for his web sites, which included apricotsfromgod.com and canceranswer.com. In its 1998 suit against him, AOL claimed that Vale sent an estimated 23.5 million junk emails to AOL members.

Vale didn't have much respect for AOL or the FDA. On his sites' home pages he explained how the pharmaceutical industry pushed the FDA to ban B_{17}, even though many people believed the compound worked as a cancer preventative. (B_{17} couldn't be patented, so, as Vale saw it, drug companies considered it a threat to their profit model.) Sure enough, the FDA had sent him several warning letters stating that Laetrile was not approved as a drug and that he was violating the law by promoting it as a cancer cure. Now it looked like their goal was to get a court order forcing him to stop selling the B_{17}.

"Do you want to stay in business, *this* business?" Harnisch asked him.

Vale stiffened. "Is that a threat?"

"It's just a question," she said.

"I would love to stay supplying seeds," he replied.

Who wouldn't? Before Vale launched the company, he was working construction and running a billiard parlor. Now, he was grossing easily $300,000 a year from his low-overhead spam business, shipping out nearly a ton of apricot pits and over 100 boxes of tablets a month.

Harnisch asked what Vale would do if the court said he could no longer sell apricot seeds or B_{17}.

"I would listen to the court if the court said that I can't sell B$_{17}$," he replied. But then he added, "If it said I can't sell seeds, that's a different story."

"Why would the seeds be a different story?"

Vale explained how the state of Arizona allowed the sale of apricot seeds as a nutritional supplement and how companies all over the place were selling them. He told her about how he called the FDA once and even it said he could do it.

"Mr. Vale," his lawyer butted in. "Just answer her questions. Just keep it to answering her questions."

"Can I go to the bathroom?" Vale asked.

Out in the hallway, Vale let out a deep breath and headed for the men's room. He'd told customers that he was in a David-versus-Goliath battle, but he'd actually faced much bigger opponents than the U.S. government. The summer after his high school graduation, Vale developed a persistent cough and a pain deep in his left side. When the symptoms didn't respond to antibiotics, doctors finally figured out there was a tumor the size of a grapefruit between his spine and his ribs. Surgeons removed the growth, diagnosed as an Askin's tumor, and left a nearly two-foot-long curved scar below his left shoulder blade. They said most people with the rare form of cancer lived only about eight months. But when Vale came home from the hospital, he did a handstand in the driveway—the staples in his back be damned—just to show everyone he was fine.

That was eleven years ago, and Vale didn't look like a cancer victim now. He was a strapping 180 pounds and had gone on to become a world-champion arm wrestler in the middleweight class. He survived a second bout with Askin's and another surgery. He attributed his success in beating the disease to eating a dozen or more bitter apricot pits every day (in addition to praying even more than usual).

When Vale returned to the conference room, Harnisch said she wanted to talk about his spam email operation.

"My forte," he smiled.

"To your knowledge, do you have a reputation in the Internet community?"

She was leafing through several pages of web page printouts. They were Nanae postings, he assumed correctly.

"I see myself in the newsgroups," he said.

"Would you say you're notorious for your spams?"

Vale's lawyer jumped in, saying he objected to the question. But he instructed Vale to answer.

"They'll do anything they can, they'll do *anything* to stop a bulk email," Vale told Harnisch.

Vale hated the meddlesome anti-spammers in Nanae who whined about his spam to the FDA and the Federal Trade Commission, and he blamed them for getting his sites disconnected by ISPs. Vale also held anti-spammers partly responsible for the lawsuit filed against him in late 1998 by America Online. The online service calculated that it had received over 47,000 complaints about Vale's spam since December 1997. Many of the junk emails bore phony AOL return addresses.

But Vale was defiant. When AOL dispatched someone to his house to serve him with the lawsuit—the Sunday before Christmas no less—Vale just threw the papers back in the man's face. After that, Vale completely ignored all of the legal proceedings and went right on spamming AOL members.

Exasperated, AOL's legal counsel assumed Vale thought he was above the law. A year later, in December 1999, they convinced a magistrate to award AOL $600,000 in damages and a permanent injunction that barred Vale and Christian Brothers from using AOL's network in the future. So far, AOL's attorneys hadn't tried to force him to pay the money. They seemed content just to keep him away from their service.

It was not at all like Jason Vale to walk away from a fight. As a teenager, he had been a master of the preemptive punch. Although it cost him a knocked-out tooth and a twice-broken nose, fighting was so much more effective than trying to reason with someone. But against the anti-spammers, Vale's pile-driver right wasn't of much use. He couldn't get to them. Antis hid behind their computers, using words to jab at him and other bulk emailers. They had taken to calling him the Cyanide Idiot in their Nanae postings, referring to one of the active ingredients in Laetrile. Some even left messages on his answering machine complaining about his spam. Their voices sounded effeminate to him. "Most anti-spammers are gay," Vale wrote to Frederick, an anti-spammer, in a May 1999 exchange.

A few months before the AOL lawsuit, Vale had annoyed spam-tracking antis with a new technique for driving customers to his sites. Instead of directly revealing the site addresses, such as apricotsfromgod.com and canceranswer.com, in his email ads—which would have made him an easy target for complaints—Vale's spams encouraged recipients to visit the AltaVista search engine and type the words "apricot seeds" and "cancer." Because Vale had hidden in his pages' source code terms like Laetrile, B_{17}, apricot seeds, cancer, holistic, and other keywords, his sites would come out at the top of the search rankings.

Vale's technique was even cited in an October 1999 article in the *Industry Standard*, which Shiksaa saw when someone posted excerpts from the article to Nanae. After reading about it, Shiksaa decided to pay Vale a little visit online. She dug up his Cianide70 screen name and contacted him over AOL Instant Messenger.

"Why do you spam, and why are you vindictive against people who complain when you spam them?" she asked.

"You should just hit delete," replied Vale, not sure who she was.

"I refuse to click delete," she said. "I will complain about every single spam I get."

Vale didn't understand why antis got so worked up about spam, which he considered to be no different than paper-based junk mail.

"There are other more important things in life that one should spend their time concerned with," he said.

"You didn't answer my question…why do you spam?"

Vale tried to dodge the question with a rare gesture of peace-making. "If you want to give me your address," he said, "I'll send you a free video and a pound of apricot seeds just cause you were nice."

"What would I do with apricot seeds?" Shiksaa asked, after thanking him.

"When you see the video your life will be changed."

But Shiksaa signed off without giving him her address.

By the time Harnisch finally wrapped up the deposition, it was quarter to two. Vale agreed to provide the government with a list of all of his web sites, their traffic stats, and documents showing his income from the Christian Brothers business dating back to 1996.

But on Easter Sunday 2000, before he'd even had a chance to pull the information together, and just as he was getting ready for church, Vale got a call from a *Wall Street Journal* reporter. She told him the government had convinced a judge to shut him down with an injunction. District Judge John Gleeson had issued an order that prohibited Vale from selling Laetrile, even in the form of apricot seeds.

"What do you think about that?" the reporter asked.

"I respect the court. I respect Judge Gleeson," he said.

Vale told her he still thought B_{17} and apricots seeds were not illegal, but he said he would abide by the court's decision. The next day, he removed the banned products from the ordering sections of his web sites. But he kept the rest of the pages online and added one soliciting donations to his legal fund.

Jason Vale wasn't planning to give up without a fight.

Hawke Concedes to an Anti

In the spring of 2000, Davis Hawke decided it was time to get out of South Carolina. In March, he and Patricia moved to Leicester,

North Carolina. They were still living in a mobile home, but now they had the Smoky Mountains right outside their door.

The charm of Chesnee had long since worn off, but there was another factor motivating Hawke's move. An Internet user in California—no one Hawke had ever heard of—had sent him a certified letter saying he was suing Hawke for spamming. The first thing Hawke did after they settled into the trailer on Serenity Lane in Leicester was to visit an attorney in Asheville. Hawke figured the lawsuit was a joke, but he wanted a professional opinion. The lawyer told him he could probably ignore the legal threat, but he advised Hawke to incorporate his Internet marketing company. That way Hawke could shield himself from personal liability should someone lob a more serious lawsuit his way.

On that day, March 14, 2000, QuikSilver Enterprises, Inc. became a North Carolina corporation. The next day, Hawke was blasting out his first barrage of spams bearing his new company name. But to keep nosy people off his back, Hawke continued to use his post office box in South Carolina as Quiksilver's mailing address. He'd make the hour-long drive from Leicester to Spartanburg a couple times each week just to gather up any checks or other mail that might have arrived.

Hawke had given up on trying to conceal the origin of his spams by routing them through open mail relays. Instead, he signed up for several accounts using bogus names at ISPs such as Blue Ridge Internet in Hendersonville, Internet of Asheville, or even Bell-South's Internet service. He paid his twenty dollars, sent a couple spam runs, and almost invariably the ISP would cut off service once it got complaints about his junk email. Hawke just chalked up the disposable dial-up accounts as a cost of doing business.

Hawke's desire for a fresh start was also prompted by a series of other business problems the previous winter. In December, bidders on his eBay auctions started leaving negative comments in the feedback section of the auction site. They complained that Venture

Alpha, as he had called his online auction business, was slow to mail out products and that emails to it sometimes bounced as undeliverable. Other winning bidders said the stuff he shipped out didn't match the photos they had seen in his auction listings.

The negative feedback was frustrating to Hawke, who had been careful to keep the wheels of e-commerce well greased by soliciting positive comments from bidders. Whenever he shipped out a knife, belt buckle, or any other item to one of his eBay customers, he sent a note requesting that the bidder leave positive feedback for him in the auction site's forum. In turn, he agreed to recommend the buyer. That way, whenever a potential bidder looked at Venture Alpha's member profile at the site, they'd see all the positive comments and feel reassured about doing business with him.

But as Hawke's sales volume grew, the complaints also started to pile up. In late December, a former customer posted a warning to buyers on the rec.knife Usenet newsgroup. "Stay away from these people they are nothing but thieves," wrote the man. "I won one of their auctions for a set of kamas ... I received the item seven weeks later! They auction things they don't have in stock and wait until they get your money in hand to order it! The quality of the item was terrible too."

The same day, eBay unceremoniously suspended Hawke's account. But he was not about to abandon the business he had come to know so well. So Hawke decided to move up the food chain and start marketing himself as an eBay auction expert. He pulled together some ideas he had seen on the Internet along with some of his own tips into a ten-page document he titled the "The EBay Home Study Course." Available only in electronic format, it walked beginners though how to choose a market niche and how to write a sales pitch. It also included details on the use of photos to spice up auction listings and advice on setting up a complementary web site. The manual even had a section on why getting positive comments from bidders is important.

"You need to have an outstanding feedback rating brimming with positive comments to really make huge profits on eBay," Hawke wrote. But he also advised auctioneers on how to deal with what he called "rogue customers" who simply can't be satisfied. "We all know that the customer is NOT always right...If they persist in causing problems, just ignore them."

The eBay manual sold fairly well. But a new Hawke venture, which he called the Banned CD, became his cash cow after moving to North Carolina. According to the spams he composed, the CD-ROM contained software programs and "contraband" information that would "teach you things that Uncle Sam, your creditors, your boss, and others just don't want you to know."

Hawke loaded the CDs with an assortment of documents he had picked up on the Internet, such as instructions on how to build a cable-TV descrambler and a directory of suppliers of explosives, silencers, and other weaponry. He also threw in a list of twenty-five million email addresses, along with a copy of a spamming program. The CD also contained a number of freeware utilities such as computer screensavers and clip art collections.

For twenty dollars, Hawke considered the Banned CD a bargain, and many customers seemed to agree. But the Banned CD spams also generated more complaints than any of Hawke's previous offerings.

In June 2000, a flood of Banned CD ads found their way into the email in-box of Reid Walker, who operated a taxi business out of his home in Crestview, Florida.

Walker had recently bought a $250 box called a WebTV that turned his television into a big computer monitor. He could sit on the couch with the unit's wireless keyboard, dial up the Internet through the box's internal modem, and look at eBay auctions or check his email between phone calls dispatching rides or handling other business details.

Walker's WebTV email account had a limited storage quota, and the unit had no CD-ROM drive, so he had absolutely no interest in the barrage of Banned CD ads. More than thirty arrived over the course of a week or two.

After Walker got the first couple of messages, he did the first thing most consumers do: complain to their ISP. WebTV admitted that its spam filter wasn't 100 percent effective and conceded that individual users couldn't customize it to block selected spams. There wasn't much WebTV could do. So Walker followed the instructions at the bottom of the Banned CD ad.

"This is a 100-percent opt-in list...we immediately honor all requests to be removed," promised the ad. So Walker replied, asking to be taken off the list. But his message was returned as undeliverable. The next day, more copies of the spam arrived, this time with a new return address, and a slightly reworked message:

> I have been receiving emails saying that I'm contributing to the moral decay of society by selling the Banned CD. That may be, but I feel strongly that you have a right to benefit from this hard-to-find information. So I am giving you ONE LAST CHANCE to order the Banned CD!

"And you just had your last chance to stop emailing me," Walker wrote back, fuming. But once again, his message bounced back undelivered.[2]

Growing more annoyed by the minute, Walked decided to visit 4publish.com, the web site advertised in the Banned CD spams. He was hoping to locate a phone number or other contact information.

"Remove my email from your distribution list," he wrote in a customer comment input form on 4publish.com.

But a few days later, in a third salvo, more ads for the Banned CD arrived in Walker's in-box. Now furious, Walker wrote in the input form at the site, "YOU CAN ALSO BE JAILED FOR SPAMMING! WHICH I AM DOING EVERYTHING I CAN

TO GET YOU TRACKED DOWN. QUIT SENDING ME THIS SHIT...IS THAT PLAIN ENOUGH FOR YOU?"

To further drive home his point, Walker sent the message over and over again. He ended up sending over one hundred copies of the message by repeatedly cutting and pasting the text into the form and hitting the submit button.

Without identifying himself, Hawke replied less than an hour later.

"Since you see fit to mail bomb me and harass me like this, I am never, ever, ever going to remove you from this list," wrote Hawke using the email account resalehighway@resalehighway.com. "In fact, I am going to distribute your email address and phone number to as many telemarketing companies and spamming companies that I know, who will in turn sell that info to hundreds, perhaps thousands, of other direct sales businesses like mine. Have fun!"

And then, a few minutes later, Hawke sent another message: "And no, asshole, I can't be jailed for spamming. Read the federal laws. It is a civil offense whereby you can sue me for $500 per message. I make $25,000 each weekend doing this. It will cost you more than $500 just to hire a good civil attorney. Go for it pal. I can afford it!"

Walker's comment about sending Hawke to jail had been a bluff. To his knowledge, there was no federal law prohibiting junk email. But he was astounded by the spammer's defiance and wondered whether there was a way to combat him. He decided to post a message on Usenet, where he had gotten good advice in the past about fishing and vacation questions.

"Can anyone help?" he asked on June 26, 2000, in a newsgroup called alt.spam.

An anti-spammer named Peter promptly came to Walker's aid. He looked up the domain registration record for resalehighway.com. Peter told Walker that the site was registered to a Winston Cross in

Spartanburg, South Carolina, who listed an email address of
hawkedw@charter.net.

On Peter's suggestion, Walker emailed a complaint to Charter
Communications, the cable company that provided Cross's Internet
account, as well as to Blueberry Hill Communications, the California ISP listed in the domain record as the host for resalehighway.
com. On both complaints, Walker sent a carbon copy to Cross's
charter.net address.

Peter warned Walker not to expect a quick response and said
that ISPs sometimes need to be reminded before they take action.
But just the next day, Walker received a terse email from Cross, a.k.a.
Hawke. "You're on the remove list, punk. You won't receive any more
ads," wrote the reluctantly repentant spammer. Walker was jubilant.

Hawke expected the incident would result in resalehighway.com
being shut down. But the site remained online and stayed nearly bulletproof to anti-spammer complaints for nearly a year. It even
escaped a nomination to the Mail Abuse Prevention System blacklist. That June, another Internet user who had received Hawke's
Banned CD ads posted a complaint to Nanae. He said that MAPS's
operators had declined his nomination on the grounds that selling
spamware was not sufficient reason to blockade the site. In reply,
anti-spammer Alan Murphy agreed the site's IP address should be
blacklisted, but he advised the user that there wasn't much more he
could do. "Move on to the next target," wrote Murphy.

After reading the complaints about MAPS's inaction regarding
resalehighway.com, Shiksaa did some brief poking around at
Hawke's site. She might have put more time into investigating the
site and its operator, but the following day a much bigger object
appeared on the Nanae radar.

A Date with a Spam Queen

The newsgroup was abuzz with word that someone had apparently
hacked into the computers of a Tennessee spam operation known as

Premier Services, downloaded over one hundred megabytes of data, and posted some of the juicier tidbits at a site he entitled Behind Enemy Lines.

"If you are an anti-spammer looking for an inside peek at the world of spamming, you have just found Fort Knox!" wrote the hacker, who identified himself only as "The Man in the Wilderness."

The hacker's site included scores of pages of chat logs and emails between Premier Services's employees and customers. The messages detailed a variety of shady practices, including pump-and-dump stock scams and AOL password-stealing schemes. The hacker's site, originally hosted at an ad-supported service called FreeWebSites. com, also included an assortment of partially nude photos of some of the company's principals.

Prior to that day in June 2000, Premier Services and its owner, 35-year-old Rodona Garst, were unknown to most anti-spammers. But they would soon become the most notorious instance of retaliatory hacking since Hacker-X targeted Sanford Wallace.

According to the Man in the Wilderness's account of events, he had been the victim of a type of online fraud referred to by anti-spammers as a Joe-job. In early 2000, Garst had forged his domain name in the return address of one of Premier Services's spam runs. As a result of the Joe-job, the hacker's mail server was besieged by thousands of error messages generated by undeliverable addresses on Garst's mailing list. The hacker also received complaints from inexperienced anti-spammers who thought he was responsible for Premier's spam. The Man in the Wilderness said he contacted the ISP Garst had used to send the messages, and the provider responded by canceling Premier's account.

"For the spammer responsible, this was warning shot number one," wrote the Man in the Wilderness in Behind Enemy Lines.

But Garst subsequently sent two more spam runs through different accounts, both of which again used the hacker's domain in their return address.

"Normally I am too busy to be bothered with the everyday activities of a small time huckster, but this one was beginning to piss me off," wrote the Man in the Wilderness, who said he worked as an Internet technology consultant. Now determined to take matters into his own hands, he managed to capture one of Garst's spams shortly after it went out. Then, after analyzing the message's header, he identified the network address of the PC used to send the spam.

"Her luck had just run out," he wrote.

At that point, the Man in the Wilderness somehow found a way to hack into Garst's PC over the Internet. His first act was to delete the copy of 1st Class Mail, a program for sending junk email, from her hard disk. Then he downloaded numerous datafiles from the PC "to determine who I was dealing with."

After studying the files, the Man in the Wilderness determined that Premier Services was apparently being hired by a variety of firms to market dodgy offerings via spam, including college diplomas, credit repair services, government grants, and pornography. According to the hacker, Garst ran the business out of her home in Clarksville, Tennessee, coordinating a handful of associates located around the U.S. Over the course of a couple of weeks, the hacker "spread like a silent wildfire through Rodona's computer network" and hacked his way one by one into the company's computers.

"What I wanted," he explained, "was unrestricted access to the data on their hard drives, and computer by computer I got it."

The Man in the Wilderness uploaded over six megabytes of the purloined files to his Behind Enemy Lines site, including over two megabytes of log files of online chats between Garst and her five spamming associates. At first, many of the more technical readers of Nanae were skeptical. Something about the hacker's account of events stuck in their craw. He provided no details about how he had managed to break into Garst's computer but instead glossed over it with what sounded to them like a Hollywood account of hacking: "I silently came across the Internet from thousands of miles away and hacked my way into the spammer's computer."[3]

But the copious details in the stolen files convinced many that Behind Enemy Lines was not fiction. Included was an incriminating exchange of emails in late 1999 between Garst and a Texas man named Mark E. Rice. The messages discussed a stock pump-and-dump deal under which Garst would be paid $1,500 per million junk emails to send spam touting the stocks of four microcap companies. Rice authored the spams, which typically included fraudulent press releases about the companies and their prospects. Soon after Garst sent off a load of spam, Rice would sell large blocks of the stocks, hoping to profit from the uptick generated by the messages.

"The thing I like about emailing at night is that the rush in the morning is very good for a stock...And if we can keep the momentum going through out the day, we win," wrote Rice in an October email to Garst The email exchanges also indicated that Garst wanted to reap more from the scam than Rice's regular payment checks, sent to her via Federal Express. At one point she asked his advice in setting up a brokerage account so that she too could trade shares of the manipulated stocks.

"Since I have an inside of sorts it seems it would be wise if I purchased some stock that we are promoting. Do you have any recommendations?" she inquired.

Rodona Garst puzzled many spam fighters because she didn't fit their trailer-trash image of spammers. Garst and her associates lived in middle-class neighborhoods in three-bedroom, two-bath colonials. Like other white-collar office workers, they chatted about work, relationships, chocolate, their hair, and family. Shattering that veneer of normalcy, however, were the women's conversations about ways to defeat ISP spam filters or about places to find pirated ("cracked") spamware programs. They also freely traded tips on stealing ("fishing") AOL accounts from gullible users and on fudging their income tax returns.

The Man in the Wilderness acknowledged that the information he found could be quite embarrassing if made public. He also noted that he'd done some soul searching before deciding whether to post the files. But ultimately, he concluded, Premier Services had abandoned its right to privacy by conducting its business so unethically.

"So, without further delay, let's get brutal!" he wrote.

The Man in the Wilderness proceeded to post revealing photographs of Garst apparently pilfered from her computer. One depicted her from behind in a bathroom, wearing nothing but a T-shirt. The hacker had captioned the photo, "The Number of Freckles on Rodona Garst's Ass."

The second shot showed Garst in her office, pulling her shirt up to her chin and baring her chest. "Rodona's Breast Size" was the hacker's title. Another set of photos, labeled "A Date with a Spam Queen," displayed Garst's business associate, 58-year-old Shary Valentine. The photos showed Valentine posing in corny studio settings wearing a variety of teddies and other revealing outfits. Also included at the site were two erotic short stories also reportedly gleaned from Premier Services's hard disks.

The appearance of Behind Enemy Lines touched off a new debate in Nanae about the ethics of hacking spammers.

"While that is exactly what we all dream about, the way these spammers' plugs were pulled is NOT, repeat, NOT the way NANAEites should conduct business," wrote one newsgroup participant. But some spam fighters, fearing that Behind Enemy Lines might be forced offline, quickly "mirrored" (copied and republished) the site on their own web sites.

One of the first to publish notice of his mirror on Nanae, a Briton named John Payne, soon received email from Garst requesting that he take down the mirror. Payne responded by contacting her over AOL Instant Messenger.

"You do know I didn't have anything to do with the content, right?" he asked Garst.[4]

But she still seemed under the impression that Payne was somehow connected to the Man in the Wilderness.

"I intend to follow through with this legally, so any information you have would show your cooperation," Garst told him.

Payne reiterated that he had no information and that his mirror was just that—a copy of the original site. "I note that you've not yet disputed the accusations," he added.

Garst took nearly a minute to reply.

"An investigator is currently on the case to discover as much information about this as he can," she said.

Her response puzzled Payne. "About you, or the hacker?"

"The hacker obviously," she replied. "Direct email is not illegal and most of what he claims my company has participated in is totally off base."

Payne tried to get her to talk about how she acquired her mailing lists and other aspects of her business, but Garst was evasive.

"Gotta run…so nice to chat," she typed and signed off.

While Rodona Garst may have been eager to discover the identity of the Man in the Wilderness, anti-spammers seemed reluctant to investigate too energetically.[5] They were focused instead on a large file lifted from Premier Services and available at the Behind Enemy Lines site. According to the Man in the Wilderness, the 1.5-megabyte file, *antifile.zip*, contained a compressed archive of addresses of anti-spammers that Garst's gang was afraid to spam. The company apparently used it to "wash" its mailing lists so that spam fighters wouldn't receive Premier's ads and complain. Nanae readers downloaded the file and pored over it, searching for their email addresses among the more than 200,000 listed in the file.

"Wow, this is the first time I've been officially 'honored' by a spammer. Somehow I feel…dirty," said a spam fighter named Cynthia upon learning that she made the list. "I'm so proud, one of my spam-fighting addresses made the list, but none of my spam traps," wrote another Nanae participant, who, like many anti-spammers, had signed up for email accounts specifically in the hope that they would provide fodder for abuse reports.

Others saw the list as a sure sign that junk emailers were fearful of anti-spammers. "Someone went to a lot of effort to put together that list. If fighting spam was as ineffective as people claim, no one would go to the effort," was the conclusion of one anti-spammer.

Although Shiksaa had only been in the spam wars for little over a year, her AOL and Hotmail email addresses both made Garst's anti list. She realized that many of the addresses apparently had been compiled simply by harvesting Nanae addresses; even emails belonging to retired spammer Sanford Wallace and spamware vendor Andrew Brunner made the list. And a good portion of the roster seemed to have been compiled from previous compendiums of anti-spammer addresses and was thus out of date. Shiksaa's newest email, *shiksaa@etherboy.com*, which she had been using on Nanae since February, was not included. (She was given the account at Etherboy.com as a gift by its administrator, Dave Lugo, an admirer and longtime spam fighter.)

As a further sign that Shiksaa had become a veteran spam fighter, she was invited to join #Nanae and #Lart, two Internet Relay Chat (IRC) channels where anti-spammers could more privately trade quips and information. While Usenet had little of the immediacy of in-person conversation, IRC was often confusingly fast-paced, with comments from participants scrolling dizzyingly down Shiksaa's screen.

Sometimes, such as occasions facetiously known as Nanae Beer Nights, more than a dozen spam fighters, from all over the U.S. and Europe, would be in the chat room at the same time. It was on IRC that Piers Forrest, a 43-year-old computer technician from England, known on Nanae as Mad Pierre, began doting on Shiksaa. Usually all business on the Nanae newsgroup, Mad Pierre was a master of the humorously flirtatious IRC remark. In August, Shiksaa began using one of Mad Pierre's more memorable utterances in the signature line of her newsgroup postings: "I worship at the feet of Shiksaa…I'd worship higher up if the straps weren't so tight."

While Mad Pierre was not alone in his hyperbolic adoration—several of the male members of Nanae had jokingly been referring to her as the Spam Goddess—Shiksaa particularly enjoyed playing along with Mad Pierre. Once, after a spammer trolled Nanae, accusing antis of having no life, Mad Pierre sarcastically responded that the spammer was correct.

"Damn, you've got us bang to rights. We have no lives. None. At all."

To which Shiksaa responded, "Your life is the worship of *moi*."

But because of her investigative skills and dedication to anti-spamming, Shiksaa continued to be a magnet for harassment from bulk emailers, who sought her out on AOL Instant Messenger (AIM) or anonymously posted insults about her on Nanae. While she could handle the occasional run-in with kooks, Shiksaa was livid over a stunt pulled by Brunner in the late summer. As part of her self-education in the ways of spamming, she had downloaded a demo copy of CyberCreek's Avalanche spamware program. Her plan was to install and test it out. But as she was skimming the ReadMe file that came with the software, Shiksaa froze.

Near the bottom of the document, which invited users to contact CyberCreek with questions or suggestions, was a section called the Net-Nazi Hall of Shame. Below a disclaimer that stated that he was not responsible for "actions/misdeeds committed unto the following persons or entities," Brunner had listed Shiksaa's first name and her phone number. Beside them, Brunner had added an appeal to all the hundreds of spambags who would install his program: "If you have her address please drop us a note, as she is going to be the first Net-Nazi to be held accountable in a California civil court for defamation."

The spam goddess was now a target.

Bubba Catts and the Crank Callers

Brunner's legal threats didn't really worry Shiksaa. He had filed defamation lawsuits in small-claims court against three other anti-spammers, none of whom took the suits very seriously. But Shiksaa didn't relish the idea of spammers harassing her by telephone. Brunner had apparently captured her number when she called him on his cell phone the previous year. Now she had no choice but to contact Pacific Bell and get a new one. But as Shiksaa glanced again at Brunner's file, her face brightened, and she burst into laughter. That wasn't her phone number; Brunner had accidentally transposed two of the digits.

It was a classic Brunner gaffe. Just to be safe, Shiksaa went ahead and had the number changed anyway. But to show Brunner she wasn't worried about his threats, she published two new photos of him at her new web site, Chickenboner.com. (She had acquired the domain name the previous March when the original owner, an Internet businessman in New Brunswick, Canada, failed to renew the registration.)

Shiksaa got the photos from anti-spammers who had doctored a picture of Brunner that appeared in a *Fortune* magazine article about spam. In the first image, they grafted Brunner's head onto Rodona Garst's naked torso. The other depicted Brunner's head pasted onto the scantily clad body of a Louisiana-based spammer named Robert "Bubba" Catts. Shiksaa had stumbled upon the original Catts photo earlier that year in his AOL member directory listing. The stocky Catts smiled sheepishly, sporting only a pair of skimpy, flowered underpants. He had captioned the photo "This is a pic of me on a WILD NIGHT!!"

Like Brunner, Bubba Catts had become a favorite target for anti-spammer vengeance. He got his start in the spam business in 1997 at the age of forty, after purchasing some bulk email software and launching an ad campaign for a popular marketing scheme. The spams instructed recipients to send five dollars to each of four people listed in the email, including Catts, whose post office box in Shreveport was second on the list. Recipients were supposed to put their own name and address on the top of the list, bumping the fourth person off, and then send the list to as many people as they could. In his spam, Catts said the income he made from the program enabled him to quit his day job selling cars.

"I was not prepared for the results," wrote Catts. "Everyday for the last six weeks, my post office box has been overflowing with five-dollar bills. I am stunned by all the money that keeps rolling in!"

But soon Catts received something else in his mailbox: threatening notices from several states' attorneys general. Catts was forced to abandon the chain-letter scheme, but he was hooked on the spamming business. Soon he had installed four computers in his home office on Richmond Street, just a block off I-49 and the railroad tracks in the center of Shreveport, and was pumping out spam for items ranging from software and cigars to condominiums and cruise trips.

One night in late 1999 Catts was watching TV in his living room. His 12-year-old daughter was asleep in the room he kept for her when she lived with him (Catts was divorced in 1991).

The phone rang. It was some guy who said his name was John. He said he was sick of receiving junk emails from Catts, and he was on his way over to Catts's house with a friend.

"Me and my buddy Junior here, he's an awful mean drunk … he's been drinking all day."[6]

"And what are you trying to do now?" Catts asked.

"We're trying to get to your house. We're going to come down and whup your damned ass because you're sending all this shit email to us."

Catts rode bulls professionally for two years. He might have been short, but he grew up in the tough town of Cedar Grove in Caddo Parish and never lost a fight in his life. Still, he didn't want two drunken rednecks showing up at his doorstep.

"I aint sent nothin'," he said.

"Every God damned time I get on, I got fourteen fuckin' emails and I'm sick of this shit," John shouted into the phone.

"Well, I don't know who you're getting it from," said Catts, his tenor voice rising.

Then Junior's voice came over the line. It was louder and clearer than John's, as if he was on another phone. He didn't have John's southern accent either.

"Take a right. Take a right!" Junior stuttered into the phone.

Catts had an idea. "Does it say it's from Bubba Catts?" he asked John.

"No, it's got some bogus email address on it. Every time I try to reply to it..."

Bubba cut in. "Have you tried Jon Scott? He's the one does my bulk mailing for me."

John paused, as if taking in the information. "So, you don't do it yourself?"

"No, I pay him to do it."

Junior interrupted again. "Take a left. Take a left on Maryland."

"Are we anywhere near your house?" John asked Catts.

Maryland Avenue was just two streets over from Richmond. "You don't want to come over here, I'm telling you right now," warned Catts.

"Why not?"

"Because the sheriff lives next door. My little girl is here. And I will go next door and get him," said Catts rapid fire.

"Oh, well, you might have to," said John, a note of bemusement in his voice. "Because Junior here wants to whup somebody's damn ass."

"He don't want to come in this house, unless he wants to go to jail," said Catts.

"Junior, you don't care about going to jail, do you?" asked John. "He's been wanting to whup somebody's damn ass, and you're the only one I could think of tonight."

"Oh yeah, go get 'em," said Junior.

"We'll be there in a minute," said John. "You better have more than him, because there's at least two of us comin'."

"Well...well, that's fine," said Catts.

"O.K., here's Richmond!" shouted Junior. "Go! Go fast!"

Bubba hung up the phone, so he couldn't hear the chuckling on the other end of the line. He had just been the victim of a spam fighter's version of the TV program *Candid Camera*. A few weeks later, a recording of the conversation appeared on the Internet, joining other crank calls made to junk emailers at a site called Spammers Speak.

When anti-spammers heard the recording, they cackled with delight. Shiksaa especially enjoyed Catts's attempt to redirect the good old boys' wrath at Jon Scott. She'd had several encounters with Scott, who sold mailing lists containing millions of email addresses. One morning the previous year he had sent her an ICQ message that stated, "Let's get naked." Shiksaa forwarded the note to the Internet service provider that hosted Scott's web site, and requested that the ISP advise Scott to stop harassing her. Then, in an open letter on Nanae, she responded to his advances.

"You are on some serious psychiatric drugs if you would even think I would have any interest in seeing you naked, much less being in the same room with you," Shiksaa wrote.

Scott, a 40-year-old resident of Chico, California, seemed hurt by her response. He posted this reply: "Many of the people in this newsgroup have anger control problems. They have so little power and control in their own lives that they try controlling others...Susan, you have my deepest love and sympathy. May God bring calmness to your angry soul."

But Scott's attempt to take the moral high ground was short-lived. A few weeks later, he sent out a batch of spam that included Shiksaa's username, along with that of anti-spammer Frederick, in the headers. The messages advertised a home-based business opportunity. Technically, it wasn't a Joe-job, since Scott had added after their usernames the network address @ddt.net, a service on which neither spam fighter had accounts. But Frederick was unable to ignore the veiled attack. He fired off a note to the Federal Trade Commission, requesting that it investigate what he considered Scott's attempt to defame him and Shiksaa.

But Shiksaa had much bigger fish to fry.

cHapTer
4our

Spamhaus Takes on Sue You Net

Steve Linford, the operator of the Spamhaus Project, a blacklist of spamware vendors and the ISPs who host them, asked Shiksaa in October 2000 to join an elite team of spam fighters in a new project he was launching. Her mission would be to help compile detailed dossiers on the Internet's biggest junk emailers. The research would be published at Spamhaus.org as part of a pioneering effort Linford had dubbed the Register of Known Spamming Operations, or Rokso. His plan was to turn Rokso into an Internet hall of shame that would put pressure on shadowy spam operations by exposing them to the light of day.

More importantly, Rokso would provide Internet service providers with a much-needed clearinghouse for screening new customers. The Rokso list would include searchable records on each of the spammers, including descriptions of their junk email operations and spam samples, as well as contact information including aliases, business addresses, phone numbers, and email addresses. To be included on the Rokso list, a spammer had to have been thrown off at least three Internet service providers. To get off the list, a junk emailer simply needed to refrain from sending spam for at least six months.

Rokso wasn't the first effort to focus public attention on the Internet's egregious bulk emailers. In 1995, Alex Boldt, a mathematics graduate student at the University of California in Santa Barbara, launched the Blacklist of Internet Advertisers. Boldt compiled a small who's-who list of chronic Usenet and email spammers, including their contact information. But Boldt stopped regularly updating his list around 1997, and nothing permanent had arisen in its place—until Rokso.

While the Rokso list would eventually swell to over two hundred, the inaugural edition included just twenty-five spammers. Among them was Jason Vale, who had stopped sending Laetrile spams after the court order and instead had been blanketing the Internet with ads for products such as Willow Flower, an herbal treatment for urination problems and other symptoms of prostate disease. The first version of Rokso also had an entry for 29-year-old Ronnie Scelson, a junior high school dropout who led a group of spammers based in the New Orleans suburb of Slidell.

Linford coordinated the Rokso effort from his houseboat, moored off an island in England's Thames River. Forty-two at the time, with a trimmed grey beard and a full head of grey hair, Linford had a hip worldliness that differentiated him from the more nerdy spam fighters. Born in England, Linford had been raised in Italy, where his father operated a factory in Rome that produced industrial platinum. Linford studied photography in college, but he dropped out to pursue a career as a rock musician. His singing and songwriting attracted the attention of GM, an Italian record label, which signed him to a five-year contract. The Italian composer Ennio Morricone even used him as a vocalist on the soundtrack for the 1982 Roberto Faenza thriller *Copkiller*, featuring Harvey Keitel. But a few years later Linford had a falling out with GM over the direction of his music, and he decided to stop performing until the contract expired. In the meantime, he worked as concert manager for much bigger artists, producing shows for the likes of Pink Floyd and

Michael Jackson when they toured in Italy. He became an early user of Apple computers and was intrigued by how technology could revolutionize music production.

Linford decided in 1986 to move back to England, where he started a Macintosh software-development firm with his brother Julian, a talented programmer. Together they created UltraFind, a personal search engine utility capable of locating information in any Macintosh file. It sold briskly for nearly a decade, until Apple built a search tool called Sherlock into its operating software. As a result, Julian decided to return to Italy and take a job with the European Space Agency. Linford remained behind, morphing UltraDesign into an Internet design and hosting business.

It wasn't long before lots of junk email, much of it originating from Sanford Wallace's Cyber Promotions business, began arriving at Linford's various email accounts. He set up a special filter in Eudora, his mail program, to automate the task of forwarding incoming junk emails to the spammer's ISP, with a carbon copy to the Federal Trade Commission. Linford felt at the time that irresponsible ISPs were as much to blame for the emerging junk email problem as the spammers themselves. At one point, he added a signature line to the bottom of his Usenet postings that stated, "Spam would not exist if not for the greed of a few carriers. This site sends all spam back to spam carriers."

Although he stopped short of making it a personal crusade, Linford believed that if others joined in this task, ISPs could no longer ignore the spammers using their networks. In a 1998 posting to Nanae, he wrote, "Beneath Nanae is an iceberg so big it has the force to terminate spam simply by stuffing a terabyte of complaints up every ISP that gives you connectivity."

Linford was an early proponent of the idea of blacklisting Internet service providers and domains used by spammers. Although he was no fan of America Online, in early 1997 Linford found himself defending AOL's PreferredMail service against criticism from an anticensorhip activist. The AOL feature, a precursor to the service's current Mail Controls system, enabled users to turn on a filter that blocked all emails from a list of domains determined by AOL to be sources of spam.

"Although filtering them won't stop all spam, it will reduce it by ninety-five percent," Linford argued in a newsgroup for subscribers of Demon, a big ISP in the United Kingdom. "More importantly," he said, "the ISPs that stand up to Cyberpromo and Cybergen now ensure that the Net in a year's time is not just a load of spam with the occasional mail item."

In 1998, Linford continued to be a gadfly to what he considered spam-friendly ISPs. But his criticism of UUNET Technologies, one of the largest service providers on the Internet, almost cost him dearly. At the time, spam fighters on Nanae were keeping a running tally of the number of spam complaints unresolved by Virginia-based UUNET. As reports of abused dial-up accounts and open relays approached one million in March 1998, Linford and others grew frustrated with the firm's sluggish enforcement of its network abuse policies. To call attention to the situation, Linford created a banner graphic atop Spam Combat, a popular page at the UltraDesign site where he offered a variety of free, anti-spam tools. The image consisted of the UUNET globe-and-lightning-bolt logo, with the word SPAM inserted in the middle. Beneath the logo were the words, "We're behind 50% of the spam in your mailbox." Clicking on the banner would take visitors to the UUNET home page.

In the middle of March 1998, the fax machine in Linford's houseboat buzzed to life and slowly spat out a two-page letter from Taylor Joynson Garrett, UUNET's London-based legal counsel. According to the letter, UUNET was "extremely angry" at the blatant infringement of its rights and reputation, which the company considered libelous. The ISP's lawyers ordered Linford to immediately remove the banner or amend it so that it made no reference to UUNET. They also demanded that he turn over the offending graphic to them within forty-eight hours. If Linford failed to comply by the deadlines, UUNET would sue him in High Court.

Linford wasn't sure whether his little logo parody violated any laws, but he was quite confident of the facts behind his claim. So he decided to meet UUNET halfway. He removed the banner and replaced it with the words, "Yeah, ok, it's gone. But tell UUNET to stop spamming and start enforcing an AUP [acceptable-use policy]."

Linford figured that would send UUNET's lawyers on their way, but six days later Garrett faxed him another letter. Linford's site still infringed on UUNET's rights, said Garrett, who gave Linford until noon the next day to remove any mention of UUNET, "whether expressly or implied," from his site or risk further action from UUNET.

Linford thought the new demand was outrageous. He hadn't spoken of UUNET's threats on Nanae until this point, but he decided it was time other anti-spammers knew about the attempts to silence him. He posted a letter to the newsgroup with a link to a web page he had created that included scans of the UUNET threat letters. Soon, mirrors of Linford's "Sue You Net" page sprang up at other sites, and spam fighters began discussing a protest rally outside UUNET's headquarters. Linford was on the verge of making plane reservations to Virginia when cooler heads prevailed at UUNET, and the company pulled back its lawyers. Even better, UUNET shook up its network-abuse department, launched an initiative to close its mail relays, and finally began acting on its spam-related trouble tickets.

The banner incident was a big victory for Linford. Even though UUNET hadn't a legal leg to stand on, it did have significant legal funds, and Linford knew he might have gone bankrupt trying to defend himself. As he saw it, UUNET had decided that suing people who protested against its spam was a fast track to a public relations fiasco. Linford's innocuous little graphic had forced the Internet's biggest ISP to change course.

Following up on his success against UUNET, Linford moved his spam-fighting resources page to its own site, Spamhaus.org. For the first couple of years, it remained a relatively obscure resource known only to anti-spammers and their opponents. But soon it would become the tip of the spear in the fight against spam.

Shiksaa was thrilled by Linford's October 2000 invitation to join Spamhaus. After nearly eighteen months of haphazard spam fighting, much of it against chickenboners, she was eager to focus her energies in a more structured way against the biggest sources of spam. Perhaps it was just his British reserve, but Linford had always seemed to Shiksaa a voice of reason among the frequently strident participants on Nanae. Since he didn't charge for access to the Spamhaus information, Linford couldn't pay her or the handful of other volunteers for their efforts. But he did provide Shiksaa with a new, spam-filtered email address that she proudly used in her Nanae postings: *shiksaa@spamhaus.org*.

Shiksaa and the Pink Contracts

One morning in late October 2000, Shiksaa's phone rang, and the twangy New Orleans voice of Rokso-denizen Ronnie Scelson was on the other end of the line. Shiksaa had exchanged instant messages with him several times in the past. Scelson had dropped out of school after eighth grade, and it showed in his messages, which were full of misspellings and tortured syntax. But Scelson had the gift of gab and a rare trait among junk emailers: a tendency to tell the truth about his spamming tactics. So despite her revulsion for his line of work, Shiksaa found herself enjoying their online and telephone conversations.

"How would you like to see a pink contract?" Scelson asked her cheerfully that morning.

Taking its name from the color of the Hormel luncheon meat (and thus from spam), a pink contract was a tacit deal by ISPs to allow spammers to use their networks as long as too many complaints weren't generated. Scelson had previously boasted that big ISPs, despite their public posturing about opposing spam, were perfectly happy to provide services to him and other high-volume bulk emailers. Indeed, the previous June a spam fighter had reported on Nanae that a supervisor at AT&T admitted that the big company did business with spammers. But spam opponents had no hard evidence to prove the existence of such deals.

That was about to change with Scelson's offer to Shiksaa. He said he had a copy of a pink contract signed in February between AT&T and Nevada Hosting, a Delaware company run by one of Scelson's partners in spam. The contract would show, he promised, that AT&T was aware that Nevada Hosting would be providing web sites to spammers and that AT&T had agreed to look the other way.

Shiksaa was wary of Scelson's generosity and suspected there were strings attached. The previous April he had tried to blackmail anti-spammers into leaving him alone. If antis didn't back off, he threatened, he would give away his custom-made mailing program to other spammers for free. He claimed the program was able to squeeze messages past filters at AOL and pump spam out onto the Internet at the rate of eight million messages per hour.

"I would much rather find a way to work together than have this software all over the Web. Due to its power I've never sold it or given it away, but if the antis play unfair then so will I," Scelson had threatened.

When Shiksaa asked Scelson why he was willing to leak the AT&T pink contract to her, he told her the big ISP had "screwed over" Nevada Hosting—and, indirectly, him—by canceling the deal early and yet requiring that Nevada Hosting pay the remaining balance. Scelson's revenge would be to expose AT&T's secret collusion with spammers, and he could think of no one better than her to do it.

After Shiksaa agreed to examine the contract and share it with other Spamhaus volunteers, Scelson faxed it over. The one-page document had a title across the top that read, "Agreement Concerning the Operation of Bulk Hosted Web Sites" and was signed by a general manager at AT&T. Under the arrangement the two parties mutually agreed that Nevada Hosting would not send any spam through AT&T's gateways and that doing so would result in termination of services. But the contact specifically stated that AT&T knew Nevada Hosting would be operating web sites "spammed from other gateways" and that it would not terminate Nevada Hosting for hosting such sites.

Finally, anti-spammers had the smoking gun they needed. Shiksaa placed the contract in her scanner and made a digitized file of the document. Then she attached it to an email message to Linford. The next day, October 31, Linford put the contract up at the Rokso section of Spamhaus.org and sent email to AT&T's abuse department notifying the company that he was making the information public.

"This fax proves that AT&T knowingly does business with spammers," he stated, and requested that his message be forwarded to AT&T management. Linford also posted a copy of his letter on Nanae.

Within twenty-four hours, word of the pink contract was making front-page headlines at CNET.com and other technical news sites across the Web. In the articles, an AT&T spokesman tried to explain away the legal agreement as an aberration, stating that it was inconsistent with corporate policy and the work of a rogue salesperson. In a message on Nanae, a company official assured spam opponents that AT&T was making efforts to ensure that such deals never occurred again in the future. But the pink contract proved an embarrassment for AT&T as it propelled Spamhaus into the limelight for the first time. (While most of the news accounts quoted Linford, there was no mention of Shiksaa or Scelson, or how Spamhaus came into possession of the contract.)

Just as the furor over AT&T began to die down, the story gained new legs. An anti-spammer provided Shiksaa with a copy of a contract between top-tier backbone provider PSINet and a Scelson-run spam service called CajunNet. To Shiksaa and her cohort, this second contract was even more revealing of the profit-driven, back-room deals between ISPs and spammers.

Virginia-based PSINet, struggling financially at the time, had agreed to sell CajunNet a high-speed DS3 line, capable of data speeds over forty times greater than a cable modem or DSL line. The contract said CajunNet would use the line to send commercial emails "in mass quantity," with the exception of ads for pornography. In addition, PSINet would not be required to handle any complaints of spams originating from CajunNet's leased line; instead, the big ISP would forward all complaints to CajunNet. In recognition of the deal's high risk, CajunNet agreed to pay PSINet a nonrefundable deposit of $27,000.

Armed with a big pipe such as a DS3, a bulk emailer could pump out devastatingly large amounts of spam in a short time. Chickenboners who routed their spam through proxies and open relays were limited to sending a couple million emails per day. But with a dedicated DS3 circuit, a big-time spammer could crank out over 200 million spams in a twenty-four-hour period without breaking a sweat. The price was steep, however: Scelson reported to Shiksaa that he paid $40,000 per month for a DS3 circuit.

Shiksaa knew she could blow another spam-friendly ISP out of the water. But she and Linford were hesitant to publicize the PSINet contract. For one thing, the document was not signed, so there would be questions about its authenticity. Secondly, the spam fighter who obtained the contract admitted he stole it from one of Scelson's PCs. As Shiksaa understood it, Scelson had configured the computer to allow file sharing with others on his network. Using a Microsoft Windows command called *Nbtstat*, the anti-spammer was able to view the remote machine's networking apparatus over the

Internet and proceeded to access its hard disk. (Shiksaa had learned how to use *Nbtstat* as a tool for viewing the names spammers had assigned to their computer networks, but she felt it was unethical to go the extra mile and access files left exposed by the spammers.)

Shiksaa couldn't bring herself to tell Scelson about how she got the CajunNet-PSINet contract. So Linford decided to provide a copy to a reporter and see whether he could confirm its authenticity. Amazingly, both the ISP and CajunNet fessed up to the deal. PSINet issued a statement that blamed the contract on a junior salesman who overlooked the company's network abuse policy. And a CajunNet spokesman freely admitted that the company was a bulk emailer and previously had contracts with AT&T, Sprint, and UUNET. Seeing blood in the water, other news outlets picked up the story. Most quoted a letter Linford had written about the incident in a message to SPAM-L, an email list for discussing spam: "I think the ISP community as a whole needs to reexamine its ethics."

Pink contracts, however, would remain a big source of income for ISPs. In 2004, deals with known spammers would earn UUNET (renamed MCI Wholesale Network Services) the top position in Spamhaus's list of the most spam-friendly ISPs.

Mad Pierre's Homage to Shiksaa

One day after news broke of the PSINet pink contract, Shiksaa's not-so-secret admirer Mad Pierre posted a detailed spammer exposé on Nanae. The report represented the culmination of several days of work he had poured into researching a particularly persistent and cocky junk emailer. In some respects, it was Mad Pierre's homage to the consummate anti-spam researcher, Shiksaa. The dossier even cited some of the sleuthing groundwork she had previously laid.

Ordinarily, such an exposé would have spawned a long thread of discussion. But few spam fighters, Shiksaa included, paid much attention to his little opus at the time. They were still up in arms over the shady ISP deals and were busy congratulating Shiksaa for her role in exposing them. (Mad Pierre had showered her with his customary praise as well, exclaiming on IRC that she made him behave "like a testosteronal teenager in an AOL chat room"—a line that Shiksaa was quick to appropriate for use in her Usenet signature.)

Mad Pierre knew that the subject of his early-November exposé was just a penny-ante chickenboner compared to big-time Rokso spammers such as Scelson. But Mad Pierre felt someone in Nanae should focus on the brazen bulker who had been boasting, "I'm a college dropout. I work about two hours a day. I'm ambitious, but extremely lazy, and I make over $350,000 a year. Are you curious yet?"

"Well, I got curious," wrote Mad Pierre in his report.

The spammer proclaimed that his twenty-dollar CD not only included spamming software but could also enable Internet users to find confidential information on anyone in thirty minutes or less.

"I decided I couldn't wait that long," Mad Pierre wrote. Like other spam fighters before him, he began reviewing the registration information for PrivacyBuff.com and other domains mentioned in ads from QuikSilver Enterprises. But unlike even the incomparable Shiksaa, Mad Pierre laboriously did Internet searches on the various names and addresses listed in the registrations. After trying unproductive searches on James Kincaid, Winston Cross, and other aliases, Mad Pierre plugged the name "Davis Hawke"—the registrant of QuikSilver's resalepalace.com—into a search engine.

Mad Pierre hit pay dirt. He located a *Washington Post* article from August 1999 that mentioned Davis Hawke's leadership of the American Nationalist Party, the neo-Nazi group he started during his student days in South Carolina. The article noted Hawke's failure to coordinate the march on Washington by various white-supremacist groups. To be sure he had found his quarry, Mad Pierre ran other searches and pulled up corroborating data, such as the *hawkedw@charter.net* email account used to register some QuikSilver domains. Mad Pierre even found a small photo of Hawke from his

Nazi days, published at Overthrow.com, a site operated by a Hawke antagonist and anarchist named Bill White.

"Many of us have been accused of being spam Nazis, but it looks as though Davis Wolfgang Hawke really is one," Mad Pierre concluded with a flourish.

He also wryly noted that Hawke was Jewish and had changed his name in 1996 from Andrew Britt Greenbaum. "You can see his dilemma, can't you?" Mad Pierre asked in the article, which he titled "The extraordinary story of Davis W. Hawke."

If Mad Pierre had published his exposé twelve months earlier, Davis Hawke might have been ashamed for the world to learn of his transformation from a neo-Nazi leader into a spammer. But by November 2000, the only dilemma Hawke had was keeping his web sites and credit card merchant account from being shut down. He wasn't directly aware of Mad Pierre's article, but Hawke indirectly felt the impact. Verio, the Texas-based ISP, shut down PrivacyBuff.com in response to Mad Pierre's report, forcing Hawke to scramble to line up a new host. He had set up mirror sites, with names including MerchantAccept.com and CompuZoneUSA.com, at other ISPs to minimize the revenues lost from such outages. Hawke also tried to erase all evidence of his connection to South Carolina. His new spams listed a rented post office box in New York City and a phone number in Boston that were both forwarded to his new mailbox and phone in Cosby, Tennessee.

Hawke and Patricia had moved at the end of the summer to the eastern Tennessee town of 800, which was just across the mountains from their old place in Leicester, North Carolina. To keep them company, they acquired two dogs that were half wolf. Nemesis, a female, was Patricia's pet. Hawke named his male Dreighton.

Patricia, who had earned her black belt, was starting up her own karate studio in a strip mall off Dolly Parton Parkway in nearby Sevierville. Hawke carved out a niche marketing to people in circumstances similar to his. Across the top of the PrivacyBuff.com site were the words, "Because sometimes…you need a fresh start." The site offered a couple dozen printed books with titles ranging from *How to Make Fake Driver's Licenses and Other Identification Cards* to *Be Your Own Dick: Private Investigating Made Easy* and *How to Use Mail Drops for Profit, Privacy, and Self-Protection.* Hawke charged between twenty and thirty dollars per title for the books, which were originally published by a variety of small presses.

At the site, Hawke introduced himself to visitors. "My name is Dave. Yours is John Smith, right? Nice to meet you," he wrote with a wink. The welcome message, which was signed "Dave Milton," acknowledged that shoppers probably wondered why he was offering to sell "such outlandish, anti-establishment titles." The first reason was simple, he wrote. "We want to make money." But rather than marketing cars, real estate, jewelry, and other products, PrivacyBuff.com was interested in spreading the word about "the unjust system of government in America and throughout the western nations," said the note. Milton and his staff were libertarians, he said.

"We believe that Government has only two mandates: national defense and public works. All other functions should be performed by the private sector, including education, welfare…we also favor the legalization of all drugs, an end to all taxes, and the abolition of the criminal justice system," he said.

While espousing such an ideology was a convenient marketing ploy, Hawke was genuinely intrigued by libertarianism. In many ways, the antigovernment political philosophy now fit him more comfortably than the racist, neo-Nazi views he had embraced during college. Starting as early as his freshman year in high school, Hawke grew disillusioned with the U.S. government. The catalyst was when international chess champion—and Hawke's personal hero—Bobby Fischer was charged by the U.S. in 1992 with defying a trade embargo against Yugoslavia. Fischer's crime consisted of traveling to the war-torn country to face Boris Spassky in a rematch of their 1972 meeting, which many had referred to as the "chess match of the century." Ignoring a cease-and-desist letter from the Treasury Department, Fischer won the match and a prize of $3.3 million but was immediately forced into exile when the U.S. issued a warrant for his arrest. (Fischer didn't help his case by boasting at a news conference before the match that he hadn't paid any federal income taxes for sixteen years.)

Around the same time, Hawke also latched onto Texas millionaire Ross Perot, who was making his bid for President. Perot had tapped into the national distrust of politicians and dissatisfaction with Washington bureaucracy, and in the summer of 1992 he was polling neck and neck with candidates Bill Clinton and George H. W. Bush. That autumn, Hawke arrived at the high school early to stand, usually alone and sometimes in the rain, with his Perot For President sign. Although Perot received an impressive 19 percent of the popular vote, Hawke was crushed when Bill Clinton won the general election.

Hawke had come to believe that spamming was a profession ideally suited for an underground economy free from government regulation and taxes. So, too, did lots of other Internet users. The best-selling title offered by QuikSilver wasn't *How to Start Your Own Country* or *SCRAM: Relocating Under a New Identity*, although each did pretty well. Hawke's top item was *The Spambook*, a kit that included an eighteen-page booklet he had found on the Internet along with an eight-page manual he authored himself: *Seven Days to Spam Success*.

Hawke's prose in *Seven Days* was clear, personable, and persuasive. Not surprisingly, the manual said writing good ad copy was the crucial element of spamming success. Hawke offered several tips, ranging from the schoolmarmish ("Use active verbs rather than passive verbs") to the more psychologically oriented ("Ask rhetorical questions frequently in your ad copy, as it engages their mental processes and encourages them to keep reading"). *Seven Days* advised spammers to tell customers what they wanted to hear but not to exaggerate too much, or they would risk losing customers' trust.

"I make $25,000 per week, but I'd NEVER claim that the *Spambook* will allow my customers to make that much money, because no one would ever believe me. I set the figure at a few thousand dollars a week because you can grab that amount much easier," he wrote in the booklet.

To take in that kind of income, a bulk emailer needed the ability to accept credit card orders, Hawke advised. Credit card buyers were mainly impulse buyers, he explained. Although setting up a credit card merchant account was fairly easy, Hawke warned that hassles and frustration were part of the business, and one merchant account provider had tried to steal over $6,000 from him by withholding funds he had processed. "Never keep more than a few thousand dollars in a bank account attached to your merchant account," he advised. "Make frequent withdrawals to keep it below $2,500 or you will be sorry."

Seven Days also included practical advice on obtaining email lists. Hawke counseled beginning spammers to avoid purchasing addresses in bulk on CDs and instead to harvest them fresh from web sites using one of the two programs included with the *Spambook* kit. Steer clear of harvesting from newsgroups, he advised: "These emails are usually very poor with professional anti-spammers included in the mix."

The manual also addressed the issue of targeting America Online subscribers. "If a spammer is like a hunter, then an AOL user is a twelve-point deer with a red ribbon on its head," observed Hawke. In general, AOL customers were new to the Internet, less knowledgeable, and more likely to waste their money, he noted. But because of the big ISP's spam filters, it was almost impossible to send email into AOL. "I have tried many methods and failed," he admitted.

As for bulk-email software, Hawke said he personally used Cybercreek Avalanche. "I have found it to be the best product of its kind on the market," he stated, although he conceded the program was pricey and "recommended for the serious spammer." *Seven Days to Spam Success* also recommended Send-Safe, a fairly new mailer program written by Russian programmers. Hawke included a copy of Send-Safe with the *Spambook* kit, pointing out that spammers first needed to purchase credits at the Send-Safe web site in order to use the software.

Hawke had discovered the Send-Safe site that summer. He liked the company's mailer, which was faster and less prone to crash than other programs he tried. As a registered user of the software, Hawke was also able to access a customer forum at the Send-Safe site, which served as a sort of Chamber of Commerce for bulk emailers. On the message boards there, spammers traded mailing lists, advertised affiliate programs, and made other business deals. Even though they were his competitors, Hawke enjoyed networking with people who faced the same obstacles he was dealing with every day.

As autumn took hold in the Tennessee hill country, Hawke grew weary of his lone-wolf existence. Aside from Patricia, he had no real friends or even business colleagues in the area. He got back into playing chess, initially in games against himself and then versus opponents over the Internet. For his first over-the-board competition since high school, Hawke drove to Nashville in October, entering a small tournament held in a bungalow owned by the local club. He introduced himself as Walter Smith to the five players who showed up and filled out a card to register with the U.S. Chess Federation under that name.

In high school Hawke, under the name Britt Greenbaum, had achieved a USCF rating of nearly 2000, which put him in the top 10 percent of chess players nationwide. Hawke, playing as Smith, easily defeated his two weaker opponents in Nashville, both of whom had sub-1600 USCF ratings, and he came away the winner of the tournament.

After the victory, Hawke entered weekend tournaments every week for the next month. He placed third in a tournament in Crossville, Tennessee and then came in second in the Under-2000 section of the North Carolina Open. His playing there lifted his USCF rating as Walter Smith to 1949, just fifty points below his peak rating of 1998 as Britt Greenbaum, which he had reached when he was fifteen. Hawke had always wanted to break the 2000 barrier, and his strong return to chess at the age of twenty-two made that goal now look attainable.

Hawke's heady rise was stalled, however, by a couple of lackluster performances in November, including a twenty-first place finish at the National Chess Congress. He had traveled all the way to Philadelphia to compete in the tournament, beating his first two opponents in the Under-2000 section. But he lost his third match, and then drew against his final two opponents, whom he considered mediocre players. His USCF rating dropped below 1900 after the poor showing. But Hawke was determined to finish his comeback year with a flourish.

A week before Christmas, Hawke returned to Nashville and entered a quick-chess tournament, again using the alias Walter Smith. Players were limited to just fifteen minutes of clock time, which gave nimble competitors an advantage. The favorites in the field of thirty-two were Jerry Spinrad, a computer science professor at Vanderbilt University who entered with a USCF rating of 2069, and Dale Rigby, an English professor at Western Kentucky University who had a USCF rating of 2031.

After he beat his first two opponents, Hawke faced Rigby in the third round. Rigby regarded "Smith" with suspicion. The newcomer entered the tournament without an official USCF rating, yet Smith obviously was no beginner. Rigby's intuition told him Smith was a sandbagger who had competed in plenty of tournaments before, perhaps under a different name. His suspicions were confirmed when he struggled before ultimately defeating Smith.

After the loss to Rigby, Hawke rebounded, winning his next three games, including one against a high school player who had been in the hunt for the tournament lead. That set up a showdown between Hawke and Spinrad in the seventh and penultimate round. Spinrad had won all of his matches until that point, including one against Rigby. He had watched the unknown "Smith" play in the early rounds and spoke with him briefly between matches. Smith struck him as friendly but not at all intimidated by the field, extremely confident of his chess skills. Indeed, Smith jumped out to a small advantage as their match began. While Spinrad never felt in danger of losing, he was relieved when time ran out, and he was able to come away with a draw. Smith, however, seemed disappointed with the outcome, as though he had expected to defeat the stronger player.

In the contest's final round, Hawke pulled off a win over a solid player, which gave him six and a half points in the tournament. But Spinrad also managed to defeat his final opponent, earning him a total of seven and a half points and the tournament title. Still, Hawke, playing as Smith, took a surprising second place and a forty-five-dollar prize, while Rigby finished third, just a half-point behind him.

As a kid, Hawke would have reviewed each round of the competition with his parents on the ride back home. Chess tournaments had always been a family activity for the Greenbaums. Both parents usually traveled with Hawke to chess competitions, and not just as spectators. Even his mother, who had originally taught him the game, would enter the tournament in the novice section. Hawke's father was rated slightly higher than she, though he never came close to beating his son. But neither parent entered a chess tournament again after Hawke went off to college.

Following his strong showing in Nashville, Hawke drove home to Cosby alone. Then, on the evening of December 24, 2000, as families all around the country gathered to celebrate the holidays,

Hawke was in his trailer, using a UUNET dial-up account to send out a new batch of spam advertising the Banned CD. He knew some people might consider it a depressing way to spend Christmas Eve. But Hawke refused to indulge in such sentimental thinking.

The next day, a spam fighter filed complaints with UUNET and Hawke's web site host about the Banned CD ads. Hawke found out about the anti-spammer's reports a few days later. Now *that*, thought Hawke, was a depressing way for someone to spend Christmas morning.

Ch@pter
five

Tracking Empire Towers

There's no Guinness world record yet for the greatest number of spams received in a two-day period. But Karen Hoffmann would surely be a contender. A self-proclaimed soccer mom from the suburbs of Toledo, Ohio, Hoffmann was inundated with over 100,000 junk emails over the course of forty-eight hours in January 2001.

The messages advertised a multilevel marketing program run by an outfit called the Institute for Global Prosperity (IGP). At the height of the spam attack, ads bearing the subject line "Be Your Own Boss" flowed into her email server at the rate of over thirty per minute. Hoffmann tried to keep her head above water by quickly downloading and deleting the messages. But she unavoidably fell behind, and before long the volume of spam overwhelmed her account's storage capacity. Hoffmann's ISP disconnected its mail server to weather the flood.

Prior to the incident, the 41-year-old Hoffmann had never paid much attention to junk email. She had been operating Toledo CyberCafe, her web-page design business, from her home since 1996. A computer science major in college, Hoffmann had started the small company after the collapsing savings-and-loan industry took with it her career as a systems analyst for banks. She had openly published her email address on the web sites she designed for clients, so

Hoffmann was accustomed to deleting a couple dozen spams each day. But the onslaught that winter suddenly turned her into a vehement anti-spammer. She wanted to know who was responsible, and she wanted the criminals to pay.

For several days following the attacks, Hoffmann was unable to concentrate on real work for clients. While her son was at high school and her husband was at his office in Toledo, she cleaned up after the spam avalanche. After doing a bit of research, Hoffmann learned that she was the victim of a dictionary attack. The spammer's mailing program had latched onto her toledocybercafe.com domain and fired off thousands of messages to nonexistent accounts, such as *Dominiquex@toledocybercafe.com*, *Jl@toledocybercafe.com*, and *ashiab@toledocybercafe.com*. The technique might have made sense against a big ISP such as AOL or EarthLink, but Hoffmann had fewer than a half-dozen active email accounts using her domain. The spam attack was so damaging because her ISP had configured the domain's mail settings with a catch-all feature so that it accepted and forwarded to her main account any message sent to a toledocybercafe.com address.

Hoffmann had no prior experience in spam tracking, but drawing on her technical skills, she was able to trace the spam attack to dial-up accounts at UUNET. To conceal his identity, the spammer had used bogus return addresses in the messages' "From" lines. He also bounced them off open mail relays in China, Thailand, and Columbia. But after studying the message headers, Hoffmann was able to determine that the emails originated from a computer using numerical Internet-protocol addresses registered to UUNET. She copied the IP addresses into an email and sent it off to the big ISP's network abuse department.

A few days later, she followed up by phone and was able to get a UUNET representative to confirm that one of its customers in Clearwater, Florida, was responsible for the spam. But he said UUNET couldn't divulge the identity of the spammer without a court order. Hoffmann was close to tears as she pleaded with the rep to help her, but he was adamant.

Hoffman turned to Internet newsgroups for more information about IGP. From searching Nanae, she discovered that the company's sales associates had generated many spam complaints in recent years. Their messages invited recipients to buy expensive audiotapes or to attend costly seminars that provided investment advice. Prospects were also told they could pay a fee to become an IGP sales associate and earn commissions of up to $5,000 per week from new clients they brought in.

Officials from several states, including Massachusetts and Michigan, decided IGP was an illegal pyramid scheme. To protect consumers, the states issued cease-and-desist orders prohibiting IGP from operating in their jurisdictions. In an odd coincidence, just days after Hoffmann's email bombing, the CBS television newsmagazine 48 Hours aired an exposé on IGP that included interviews with several people who claimed the company scammed them out of thousands of dollars.

Hoffmann decided to notify the FBI's Toledo office about the spam attack, which she calculated had cost her at least $15,000 in billable time. A few weeks later, an agent showed up to interview her at her house, which was just down the road from a golf course in one of Sylvania, Ohio's better neighborhoods. With Hoffmann's husband—an attorney—at her side, the three of them sat in the living room, going over the stack of evidence she had printed out about the incident. The agent was very professional and seemed interested in her case. But he admitted his experience in spam investigations consisted of a one-week course at the FBI's Quantico training center. He said the Toledo office had only one Internet-connected computer and a lone agent working computer-related crimes, who spent most of his time disguised as a 12-year-old, chasing pedophiles in online chat rooms. But the agent promised to submit a report about Hoffmann's email bombing to the better-equipped Cleveland office for further investigation. He explained that he probably wouldn't be able to write it up right away, since he was going on vacation to Florida the next week.

Unsure about what to do next, Hoffmann wrote up her own report on the attack and posted it to Nanae. Besides recounting her technical findings and the FBI interview, Hoffmann used the report to pontificate a bit about spam.

"There are thousands upon thousands of small-business owners on the Internet that are vulnerable to this malicious, illegal, unauthorized use of their computer equipment," she wrote. "The spammers must be stopped now…By prosecuting to the fullest extent of the available laws, we can send a message that we won't allow these unscrupulous vermin to deny others the right to life, liberty and the pursuit of happiness."

That might have been the end of Hoffmann's brief spam-fighting career but for two things. First, she was subsequently hit by smaller but similar dictionary attacks. (Her ISP took several weeks to turn off the catch-all setting.) And then there was the warm way that anti-spammers received her report on the incident. A Nanae participant in Massachusetts named Steve complimented Hoffmann for being such a quick study.

"I can't tell you how much I respect you for following through on this knowing that your effort might just be a drop in the proverbial bucket. You ever get to Boston? Email me, dinner's on me," he wrote.

In early March 2001, Shiksaa patiently worked with Hoffman on another spam problem. Hoffmann was outraged after learning her ISP hosted a company that was selling Stealth Mail Master and was listed on Sapient Fridge's spamware-sites roster. Hoffmann fired off an email to Host4U.net, reminding the firm that berserk spamware had caused her recent dictionary attacks and warning the ISP to cut off service to the spamware vendor, or she would take her business elsewhere. Hoffmann posted a copy of the letter on Nanae, prefaced by the words, "I hope my fury is showing."

The next morning, Shiksaa gently told Hoffmann it was unrealistic to think Host4U would quickly give the boot to the spamware vendor. After all, Shiksaa pointed out, Host4U had been sluggish to respond to complaints about other bulk emailers, including Empire Towers, a major spam outfit listed in Rokso.

Hoffmann had never heard of Empire Towers, so she visited Spamhaus.org and reviewed the entry on the company. According to the Rokso listing, Empire Towers was "a hard-line stealth spamming operation" that "goes to elaborate lengths to hide spam origins and obfuscate URLs." 32-year-old Thomas Carlton Cowles headed the company, which also went by aliases including Leverage Communications, World Reach Corporation, and PopLaunch.

The last name rang a bell. In February 2001, Hoffmann had received several pornography spams that advertised sites with bizarre addresses full of numbers, percent signs, and other code. The messages also contained the first copyright notice she'd ever seen in a spam. It warned recipients against "attempting to infringe upon the copyrights of PopLaunch or attempting to harm the natural course of business of PopLaunch" by hacking, performing denial-of-service attacks, or publishing "the location of client sites."

That final bit about the concealed location of sites was apparently the raison d'être for the odd format of web addresses advertised in the spams. After Hoffmann posted a copy of the messages, an anti-spammer on Nanae using the alias Spamless explained how Empire Towers deployed an array of technical tricks, such as doubly encrypted JavaScript and browser redirects, to quickly shunt spam recipients through a series of temporary sites. When the user finally landed at the ultimate destination page, the browser's location bar, which ordinarily displayed the site address, would be hidden. In addition, the right mouse button would be disabled in an effort to prevent users from viewing the web page source code. All the sleight of hand was intended to make it extremely difficult for the average person to identify, much less complain about, the sites advertised in the messages.

Hoffmann poked a bit further into the Rokso record on Empire Towers. Under the section listing the company's known addresses, she was startled to read that it was based in her home state of Ohio. Empire Towers even maintained offices in Toledo, as well as one just across town from her in Sylvania.

Moments later, Hoffmann was in her blue minivan headed south on McCord Road. She was looking for 8505 Larch Road, the Empire Towers address listed in Rokso. After the frustration of being unable to positively identify the IGP spammer who had mail-bombed her, Hoffmann couldn't believe the ease with which she was closing in on one of the Internet's biggest spammers.

As she turned onto Larch Road and rolled slowly down the wooded street, Hoffmann spotted a mailbox just ahead with the number 8505. It belonged to a large, white house on the corner. The place had the look of a 1970s dream home gone to seed. Peeling paint on the exterior walls of the modern structure revealed large patches of grey stucco below. The bushes in the yard were over-grown and the lawn was unkempt. A camper trailer was parked in the side yard, and a Buick with weathered red paint sat beside the gravel driveway.

Hoffmann would later learn that the house was where Tom Cowles was raised and that his parents still lived in the place. But on that afternoon in early March, Hoffmann, who was just five-foot-two and had a tendency to avoid confrontation, didn't even come to a full stop, let alone get out of her van and knock on the house's front door. Instead, she drove quickly home and posted a note to Nanae about her findings.

"My God, what a small world," she wrote. Then Hoffmann fin-ished her post with a nod to Shiksaa, "Thanks for all you do."

Shiksaa responded by publishing the most current address she had for Cowles—which turned out to be a mailbox rental place in Toledo—as well as the man's physical description, which she had received from former Cowles business associates. Cowles, she reported, was around six-six, skinny, dark-haired, and geeky looking.

"If you see a similar creature strolling down the street in your town, it may be him," said Shiksaa, not realizing at the time that she was planting the seeds for what she would later consider Hoffmann's obsession with Tom Cowles.

Although Cowles and his company had begun to occupy a lot of her time, Hoffmann didn't consider herself overly preoccupied with them. True, a week later, she dialed the number listed in Nanae as Cowles's cell phone and hung up as soon as he answered. But she simply thought of herself as part of a team of people investigating one of the Net's biggest spammers. Since Hoffmann was local to the Empire Towers operation, she figured she could contribute in ways others couldn't. Shiksaa was using the Internet to dig up court records that showed Cowles had prior convictions in Indiana for burglary and in Ohio for passing bad checks. An anti-spammer named Mark had built a site that included details on how PopLaunch worked. Hoffmann, in turn, could physically visit the county courthouse or other places with information about Cowles and his gang.

To publicize the results of her Empire Towers investigations, Hoffmann put up a special page at her ToledoCyberCafe.com site. It also featured photographs she had taken of several area buildings used by Empire Towers, as well as links to other sources of information about the spam operation and to her Nanae postings about the IGP mail-bomb attack. Hoffmann's hope was that the local media or law enforcement would pick up the story if she handed it to them on a silver platter. But none ever did.

A few weeks later, Hoffmann learned from Shiksaa that Cowles was keeping a low profile as the result of a big falling-out with a partner-in-spam. Shiksaa told her that Cowles had been sharing a data center in Florida with Eddy Marin, a notorious spammer-for-hire added to the Rokso list the past December.

Marin's Boca Raton–based company, OptIn Services, was known to offer Internet users a free pornographic picture in exchange for providing a working email address. The trick enabled Marin to claim the users had "opted in" to receive his spam. Besides advertising porn sites, Marin had a history of sending spams touting Viagra and other drugs without prescriptions, as well as loans and cheap computer software.

Like Cowles, Marin had a criminal rap sheet. He was convicted in 1990 for cocaine trafficking and again in 1999 for money laundering. When Hoffmann learned about him in March 2001, Marin was halfway through his twelve-month money-laundering sentence at Eglin Federal Prison camp, a minimum-security facility on Florida's Gulf Coast, also known as Club Fed.

The partnership in 2000 between Marin and Cowles seemed like a synergistic deal at the time. Marin had been running Azure Enterprises, a webcam pornography business, out of an office in Pompano Beach, Florida, and wanted to get into serious bulk emailing. Cowles was interested in setting up operations in South Florida to be closer to his many clients in the area. Through a third party, the two men worked out a deal by telephone under which Marin would get unlimited access to Cowles's proprietary Massive-Mail spamware system. (Empire Towers normally charged $20,000 per month for each server capable of sending a million spams per day.) In exchange, Marin would give Cowles half of any revenue from the mailings. In addition, Marin agreed to share his computer data center in Palm Beach, including the facility's high-speed DS3 line, with Cowles.

Marin wasn't the first spam king Cowles had tutored in the business. A few years back, he had driven up to West Bloomfield, Michigan and spent a couple days teaching a convicted fraud artist named Alan Ralsky the ins and outs of bulk email. Soon, the 57-year-old Ralsky was big enough to earn a top spot on the Spamhaus Rokso list—and a lawsuit in 2001 from Verizon Online Services, which accused Ralsky of bombarding its mail servers with fifty-six gigabytes of spam in one day. (Ralsky and Verizon later settled the lawsuit, and Ralsky returned to spamming.)

But when Cowles arrived in Florida, he felt like he had been dropped into a pool of sharks. The clients who had seemed like respectable business people on the telephone turned out to be coke-heads, pornographers, and petty thugs. Everyone seemed to be looking for a scam. Even Marin was quick to use his new affiliation with Empire Towers to position himself as a big player in the email business. As the weeks went by, Cowles suspected Marin of trying to steal Empire Towers's clients by telling people he was one of the firm's executives. (Marin's lawyers later registered a Florida company named "Empire Tower Group" on Eddy's behalf.)

In December 2000, a disgusted Cowles finally decided to pack up his equipment and move back to Toldeo. With Marin incarcerated, and Marin's wife Kimberly running the spam operation, Cowles had an employee box up a load of servers and other computer gear from the shared data center and haul them to Ohio.

When Kim Marin found out, she filed a police report claiming that Cowles had stolen $16,000 of her company's equipment.

In June 2001, the Broward County Sheriff's Office told Marin an arrest warrant for Cowles was on its way, and she passed the word along via email to Shiksaa. (The two had previously exchanged messages about OptIn Services's spamming. Like Ronnie Scelson, Marin had impressed Shiksaa with her tendency to tell the truth about her business.)

"Rest assured that this scum bag will be around for only a limited time," wrote Marin. "Once they issue arrest warrants he will be extradited and held without bond. A day I look forward to."

When Shiksaa posted the email to Nanae, with Marin's name redacted, spam fighters chuckled at the spammer soap opera. Meanwhile, Hoffmann updated her Empire Towers site with the new information. Little did she know that her preoccupation with the company and its founder would eventually lead her right into the crossfire of the spam wars.

Terri Tickle Descends on Nanae

Just as Hoffmann was launching her Empire Towers page in April 2001, an anti-spammer who called himself Rob Mitchell was putting the crowning touches on a spammer-tracking web site he had been building for three years.

Mitchell was also considered obsessive by some Nanae participants for his painstaking research into the subject of his site: a chronic spammer who used the online nickname "Terri DiSisto" and claimed to be a female college student in Massachusetts.

Unlike most junk emailers, DiSisto wasn't littering the Internet in hopes of selling something. Instead, her ads offered payment in the form of cash and computer or audio equipment to young men between eighteen and twenty-three who mailed her videos of themselves being tickled.

DiSisto's bizarre story began around 1996, when she started spamming obscure newsgroups including alt.sex.fetish.tickling with her ads. "No sex or nudity are ever wanted in my videos," stated the spams. "I just want to see guys tied up and mercilessly, relentlessly TICKLED!" DiSisto claimed she enjoyed tickling as a hobby and was not interested in real-life encounters with her video subjects.

"I have a boyfriend, full cadre of friends, and plenty of guys to tickle already. I AM NOT LOOKING TO MEET OR TICKLE ANY GUYS ENCOUNTERED FROM CYBERSPACE!" stated the ads. College-aged men who stepped up to the offer were told to send the finished products to post office boxes in New York or Massachusetts and were given elaborate instructions on how to produce the videos.

"When laughter begins, the tickler must ask the question, 'How ticklish are you here?'" explained DiSisto's instructions. "The tickled guy—while still being tickled—must respond in as much of a complete sentence or sentences as possible (e.g., avoiding responses like 'very' or 'not too much' in favor of 'I'm totally ticklish under my arms...'). No one- or two-word answers."

DiSisto also detailed her offer, as well as excerpts from videos and audiotapes she had received, at her web site, tickling.com. The site featured a photograph of an attractive young blonde woman, purportedly DiSisto, in an over-the-shoulder, yearbook pose.

In a misguided effort at target marketing, DiSisto began repeatedly posting her ads in newsgroups frequented by young men, such as rec.sports.paintball and rec.music.phish, a discussion board for fans of the rock group Phish. To avoid complaints that her messages were off topic and inappropriate, DiSisto posted offers of free tickets to Phish concerts in New York City to qualified young men who sent her videos.

But participants nonetheless began to complain about DiSisto's flagrant violation of newsgroup etiquette. As the complaints piled up, anti-spammer Morely Dotes declared a Usenet Death Penalty against DiSisto in 1997, which meant that newsgroup administrators all over the Internet would immediately cancel any of her postings to Usenet.

Consumed by a belief that she had a right to act out her fetish anywhere in cyberspace, DiSisto began to fight back.

First, she started indiscriminately spamming her ads to email users all over the Internet. Then she dropped "binary bombs"—encoded messages designed to flood and disrupt a discussion group—on rec.music.phish and other forums where regulars had told her she was unwelcome. DiSisto also retaliated directly against individuals who griped about her tickling ads, deluging them with thousands of emails over the course of a few hours. She similarly used email bombs to take revenge on people who had second thoughts after agreeing to make videos for her.

When a Massachusetts high school student named Sean Gallagher stopped sending her videos after he graduated and went off to college, DiSisto bombed his personal email account and that of Gallagher's friend, who was attending Suffolk University in Boston. DiSisto similarly bombed the email account of Suffolk administrators, forging the messages so they appeared to come from Gallagher's friend. The attacks completely disabled Suffolk's email system on three occasions. Similar retaliatory bombings knocked out the mail servers of at least two other universities.

Rob Mitchell was dragged into the bizarre world of "Terri Tickle" in early October of 1998. Thirty-nine at the time and a public school teacher in Huntsville, Texas, Mitchell had heard about DiSisto's spamming and email bombings on a web-based message board. In a posting on his own board, which Mitchell had created for discussions of humorous fiction, Mitchell criticized DiSisto for harassing people who had no interest in providing her videos.

Somehow, DiSisto learned about Mitchell's comments and decided to retaliate. She sent thousands of spams with the subject line, "A message board for TICKLISH GAY GUYS." The body of the messages invited recipients who "would enjoy conversing and sharing stories/experiences involving tickling" to visit a web address—Mitchell's—listed in the spam.

Within an hour, complaints began appearing on Mitchell's board from people livid over receiving the spam. In the course of an afternoon, people posted over 200 angry comments. Meanwhile, reports about the spam were appearing on several Usenet newsgroups, including alt.kill.spammers. The next day, when Mitchell tried to access his board, he learned that the ISP hosting the service had terminated his account.

That was when Mitchell became DiSisto's most formidable opponent and an ardent anti-spammer.

Over the course of nearly three years, Mitchell tussled with DiSisto in newsgroups and eventually over IRC chats and emails.

As he tried to warn Internet users about the dangers of getting involved in DiSisto's fetish, she publicly accused him of being gay and being jealous of her video collection. All the while, Mitchell was compiling evidence of her spamming and other Internet abuses. He studied every DiSisto email message header he could get his hands on and determined that she used accounts with at least sixteen different ISPs to send her ads and her mail bombs.

Mitchell posted his findings to Nanae and other groups under the title "Terri DiSisto: a History in URLs." Yet his initial reception in Nanae was decidedly hostile. Many anti-spammers considered both DiSisto and Mitchell kooks cut from the same cloth.

"Why don't you just marry her or shoot her or do something else reasonable?" suggested a veteran anti-spammer who used the online nickname Rebecca Ore. "Really, we know she's bad. Just some of us think there are spammers who are several orders of magnitude worse," Ore added.

Mitchell realized that DiSisto was a relatively small-time spammer who bulked out messages by the tens of thousands, not by the millions like some of the big players. But her crimes went well beyond spamming and made her, in his opinion, one of the worst individual abusers of the Internet.

But that argument mostly fell on deaf ears in Nanae. Even Steve Atkins, a veteran spam fighter and creator of the SamSpade. org site, which Mitchell relied on to analyze and track DiSisto's spams, dismissed his explanation: "Bollocks…You just have a thing about tickling."

Eventually DiSisto began visiting Nanae and became a regular participant. She alternated between trying to engage anti-spammers in rational discussions about her online behavior and taunting them with S.S. *Titanic*–derived metaphors about their inability to get her web site disconnected for more than a few days at a time.

"Tickling.com remains, I assure you, UNSINKABLE," DiSisto bragged in a January 2000 posting to Nanae. "But like any great ship," she added, "there can be periodic difficulties in the engine room."

Shortly afterwards, DiSisto announced that she had located two television production firms in California that were making the videos she wanted. As a result, she claimed she no longer would advertise for tickling videos via email or Usenet spam.

"There is NO NEED to look for guys randomly out here in cyberspace. I haven't done it in months. I don't intend to do it any-time soon. I think my disappearance from the spam scene deserves notice," she wrote.

If DiSisto believed the public announcement of her retirement from spamming would somehow erase her past, she was wrong. In fact, her Internet notoriety had already caught the attention of *Reader's Digest* magazine, which planned to include her in a forth-coming article about online harassment. Hal Karp, a reporter for the magazine, contacted Mitchell that January after encountering his "History in URLs" postings to Nanae.

Karp said the story would focus on a group called Cyber Angels, which had assisted one of DiSisto's mail-bombing victims. As Mitchell traded notes with Karp, he sensed the reporter was sitting on information that would blow the DiSisto case wide open. But Karp was keeping his cards close to the vest, and at one point he even said he had to be careful so as not to jeopardize an investigation by law enforcement.

When the April 2000 issue of *Reader's Digest* was published, Karp's article didn't cite Mitchell or his Nanae postings. Nor did it mention tickling.com or the surname DiSisto, referring instead only to "a woman named Terri." According to the article, the woman cyber-stalked a young Internet user, pseudonymously named Gary, hoping to get him to sell her a video of himself bound and tickled. When Gary refused, she bombed him with over 30,000 emails. Then, one night as Gary was discussing his situation in a chat room, someone claiming to be a Cyber Angel offered to help him track and research his stalker.

"The hunter was now the hunted," wrote Karp, who reported that the anonymous Cyber Angel helped Gary uncover some shocking information. According to the article, "he learned that Terri was not a female college student, but a man...One night Gary tracked Terri online and revealed what he knew. The harassment screeched to a halt."

The article left Mitchell stunned. All along, he had occasionally wondered about DiSisto's gender, but how was Gary able so quickly to dig up information that Mitchell and others had failed to find over several years?

While unsatisfying to Mitchell, the article gave him hope that DiSisto was about to be publicly unmasked. Surely if Gary knew her real identity, it would just be a matter of time before federal authorities would act on the information. To assist in that process, Mitchell gathered up his "History in URLs" pages from Nanae and published them at a web page he created, which he entitled "Project Iceberg."

What Karp hadn't revealed in his article was that DiSisto's victim Gary had provided the reporter with an archive of electronic files apparently stolen from DiSisto's computer by a hacker in late 1999. The files included a trove of incriminating data such as a resumé bearing DiSisto's true name and address, a file containing her social security number, and correspondence and other personal documents. Also contained in the archive was a newsgroup posting Mitchell had made with instructions on how to report DiSisto for spamming.

Karp hadn't disclosed the information, or how he obtained it, primarily because of the liability concerns of the magazine's lawyers. But he handed over the files, as well as a pile of other evidence he had dug up on DiSisto, to the FBI shortly after his article was published.

Meanwhile, DiSisto tried in public to spin the *Reader's Digest* article as a work of fiction aimed at entertaining readers.

"I think you'll find the overall impact of the article rather disappointing," she told Nanae participants.

But clearly the piece had staggered DiSisto. Soon after it appeared she stopped posting to Nanae and retreated instead to newsgroups devoted to tickling, including one she had created herself, alt.multimedia.tk.terri-disisto.

Mitchell was ready to move on. He turned his attention to spamware vendor Andrew Brunner, on whom he composed a series of Nanae postings familiarly entitled "Andrew Brunner: A History in URLs." The articles documented the combative Brunner's online machinations since 1998. For his efforts, Shiksaa offered Mitchell a new email address using her domain: *spicy_crust@chickenboner.com*.

But Mitchell had not heard the last from "Terri Tickle."

Hawke Rips Off Dr. Fatburn

In their battles against junk emailers, anti-spammers constantly remind themselves of a bit of folklore known as "The Three Rules of Spam":

Rule #1: Spammers lie.

Rule #2: If a spammer seems to be telling the truth, see Rule #1.

Rule #3: Spammers are stupid.

In January of 2001, Davis Hawke got a rude introduction to Rule #3. He had accidentally left a sensitive file exposed at one of his web sites. When Shiksaa stumbled upon it and announced her discovery on Nanae, a fellow anti-spammer cried out, "Rule number three shining bright!"

Shiksaa had been poking around at CompuZoneUSA.com after someone on Nanae called attention to Hawke's *Spam Book* ads, which included a link to the site. Shiksaa had taken to referring to Hawke on Nanae as "that neo-Nazi idiot" or "the creep Mad Pierre exposed." So she was pleased to discover Hawke's server had been improperly configured and allowed any Web surfer to view files not intended for the public. (She had used the same trick two years before to find unprotected customer order logs at a site run by computer seller and convicted stock manipulator Glenn Conley.)

Shiksaa didn't uncover any order logs at CompuZoneUSA.com, but she did stumble across something known as a file transfer protocol (FTP) log. It included a list of over two dozen web sites operated by Hawke, most of them previously unknown even to anti-spammers such as Mad Pierre, who had been tracking Hawke closely.

Hawke wasn't the first spammer to fall victim in that way to Rule #3. In the past, the discovery of FTP logs had helped anti-spammers notify ISPs that they had a chronic spammer in their midst. And this time was no different. An anti-spammer volunteered to report all of the sites on Hawke's FTP log. A few days later, he proudly announced "Nuked and paved!" after the ISP hosting CompuZoneUSA.com shut down the site.[1]

It wouldn't be the last time Hawke was susceptible to dangerous lapses in his site security. But on this occasion, he was able to shrug it off without major damage. Following some downtime, he lined up new ISPs to host his sites. Soon, the refurbished CompuZoneUSA.com would become the online storefront for his newest spamming endeavor: androstenone pheromone concentrate.

Hawke had first heard about pheromone concentrate from the discussion forums at the Send-Safe spamware site. A company in Kansas called Internet Products Distributors had been spamming pheromones for nearly four years. The owner of the Wichita firm was looking to get out of spamming and instead wanted to wholesale the compound and other herbals to "bulkers," a term many spammers used to describe themselves.

Androstenone came in little bottles and was worn like cologne. The substance was essentially odorless, despite that fact that trace amounts are present in human sweat. But according to the supplier, wearing androstenone concentrate would make any guy into an instant babe magnet. It supposedly caused a special receptor in a woman's nose to send a powerful signal to her brain, announcing the wearer as a highly desirable sexual partner.

Hawke decided to buy a couple cases of concentrate and see how well it sold. He paid just over five dollars per bottle and planned to sell them for twenty-nine dollars each. Hawke wasn't crazy about shipping and handling the little glass vials. But it was time for a change. The *Spam Book* and the Banned CD he'd been offering from PrivacyBuff.com were profitable, but the sales volume had stalled, and the books about becoming a private investigator and other topics weren't selling at all.

Hawke had a feeling androstenone could take off, though. As he was writing the ad copy, he imagined some lonely guy just out of college, sitting at his computer, looking for love in all the wrong places:

> *In the 80's, you could visit your local bar, have a few drinks, and expect to go home with a lady. Times have changed since then, and these days picking up a woman is not so easy. Unless you're a body builder or part of the "in" crowd at college, your chances for finding the woman of your dreams are rather dim. And if you're the least bit shy about making the first move, you can forget about it. Until now...*

The ad continued for several paragraphs. In strategic places Hawke had sprinkled a call to action ("Order Now!") along with a hyperlink to his revamped CompuZoneUSA.com site. For readers who still needed convincing, the copy continued:

> *How many times have you walked past a gorgeous woman, looked into her eyes, and hoped she would notice you? If you're like most people, the answer is TOO MANY. With Androstenone Pheromone Concentrate, women will be irresistibly drawn to you without knowing why. Wearing human pheromones is like cheating because they simply CAN'T resist you.*

Hawke fired off a couple hundred thousand spams for andros-tenone in March. They carried the subject line, "Turbo charge your SEX life! Attract women FAST!"

The stuff moved quickly. Hawke sold out his supply in a week and had to get a rush order from the supplier to restock. He considered charging more for the pheromones, but from experience he had learned that there was a sweet spot in pricing spamvertized products. Even if Internet shoppers suspected you were selling snake oil, they'd whip out the plastic and take a chance as long as you kept the price under thirty dollars. Another plus to pricing right was that most people would just chalk it up to experience if the product arrived and didn't work as advertised. But if you charged too much, they'd be lining up to get their money back.

For Hawke, selling pheromones was his way of cashing in on the sex-starved people who seemed to flock to the Internet. He had briefly mulled over the idea of sending ads for pornography sites. The market for digital images of naked people was huge, with sex sites among the biggest revenue generators on the Internet. (The domain sex.com itself was said to be worth sixty-five million dollars.)

But compared to the Publishing Company in a Box and other e-books, porn spam generated many more complaints. Plus, you couldn't rip off someone's porn content for very long without expecting trouble. Porno producers policed their copyrights, and some of the sex sites, he'd been told, were connected to organized crime. Hawke did not want to be messing with them.

On the other hand, porn site operators made going to work for them very easy. They had created affiliate programs that were advertised heavily on the message boards at the Send-Safe site and at BulkBarn.com, a spamming forum Hawke joined in early 2001. Spammers could earn commissions of between ten and twenty dollars for driving a new customer to a porn site.

Bottom line, being a porn spammer meant being a middleman. And that was something Hawke never wanted to do. He was a leader, not a follower. But most importantly, spamming on commission ran against his business strategy.

As Hawke saw it, the way to stay off the Spamhaus Rokso list and the Realtime Blackhole List run by Mail Abuse Prevention Systems (MAPS)—not to mention off the radars of regulators and anti-spam litigators for ISPs such as AOL—was to keep his volume of spams as low as possible. He could do that and still make a lot of money if his net income from each spam was as high as possible. Ensuring that his mailing lists were clean—free of undeliverable addresses and those of anti-spammers—was one way to keep the response rate high. But beyond that, the best way to maximize profits with the least amount of spamming was obvious: efficiently sell his own unique, high-margin products. It was boutique spamming, and it meant walking away from spammer-for-hire jobs.

After his quick success with pheromones, Hawke decided to try another product in the herbal-pharmaceutical niche. At the time, diet pills were all the rage with many bulk mailers, but Hawke was justifiably cautious. The U.S. government had already shown its willingness to prosecute online marketers of weight-loss products. The Federal Trade Commission (FTC) had been running a sting called Operation Waistline. As part of the FTC's crackdown, seven companies had agreed in 1997 to pay a total of nearly a million dollars to settle charges of deceptive practices.

The agency followed up in 1999 with an unusual program to educate Internet users about online scams. The FTC mocked up a convincing web page for a fake weight-loss product called NoriCaLite. The ads promised to help users shed thirty pounds in a month. But clicking the site's ordering link pulled up an FTC-created page with the title "You Could Get Scammed!" It warned users to resist "the false and deceptive advertising claims made by many so-called 'weight-loss' products."

Still, by 2001 the Internet remained awash with ads for diet pills. Even eBay was full of them. During a visit to the auction site

Hawke noticed a particular glut of ads for an herbal weight-loss product called Extreme Power Plus. The pills sold for thirteen dollars per bottle and contained a mixture of over a dozen herbs. The active weight-loss ingredient was ma huang, a Chinese herbal stimulant also known as ephedra. The pills were being offered by distributors working for a company in Louisiana called Dutch International Products. Dutch had built a multilevel scheme to market Extreme Power Plus and a handful of other herbal remedies, including Extreme Colon Cleanser and Extreme Coral Calcium.

Hawke had no desire to be a foundation stone in a pyramid scheme. But he was eager to try spamming diet pills. So he made arrangements to purchase some in bulk from Peak Nutrition, a supplier in Syracuse, Nebraska. In place of ma huang, Peak's weight-loss pills contained what it called lipotropic fat burners. The ingredients supposedly produced none of the jitteriness and other side effects of ephedra. Hawke ordered a couple of cases of the ninety-tablet bottles and started working on an ad.

To speed things up, Hawke went to eBay and downloaded a web page containing the auction listing for Dutch International's Extreme Power Plus. He made a few customizations to the ad, such as in pricing. He charged twenty-nine dollars per bottle, almost a twenty-five-dollar premium over what Peak charged him. Hawke also added hyperlinks that would take buyers to his ordering site. To capitalize on the work others had already done promoting the brand, he swapped out the words Extreme Power Plus with a name confusingly similar: Power Diet Plus.

The original ads had included testimonials from satisfied Extreme Power Plus customers, which Hawke modified only slightly. This led to some contradictions with the rest of his ad that Hawke overlooked. In one testimonial, a happy Power Diet Plus user named Sheryl told how her doctor proclaimed that ma huang was perfectly safe. Yet higher up in the ad, Hawke boasted that Power Diet Plus, unlike "the other stuff," doesn't contain the stimulant.

In April of 2001, Hawke fired off his first batch of spams for Power Diet Plus. "Lose 80 pounds by June GUARANTEED! #1 Diet Pill!" they said. What Hawke didn't know as he pushed the send button was that he was about to stomp on the toes of George Alan Moore, Jr., a Dutch International Distributor.

Moore lived in Linthicum, Maryland, and referred to himself as "Dr. Fatburn." He had been selling Extreme Power Plus via eBay and his own web site, UltimateDiets.com, for a couple of years. Unbeknownst to Hawke, Dr. Fatburn had hidden a digital watermark in the source code of the web page Hawke had copied from eBay. To prevent other eBay sellers from stealing his ad copy, Dr. Fatburn had inserted the words "This diet ad is property of UltimateDiets.com" in white-on-white text in several places within the ad. When casually viewed with most web page editors, or with an email software program such as Microsoft Outlook, the watermark was invisible. But it was plain to see for anyone who scoured the source code of the ad.

Anti-spammers often examined the source code of spammer web sites and email messages in their quest for clues, and they were quick to notice the reference to UltimateDiets.com in Hawke's ads. As copies of Hawke's Power Diet Plus ads began showing up in their email inboxes, some fired off complaints to the Florida ISP hosting Dr. Fatburn's site. In turn, the ISP forwarded the messages to Dr. Fatburn.

Prior to selling diet pills online, Dr. Fatburn had made money through occupations such as delivering pizzas and selling collectible sports cards and autographs. His new weight-loss business was doing nicely, and he intended to keep it that way. In the eighteen-plus months that he had been marketing diet pills, Dr. Fatburn had never resorted to bulk email. That's not to say he hadn't contemplated it. In 2000 he purchased on eBay a bulk-emailing program capable of sending 100,000 messages per hour. But Dr. Fatburn didn't use it. He stayed with his strategy to build a network of downline distributors by word of mouth and by discreetly placing messages in newsgroups such as alt.entrepreneurs and alt.make.money.fast.

But now, some guy was ripping off his ad copy and getting Dr. Fatburn unfairly branded as a spammer to boot.

Using the email address listed in QuikSilver's spams, Dr. Fatburn sent a message warning the company to stop stealing his ads. But he never heard back, and QuikSilver continued to send out messages using the same ad copy. So Dr. Fatburn decided to do some reconnaissance: he placed an order for QuikSilver's Power Diet Plus. When the package arrived, the bottle inside was labeled "Peak Nutrition Lipotropic Fat Burners." He realized there was no such thing as Power Diet Plus. QuikSilver hadn't even arranged for private labeling; it was just selling Peak's house brand.

Dr. Fatburn located a phone number for Peak Nutrition and managed to reach one of the owners. He told her QuikSilver had ripped him off, and he wanted to know who was behind the company.

"They're using a copyrighted ad and can be sued for that," he said.

But the woman from Peak just gave him the brush-off. She refused to disclose who operated QuikSilver, although she agreed to bring up the matter of the advertisement when she had a chance. It was obvious to Dr. Fatburn that Peak was protecting QuikSilver because Hawke was making money for Peak.

In later spam runs QuikSilver used the same basic ad, modifying only the return address and the web site address for ordering. By August, Dr. Fatburn decided it was time for a change in tactics. He dusted off his bulk-mailing program and sent out his first salvo of spams for Extreme Power Plus. In a subtle jab at QuikSilver, he used the subject line "Finally A Product That Lives Up To Its Name." Like the ad QuikSilver had ripped off, Dr. Fatburn's message included a description of the product along with testimonials from customers. But Dr. Fatburn added a bonus QuikSilver didn't have. If shoppers ordered within forty-eight hours, they'd get a free trial pack of Extreme Colon Cleanser.

It was Dr. Fatburn's first foray into spam, but you'd never know it from the techniques he used to keep anti-spammers from reporting the spam to his ISP. The hyperlink to his ordering site was obfuscated, so that instead of the legible domain name (in this case, his site freecableland.com), it showed only a series of numbers. Rather than including his regular email as the message's return address, Dr. Fatburn used an account he had specially set up at Yahoo!. Then, for the message's "return path" header—the address to which bounces and other error messages would go—he listed an account he had created with a free email service in Poland.

But despite these stealthy spamming tricks, Dr. Fatburn did something junk emailers almost never do: all of his spams included his real name and home-office phone number. It wasn't out of naïveté or an oversight. Dr. Fatburn considered himself an honest businessman and wanted customers to know that his company, Maryland Internet Marketing, was on the up and up. Only time would tell whether the calculated gamble would give him a competitive edge against spammers such as QuikSilver.

But one thing was certain. Hawke was on his way to earning a reputation among other junk emailers as a scammer.

David D'Amato, the Titanic Spammer

In early 2001, anti-spammer Rob Mitchell continued to watch tickling fetishist and spammer Terri DiSisto's online activities out of the corner of his eye. When he did mention DiSisto, he referred to him as "Terrance." But Mitchell had almost given up hope that the law would ever catch up to the strange spammer.

Then, in March of 2001, Mitchell got a phone call from *Reader's Digest* reporter Hal Karp. The reporter told him that federal prosecutors in Massachusetts had quietly announced a plea agreement with David P. D'Amato, a guidance counselor and assistant principal at West Hempstead High School on Long Island.

The 39-year-old D'Amato had pled guilty to misdemeanor charges of email bombing computers at Suffolk University in Boston and James Madison University in Harrisonburg, Virginia. The U.S. Attorney's press release didn't mention D'Amato's Terri DiSisto persona or the spams for videos. But Karp assured Mitchell the feds had found their man and said D'Amato was facing up to a year in prison and fines of over $100,000 on each count, with sentencing scheduled for July.

Mitchell surfed to the West Hempstead High web site. There, at the top of the home page, was D'Amato's name. As an educator himself, Mitchell was aghast at the thought of a sadistic spammer and online harasser like D'Amato working in schools most of his adult life.

"Such a person should never be in charge of children in any capacity ever again," wrote Mitchell at his Project Iceberg site.

Newsday, a daily paper serving the greater New York metropolitan area, was among the first to publish a photograph of D'Amato. Taken from the West Hempstead High yearbook, the photo showed the plump, unsmiling assistant principal seated in his office. D'Amato's balding pate and jowls made him look older than his years.

"Ewwww. He looks like Truman Capote," was Shiksaa's response after Mitchell posted a link to the photograph on Nanae.

Karen Hoffmann chimed in as well when she saw the photo: "MY GOD, could he have been any uglier?"

Another anti-spammer used the image to create a parody playbill for the movie *Titanic*, which Shiksaa posted at her site Chickenboner.com. It showed D'Amato's head, juxtaposed with the female image of Terri DiSisto above the luxury ocean liner. Superimposed over the ship were the words "Titanic Spammer" and "A Rob Mitchell Film."

Even Rebecca Ore, who had originally expressed skepticism about Mitchell's obsession with DiSisto, had come around. She encouraged victims to travel to Boston for D'Amato's sentencing. "All that's remaining is for people who want to see him do active time to show up and let the judge know how much damage he did," she said.

To the amazement of Mitchell and many other people following the case, D'Amato continued to work at West Hempstead High for nearly two weeks after signing the plea agreement. The school district suspended D'Amato only after *Three Village Times*, the hometown paper, acted on a tip from Karp and confronted school officials about D'Amato. They admitted they had heard nothing about the charges until that point.

Karp suspected that D'Amato's attorneys had negotiated a deal to tone down the government's press release and to keep it devoid of sensational details. Clearly, D'Amato was getting good legal representation. D'Amato's father, George, was the head of a big Wall Street law firm. And his lawyer, Tracy A. Miner, was one of the top defense lawyers around and president of the Massachusetts Association of Criminal Defense Lawyers.

Karp concluded that George D'Amato was financially supporting his son, who lived in a swanky penthouse in Garden City, New York, well beyond the means of most public-school administrators.

When FBI agents raided the apartment in June of 2000, D'Amato admitted he was DiSisto and detailed how he performed the mail-bomb attacks. He said he used CyberCreek's Avalanche software to send the messages through open mail relays. He also admitted to registering numerous post office boxes and telephone numbers under false names as part of his tickling video schemes. Later, in a hearing held at the time of his plea bargain, D'Amato told the court he had been under the care of a psychiatrist since January of 2000 for Internet addiction and job-related stress.

The *Three Village Times* article revealed that D'Amato had sub-mitted his resignation to the school months prior to being exposed as Terri DiSisto. He had planned to leave in order to attend law school the coming autumn at his father's alma mater, Fordham. The news troubled Mitchell. Impersonating lawyers was one of the tricks DiSisto had used to scare off anti-spammers and others who com-plained about his spamming and abuse.

"A more unfit person to enter the legal profession I cannot imagine," concluded Mitchell in Project Iceberg.

Fordham Law School apparently reached a similar conclusion following D'Amato's sentencing in July 2001.

At the hearing, D'Amato stood up and addressed the court: "Your honor, I would like to express my remorse and sorrow." He apologized to his parents, who were present, and to "every person in this courtroom who may have been impacted." D'Amato pleaded to the court for "mercy and compassion."

Prosecutors had provided the judge with a small stack of letters from DiSisto's online victims. The letters were gathered by Charles Dirksen, a San Francisco attorney and regular participant in the rec. music.phish newsgroup, who had put out an online call for testimony on behalf of prosecutors.

"I realize there are (inarguably) far more important things to get excited about these days...than putting a twisted, deviant spammer in jail for a year or two," Dirksen wrote in an April posting to the newsgroup. "But nevertheless, as Phish fans, we have the chance to help put someone in prison who trashed our online community and harassed, threatened and insulted many of our fellow fans repeatedly and persistently."

Before sentencing D'Amato, the judge asked whether anyone in the courtroom wished to speak about his or her experiences with the defendant. But no one rose to the occasion—not even Sean Gal-lagher, the student who had been mail-bombed by DiSisto. He was present in the courtroom but apparently content just to watch the proceedings.

The lenient sentence finally handed down by the judge disappointed many who had followed the case. Noting that D'Amato had already paid over $20,000 in restitution to Suffolk and James Madison universities, the judge spared D'Amato jail time for his violations of the Computer Fraud and Abuse Act. Instead, he ordered D'Amato to spend six months in a halfway house. The judge specifically stipulated that D'Amato's incarceration should not interfere with his law school classes or mental health counseling. The order also didn't place any restrictions on D'Amato's Internet use.

But a wrench was thrown into the works when officials at Fordham, apparently awakened to the controversy surrounding D'Amato, balked and withdrew their offer to admit him. Despite protests from D'Amato's attorney, the judge revised the sentence.

Instead of spending his days at Fordham's midtown Manhattan campus—just a block from Central Park and the Lincoln Center for the Arts—D'Amato would be booked that August into the Metropolitan Detention Center in Brooklyn, where he would stay for three months until being transferred to a medium-security facility in Fairton, New Jersey. D'Amato would serve out the remaining two and a half months of his sentence in Fairton and be released in February of 2002.

For Mitchell, the conclusion of the case left many questions unresolved, such as how D'Amato had acquired his spamming and mail-bombing skills and whether he worked alone or had accomplices. Similarly, serious doubts remained for Karp about whether investigators had missed evidence of pedophilia in D'Amato's past. The assistant principal's resumé showed him to be a job hopper, having changed schools eight times in eleven years. Karp worried that D'Amato's short stints at each school were the result of his being quietly let go due to misconduct that administrators decided was best to sweep under a rug, rather than face a lawsuit from D'Amato.

But those questions would stay unanswered, and Mitchell had to be content with knowing that Terri DiSisto would never again appear online.

"The era of the Internet presence of Terri DiSisto is at an end, forever," he wrote as the final entry to his Project Iceberg site.

But then in early August, just days before D'Amato was incarcerated, Mitchell was surprised to receive a rambling email from the man. The message came from an email address he didn't recognize, and the headers showed it was sent from a public library in Brooklyn.[2]

A history major in college, D'Amato had frequently compared their online battles to those of opposing generals in the American Revolutionary War, and in his message that day he acknowledged that Mitchell had been a worthy opponent.

"Everything is going to turn out just fine," said the former guidance counselor, noting that he still had his permanent certification from the New York State Education Department.

Annoyed, Mitchell sent a terse reply stating that he had grown weary of D'Amato's analogies. He said D'Amato seemed in denial about what he had done and what lay ahead of him. But D'Amato apparently had no desire for introspection. He wrote back to say he was disappointed not to see Mitchell at his sentencing in Boston, and he invited Mitchell to meet him someday in New York.

When Mitchell finally responded, he said he'd try to look up D'Amato if his travels ever took him to the Northeast. But Mitchell never received a reply.

CHAPTER *SIX*

Nanae Battles over Block Lists

Although she appreciated the sentiment, Shiksaa wasn't entirely comfortable with being called an anti-spam goddess. She knew that long before she received her first junk email message, several other women had already distinguished themselves as elite anti-spam activists. Among the established luminaries was Kelly Molloy Thompson, a Washington State resident who for several years had been the public face of spam fighting and was quoted widely in press reports on the topic.

But in the late summer of 2001, during a seismic shift in the world of spammer block lists, Thompson did something that would force Shiksaa and other junk email opponents to rethink Thompson's place in the anti-spam pantheon.

As early as 1998, with her round face, coiffed hair, and perky smile, Thompson came across more like a kindergarten teacher than an anti-spam fanatic. That made her the perfect spokesperson for the handful of spam busters who decided to picket a Seattle car dealer in May 1998. Led by the 31-year-old Thompson, the protestors stood outside Aurora Nissan on a busy suburban Seattle street. They held up hand-lettered signs to passing motorists, decrying the car dealer's use of a contract spammer to send unsolicited email ads to thousands of Seattle Internet users.

Thanks to some savvy advance PR work by Thompson, the unusual protest was covered by the national media, which quoted her on the evils of spam, and eventually resulted in a public apology from the dealer. The event also garnered lots of attention for an anti-spam group Thompson helped found earlier that year: the Forum for Responsible and Ethical Email (FREE).

Thompson's organizing abilities were showcased again in 1999, when FREE picketed Internet multimedia software developer Real Networks. The Seattle company had drawn criticism from anti-spammers for sending email advertisements to anyone who downloaded its media player software. FREE argued that responsible email marketers send their ads only to Internet users who have expressly confirmed their interest in receiving them. After Real Networks stubbornly persisted, the Mail Abuse Prevention System (MAPS) placed the company on its spammer blacklist. When that failed to change Real's practices, Thompson and a dozen or so other protestors staged a protest across the street from Real's headquarters in a downtown Seattle high-rise tower.

As the anti-spammers were handing out leaflets and displaying their signs ("Spam is theft!") to passersby, a few Real Networks representatives showed up. They invited Thompson and other organizers up to the company's offices and asked Thompson to instruct the other protestors to disperse. Thompson said they'd happily meet with company officials after the picket was over. But until then, the anti-spammers would hold their ground. At the scheduled conclusion of the protest, Thompson and two other antis rode the elevator up to Real's twenty-ninth-floor offices. They ended up spending over three hours trying to educate the firm's marketing executives about why spamming was actually bad for business.

Thompson's impromptu meeting with Real Networks didn't instantly change the company's business practices. But it did help her land a job the following November with MAPS in Redwood City, California. As associate director, she was responsible for media relations as well as for handling negotiations with companies eager to get off MAPS's Realtime Blackhole List (RBL).

Soon, Thompson was working sixty-hour weeks, trying to keep both spammers and anti-spammers at bay. She quickly discovered that being on the front lines at an anti-spam protest was nothing like working the phones of a blacklisting organization. Anti-spammers frequently emailed and phoned her to inquire why MAPS was slow to process nominations to the RBL. But her toughest job was informing companies that they were about to be placed on the RBL. Since many major ISPs, including America Online and Microsoft, relied on the RBL to filter their email, blacklisted companies were unable to exchange email with large swaths of the Internet. As a result, many firms facing the blacklist were hostile when Thompson gave them the word.

On one occasion, when Thompson warned the manager of a company that it was headed for the RBL, he snidely asked how many different fathers her children had. The representative of another firm about to be blacklisted inquired whether she was on welfare. Another time, Thompson informed a California ISP that it would find itself on the RBL if it continued providing service to Bulk ISP Corporation, a spam-support company. When word reached Saied Abdul R. Al-Zalzalah, the head of Bulk ISP Corp, he left an angry message on the MAPS hotline answering machine.

"You've caused a lot of problems for us now. I have to move the site somewhere else. That's a lot of work for me to do," said Al-Zalzalah. "I think you're a bitch. I'm going to go speak with my lawyer today … and get your site sued, you and your company, and try to get you fired."[1]

Al-Zalzalah never succeeded in his threats. But taking verbal abuse remained a regular part of Thompson's workday. Some callers to the hotline even went so far as to threaten to kill Thompson. One day, as she was getting into her car after work, she noticed someone had shot a hole in the windshield.

Soon, the attacks on MAPS came from high-priced lawyers hired by large Internet firms. In 2000, several companies, including Harris Interactive, a division of the renowned polling firm, filed separate lawsuits against MAPS after being listed on the RBL. In a news report about the Harris lawsuit, the polling company's chief executive accused MAPS of being "a group of self-appointed zealots."

Rather than circling the wagons around MAPS, Shiksaa and other spam fighters watched the attacks with a sense of detachment. Over the years, they had grown increasingly disillusioned with the service and were often frustrated with what they considered its excessive caution and lack of communication.

But the erosion of support for MAPS accelerated in October 2000. A discussion had been underway in Nanae about how the block list could improve its effectiveness. In a moment of frustration, MAPS founder and chief executive Paul Vixie crashed the conversation.

"Fuck Nanae," he wrote in a posting to the newsgroup, and then twisted the knife.

"I mean, a lot of you are my friends, but…your opinions about what MAPS should be doing are both generally and specifically worthless other than as conversation-starters."

Nanae participants recoiled, giving Vixie an opportunity to soften his remarks. But instead he dug in: "You may all fight spammers if you wish. MAPS is fighting spam itself."

The distinction was an important one to many spam opponents who believed that it was detrimental to personalize their battles with spam. But Vixie's proclamation caused a rift among spam fighters.

Until that point, Shiksaa, like many anti-spammers, still thought of MAPS as a kind of community-based project. Technically, it was a California limited liability corporation that employed over twenty people. But MAPS relied heavily on nominations from the grass roots in building its spammer blacklist. Shiksaa also tremendously admired the dedication of Thompson and other people running the organization, and she had been prepared to contribute generously to the MAPS legal defense fund. But Shiksaa announced that she had put away her checkbook after reading Vixie's comment, as did a number of other anti-spammers on Nanae.

MAPS nonetheless managed to weather its legal challenges. It was able to convince Harris to drop its lawsuit and switch to a "confirmed opt-in" system, under which Internet users would have to follow two explicit steps before Harris could add them to its mailing list. But the lawsuits also drained MAPS financially, and when the dot-com economy started to tank in late 2000, MAPS suffered as well. In response, the non-profit made a big announcement in mid-July of 2001. The block list service said it was discontinuing its practice of voluntary subscriptions and instead would require all large users to pay (up to $10,000 annually) for access to the RBL and other MAPS services.

"MAPS' purpose is to stop spam on the Internet. That purpose can only be achieved as long as MAPS can maintain itself as a corporation...MAPS can simply no longer afford to foot the bill for the bulk of the Internet community," said Margie Arbon, MAPS business development manager, in a posting to Nanae about the policy changes. Going forward, MAPS would allow free access to its data only "under limited circumstances" she said.[2]

Despite the stress, Kelly Thompson loved her stint at MAPS; and she loved making a difference in the spam fight. But two weeks after the big subscription announcement, Thompson posted a note of her own on Nanae: she had resigned her position and was looking for work.

Thompson didn't explain why she was leaving, but it was obvious to Shiksaa. MAPS had become increasingly impotent over the years, and its switch to a fee-based system was just the final death knell. In making the decision to go purely commercial, MAPS would lose the goodwill of many volunteers such as Shiksaa, who for years had felt that MAPS treated them with indifference.

The MAPS announcement set in motion other important changes in the anti-spamming world. In August, a new spam blacklist quietly appeared on the Internet. In many ways, it was the antithesis of MAPS. Calling itself the Spam Prevention Early Warning System, or Spews, the new blacklist could be downloaded for free by anyone. The operators of Spews were anonymous. (The registration record for the site, Spews.org, listed an address in the Russian Federation of Irkutsk, but most people on Nanae assumed that was a joke.)

Unlike MAPS, Spews was not interested in receiving nominations to its block list. "Think of it as one group's Consumer Reports review of portions of the billions of Internet addresses," said a notice at the site. In fact, there was no way to communicate directly with Spews. The operators simply instructed individuals to leave messages for them on Nanae.

Perhaps the biggest difference between Spews and MAPS was the ruthlessness with which Spews attacked spam. MAPS usually tried to educate companies about how to avoid being blacklisted, whereas the operators of Spews appeared to have a "shoot first, ask questions later" mentality about hard-core spammers. They never shied away from causing collateral damage and sometimes placed all of an Internet service provider's network addresses on the Spews list, even if spammers were using only a small portion.

Yet the renegade new service continued to attract supporters, with significant numbers of mail server operators using the block list to protect their users from spam. With its higher public profile, Spews became the subject of intense speculation about who was running the show.

One Nanae reader noted that the design of the Spews site was strikingly similar to one used by Xoasis.com, a free web-hosting service run by a Seattle ISP. A Nanae regular named Gary reported receiving a phone call from someone representing himself as one of the principals of Spews. The caller had revealed that Spews was run by seven people, each of whom was a system administrator at a large company. But the caller hadn't revealed his name or those of the other Spews principals.

"I suspect any attempt to back track Spews is going to run into brick walls, dead ends, land mines, booby traps…I suspect that a LOT of thought went into this," wrote Gary.

While many anti-spammers admired Spews for its boldness, Thompson found the blacklist's secrecy offensive.

"I signed my name to every single thing I did at MAPS. I took the phone calls, I answered the email, and I didn't hide," she wrote in a note to Nanae. "People know who I am, and they can decide whether to trust me or not. I owned my work. If they don't have the guts to own their work, then I don't care to consider their opinion."

Thompson also resented Spews's decision to use Nanae as its support forum. Why should the newsgroup have to be polluted with irate postings from companies blacklisted by Spews?

Among those who defended Spews was Steve Linford, operator of Spamhaus.org. Linford said he was saddened by the way some anti-spammers had greeted the new blacklist. He noted that since Spews went live, it had already caused several recalcitrant ISPs to give the boot to longtime junk emailers on their networks. Many of those same spammers had also been listed in the Spamhaus Register of Known Spam Operations (Rokso), which had grown from just twenty-four firms in 2000 to over sixty by August of 2001.

"There are suddenly a lot of homeless spammers" thanks to Spews, noted Linford. Then, in a comment directed at Thompson, Linford defended the decision by Spews's operators to remain anonymous. As he saw it, Spews was hoping to avoid the same fate as MAPS.

"The MAPS ex-staffers here know better than anyone how many people contacted you every day asking and demanding replies, wanting every ISP black holed now, sending you spam after spam, carbon-copying you on everything, not to mention the amount of spammers calling you trying to wangle off your list, " wrote Linford.

As he justified why Spews operated as it did, Linford might just as well have been describing the pressures he felt as the not-anonymous operator of Spamhaus.

"They don't want their personal details, addresses and phone numbers known to every spammer and every lawyer in town. They're in the front line, right in the thick of it, finding out who's making the connection with whom, which spambag is about to set up on which Costa Rica ISP, who's just agreed to provide haven for whom, etc. That's what it's all about," he wrote. Linford concluded with a plea for spam fighters to give Spews a chance to correct any systemic flaws.

Thompson decided to withhold further public judgment on Spews. But she felt Linford's message deserved a response. Despite their efforts to insulate themselves from criticism, she warned, the people behind Spews were sure to have some rocky days ahead.

"If the Spews folks want to do this, they had better be prepared. Because…it will never, NEVER be any easier than this. It only gets harder."

Thompson's words struck some anti-spammers merely as sour grapes. But her prediction would prove painfully true. In the years ahead, the desperate efforts by spammers to unmask Spews would eventually roil the lives of several Nanae leaders, including Shiksaa and Linford.

But at the time, September 2001, it was Thompson's life that was about to take a dramatic new turn. No one would read about it in Nanae for months, but she had quietly started working for Mindshare Design, a California company that operated a bulk-emailing service called PostMaster General.

When Thompson accepted the position as Mindshare's Standards and Practices Manager, she was well aware that PostMaster General was frequently abused by junk emailers and derided on

Nanae as a spam foundry. She realized that many anti-spammers, had they known of her plans, would have scorned her for selling out, for crossing over to the dark side. But Thompson didn't view her decision that way. Instead, she saw herself going to fight spam from the inside.

Hawke Takes on an Apprentice

After nearly two years of nonstop spamming, Davis Hawke finally started to make some serious money in the summer of 2001. Instead of earning a couple hundred dollars per week, Hawke suddenly measured his cash flow in the thousands as he racked up orders for Power Diet Plus. And it wasn't as if he was working any harder. In fact, Hawke had discovered that business operated most smoothly when he sent out spams only from Friday evening through Sunday evening. System administrators at ISPs tended to take off weekends, so they couldn't respond to complaints about Hawke's spamming until Monday. By then, his messages were already waiting in the in-boxes of hundreds of thousands of people.

The schedule essentially left Hawke with a five-day weekend. While the working stiffs of the world were chained to their desks, he was taking hikes in the woods with his wolf Dreighton, working on his knife-throwing technique, or polishing up his archery skills. Hawke also whiled away his time reading chess books and polishing his playing skills against online opponents through an interactive system called Internet Chess Club.

But as Hawke watched the ever-larger deposits from his credit card processor arrive in his bank account, he got nervous. The money seemed too vulnerable there. One day he withdrew a couple thousand dollars in hundred-dollar bills. Using rubber bands, he tightly wrapped the stack of bills in heavy black plastic sheeting and placed them in a plastic bottle. Hawke put the bottle and a small spade in a backpack and headed on foot with Dreighton deep into Tennessee's Cherokee National Park. When Hawke located a good spot, away from any trails but near some memorable landmarks, he dug a hole and buried the bottle. It would be the first of several stashes of cash that he would refer to as his "deposits."[3]

At the end of June, Hawke decided to go to Philadelphia for the 2001 World Open chess tournament. With Patricia staying behind to run QuikSilver, he headed out on the nine-hour drive north. To keep himself alert, he listened to books on tape, including *A Brief History of Time* by Stephen Hawking. Hawke had read the Cambridge University professor's book a few years before, but he still found himself mesmerized as he motored up I-81 while a British narrator read Hawking's explanation of Einstein's theory of relativity and other concepts of astrophysics.

The tournament was held in a large hotel in the northwestern suburbs of Philly. Hawke found the conference room set aside for registration and began filling out an entry form using his Walter Smith pseudonym. As he was leaning over the table, Hawke heard a loud voice behind him.[4]

"Britt Greenbaum? Yo, is that you Britt?"

Hawke winced and turned around. He recognized Mauricio Ruiz, a talented chess player he hadn't seen since he left Massachusetts. Ruiz was a good looking, happy-go-lucky guy, a couple of years younger than Hawke.

"Hey, Maury," he said cautiously.

"What have you been up to lately, Britt? I hardly recognized you."

Hawke shot a glance at the woman working the registration table and took a step toward Ruiz.

"Call me Walter now, ok?"

"No problem…Walter," said Ruiz.

Ruiz invited Hawke to join him in the skittles room down the hall, where players hung out and challenged each other in informal matches. Hawke agreed to meet him there after he finished registering.

Hawke liked to think of himself as imperturbable, but bumping into Ruiz had knocked him a bit off balance. Hawke had known Ruiz since 1991, when they met at a chess tournament in Providence, Ruiz's hometown. Hawke was just thirteen at the time, and Ruiz was eleven. But the younger boy had already established a higher USCF rating, and earlier that year had won the national sixth-grade chess championship. Still, Hawke managed to finish the tournament in twelfth place, one place ahead of Ruiz. Over the next several years the two occasionally crossed paths at tournaments in Rhode Island and Massachusetts. Mauricio's dad, like Hawke's parents, sometimes entered tournaments with his son. Rolando Ruiz played in the same division as Hy and Peggy Greenbaum, and the adults struck up a casual friendship.

Hawke didn't face Ruiz directly in tournament play until 1995. By then, Mauricio was clearly the stronger player, having established a USCF rating of around 2100, while Hawke, playing as Britt Greenbaum, had hit a plateau in the 1900s. Ruiz defeated Greenbaum in the first round and went on to place third overall, with Britt coming in tenth. They hadn't seen each other since that match.

When Hawke caught up with him in the skittles room, Ruiz was just about to sit down to a five-minute blitz match against a kid who couldn't have been older than fourteen. As Ruiz was setting up his pieces, he told Hawke he had been attending Bryant College, a business school in Rhode Island. It was boring and he wanted to drop out, said Ruiz.

Hawke replied that he had quit college after his junior year and had gone into business for himself. But before Hawke had a chance to provide the details, he was interrupted. Ruiz loudly hailed a high-school-age kid who had just walked into the room.

"Brad Bournival, meet my old buddy Walter."

Bournival, a pudgy, brown-haired 17-year-old from New Hampshire, shook hands with Hawke. Hawke asked him if he wanted to play a quick five-minute match for money.

"How much money?" asked Bournival.

"Five bucks a game," suggested Hawke.

"Nah, I think I'll pass," he said.

After someone offered to put up the money for Bournival, he relented. As Hawke and Bournival were arranging themselves at a table and setting their time clocks, Hawke scrutinized the younger player.

"What's your rating, by the way?"

Bournival hesitated. "Nineteen hundred."

"Good," said Hawke. "Me, too."

They ended up splitting two matches, with Hawke taking the first and Bournival beating him in the second game. Hawke's matches with Bournival in the skittles room would be the best he'd play in Philadelphia. After taking a draw in his first match, Hawke was beaten by his next two opponents and decided to withdraw. His play gave him a 215th -place finish out of 226 entrants in the open division. Ruiz fared better, coming in 123rd. As it turned out, Bournival had lied to Hawke about his rating, which was actually over 2100. But Bournival played above himself at the tournament. He upset several stronger players— including William Mark Paschall, who had a 2500 rating—and finished 90th overall.

Hawke and Bournival would cross paths again a few weeks later. In August of 2001, Hawke returned to the Northeast to play in the U.S. Open tournament in Framingham, Massachusetts, just outside of Boston. It was the closest he had been to his parent's house in over two years. But he didn't even tell them he was in town. Instead, Hawke surprised his grandparents on his mother's side by calling them at the last minute and asking if he could crash there. They lived in Westwood and said he was welcome any time he was in the area. (Hawke's grandfather, a vice president at the Massachusetts Institute of Technology, had always seemed more amused than upset about Hawke's neo-Nazi period.)

The Framingham event was held in a Sheraton decorated on the outside to look like a castle. Matches took place at long tables in large conference rooms lit by massive chandeliers. Hawke, playing as Walter Smith, drew a player rated 1400 in the first round and quickly dispatched him. Bournival similarly beat his first opponent, who had just a 1600 rating. The two met afterwards in the skittles room. This time, Hawke challenged Bournival to a rematch of their five-minute game at twenty dollars per game.

Bournival laughed nervously. "Are you rich or something?"

"As a matter of fact, I am."

With a flourish, Hawke pulled out his wallet and opened it wide so Bournival could see the contents. A thick collection of hundred-dollar bills was stuffed into it, easily totaling $5,000.

"Where did you get so much money?"

"I'm a spammer," Hawke said proudly.

Bournival just stared at him. "What the hell is a spammer?"

Hawke was amazed that anyone alive in the year 2001 hadn't heard of spam. He explained how he mailed out ads for diet pills and other products to email addresses all over the Internet, and a percentage of people placed orders. He told Bournival he worked only a couple days each week and spent the rest of the time playing chess or just hanging out. He even had a girlfriend who lived with him and looked after the business when he was away at chess tournaments.

Bournival listened intently as Hawke, whom he still knew as Walter Smith, described his business. The two couldn't have been more different. Hawke's long, dark hair was tied in a ponytail down his back, and his face was covered with a two-day-old beard. He wore a black T-shirt and a silver skull on a chain around his neck. In contrast, Bournival was dressed in a striped shirt with his hair neatly parted and gelled. He didn't regale Hawke with a description of his own life, besides saying he would be a senior at West High in Manchester and had been playing chess for just three years. Hawke assumed Bournival came from a boring, middle-class background, and Bournival had no desire to correct that impression. He figured Hawke wouldn't want to hear about how his parents divorced when he was ten. Or how he now lived with his half-brother and his mother, who was a crack cocaine user, along with her physically abusive black boyfriend, in a cramped two-bedroom apartment in a three-story walk-up owned by Bournival's grandmother. Or how his mom kept several Pekinese dogs in the apartment, none of which was entirely housebroken.

Yet somehow amidst that mayhem in Manchester, Bournival had taught himself to play chess. He discovered chess as a freshman in high school during a 1999 visit to the games section of the Yahoo! site. He immediately liked the game, so he joined the school's chess team. A few months later, Bournival surprised many by winning the New Hampshire high school chess championship. Soon after that, people were paying Bournival ten dollars an hour for lessons. Chess was about the only thing that kept him from dropping out of school.

Time ran out before Hawke and Bournival got around to playing their skittles match. As they headed out for the next round, Bournival said he wanted to hear more about QuikSilver Enterprises. Hawke suggested a poker game that night with Mauricio Ruiz and anyone else willing to put up some cash. Bournival balked, never having played poker for money before. But he agreed anyway. When he left the skittles room, Bournival had the uncomfortable yet exhilarating feeling that Hawke could get him to do just about anything.[5]

As it turned out, Bournival somehow managed to win ten dollars at the poker table that evening. Even better, he convinced Hawke to tutor him about spamming in exchange for half of what he earned from spam. The two traded email addresses, and Hawke said he would be contacting Bournival with instructions on how to get started.

In all other respects, it had been a mediocre tournament for Bournival. He beat the players he should have but lost his rematch with Paschall, finishing 150th out of 480 players. Hawke, competing as Smith, played solidly as well, but pulled off no surprises en route to his 270th-place finish.

But with his new spam income, Bournival would have all the money he needed to attend tournaments anywhere in the country. Even though he had managed a 3.8 GPA his junior year, Bournival departed Framingham knowing he would not return to West High that fall.

"You can call me Johnny," Hawke told him as they said goodbye.

9/11

In the spam wars, the best defense is often a good offense. That's why Davis Hawke began spiking his spams with intimidating legalese in September 2000. At the bottom of the ads he placed a notice informing recipients that QuikSilver's spam was sent "in compliance with federal guidelines governing the transmission of unsolicited commercial email."

Hawke also added a link to a page at SpamLaws.com containing the text of the Unsolicited Electronic Mail Act of 1999, also known as H.R. 3113. He closed the spams with his favorite excerpt from the Act: "Unsolicited commercial electronic mail can be an important mechanism through which businesses advertise and attract customers in the online environment."

Never mind that H.R. 3113 had died in the U.S. Senate in July of 2000. And Congress had so far failed to approve any other federal laws regulating junk email. Hawke's disclaimer did the trick: it kept would-be anti-spammers at bay. (Hawke wasn't the only junk emailer using the technique. In fact, at one point in 2001, the operator of SpamLaws.com, law professor David E. Sorkin, put up a notice explaining that he was not responsible for disclaimers included in spam emails that linked to his site.)

Before it languished in the Senate, H.R. 3113 had received support from two powerful opposing groups: the Direct Marketing Association (DMA) and a grassroots organization known as the

Coalition Against Unsolicited Commercial Email. CAUCE was led by a number of respected anti-spam veterans and boasted over 20,000 members in 2000. Thanks to efforts by CAUCE on behalf of the bill's author, Heather Wilson, and cosponsors Gary Miller and Gene Green, H.R. 3113 breezed through the House by a vote of 427–1 on July 18.

But Senators were partial to S.R. 2542, a companion bill from their Senate colleagues, and they never took a vote on Wilson's legislation. But they also failed to summon much enthusiasm for S.R. 2542. Entitled the Controlling the Assault of Non-Solicited Pornography and Marketing Act of 2000 (CAN-SPAM), the Senate bill never made it out of the Senate's commerce committee. As a result, the 106th session of Congress concluded without a federal junk-email law.

Hawke continued citing H.R. 3113 in his disclaimer well into 2001. By then, Wilson had introduced a new version of her spam bill. Like its predecessor, H.R. 718 proposed that junk emailers be required to conspicuously label their messages as spam. The new bill similarly called for spammers to include their correct street and email addresses in their ads and prohibited them from falsifying the routing information in their messages' headers. H.R. 718 also made it a crime for spammers to continue sending ads to anyone who asked to be removed from their mailing lists.

But this time, Wilson's Unsolicited Electronic Mail Act faced a new hurdle getting through the House Energy and Commerce Committee. Lobbyists from the DMA as well as the banking industry cajoled committee members to remove a provision of H.R. 718 that would have enabled businesses, schools, or Internet service providers to post a "Spam Free Zone" sign on their mail servers. Under the original language, marketers who disregarded the notice and spammed anyway would be subject to stiff fines. But that language was gone from the version of the bill approved by the committee in March 2001. What's more, the updated version required that all mail server operators install spam-filtering software or else lose their right to sue violators of the law.

Many junk email fighters who had supported Wilson's original bill suddenly withdrew their backing. CAUCE condemned the revised legislation as a "costly, messy pro-spam bill," and predicted it would result in more spam rather than less. In a statement, CAUCE said it "remains hopeful that the unfortunate changes to the bill can yet be corrected, and we remain very appreciative of Rep. Heather Wilson's efforts on behalf of consumers."[6]

Despite CAUCE's objections, the revised legislation, which now had over one hundred cosponsors, moved forward and was scheduled for debate on the House floor in the second week of September. Wilson's goal of getting a federal spam law on the books, albeit a flawed one by some standards, once again seemed within reach.

Then a group of hijackers rammed two passenger jetliners into New York's World Trade Center. Terrorists commandeered a third jet and struck the Pentagon in Washington, D.C., while another plane was crashed in a Pennsylvania field.

In an instant, controlling the junk email problem became a trivial pursuit, even for many anti-spammers. On September 11, operators of several spam block lists announced they were temporarily suspending operations in order to allow email to flow unimpeded during rescue efforts. Among them was Spamhaus operator Steve Linford, who decided that the Spamhaus Block List, which he had launched just weeks before, would go on a hiatus until further notice.

"From what we understand there are no telephone communications in or out of Manhattan but Internet communications are still working ... Therefore this is not an appropriate moment for any blacklist which may be blocking IPs of hosts in Manhattan to be operating," said Linford in a notice on Nanae.

But for some spammers and fraud artists, the 9/11 attacks on America presented a golden opportunity. In some cases, spammers sent phony condolences that were just tasteless ways to drive traffic to their shopping sites. In others, spammers looked to capitalize on the fear of additional terrorist attacks. Email ads for survival kits and anthrax treatments were all the rage in the weeks following September 11.

"The U.S. is under serious threats of Biological, Chemical and Nuclear attacks!" shouted one spam for fifty-dollar gas masks. "Don't wait until it is too late! Protect yourself and your family today!" advised the ad. A few months before, the company hawking the gas masks had been advertising credit card merchant accounts.

But more sinister ads appeared as well. On September 12, an email message bearing the subject line "Help for the Red Cross and the victims of our Nation's tragedy" began arriving in email in-boxes. The spam was sent through a computer in Belgium and solicited donations to the "Express Relief Fund" and the "Victims Survivor Fund." Recipients were directed to hand over their credit card numbers at a makeshift site. A week before, the same site had been selling what it called "Viagra for Women." Around mid-September, the site disappeared completely.

In some cases, the motives of opportunistic spammers were harder to judge. Using the Postmaster General system, a Denver, Colorado, company called SaveRealBig.com deluged the Internet with messages on the evening of September 11. The spams were identified as coming from the company's 29-year-old CEO, Scott Richter. They had the subject line "Help us support our nation" and invited recipients to purchase large nylon U.S. flags for twenty dollars at the SaveRealBig.com site. The messages said "all available proceeds" would be donated to "emergency and relief efforts."

Anti-spammers were immediately suspicious. Spamhaus's Steve Linford posted a copy of SaveRealBig.com's spam on Nanae and suggested it was a scam designed to put money in Richter's pockets.

In recent weeks, Richter's company had been using Postmaster General to send ads for products ranging from diet pills to Ginsu knives to pagers. The company was also sending out spams for an adult entertainment site Richter owned called Ejackolate.com. Suddenly those offerings were no longer listed on the SaveRealBig.com home page. In their place appeared information on ordering U.S. flags.

To fend off skeptics, Richter updated the page a few days later with a photo of himself making a donation at the Denver chapter of the American Red Cross. A note from Richter claimed that he had given $20,000 dollars to the relief agency. On a message board he had set up to take comments about the fund-raising effort, Richter posted this introduction:

> We have nothing to hide. I feel that our efforts are very sincere and genuine. If any of you have anything negative to say about SaveRealBig. com and its present actions, then please show us what you have done to make a difference in this time of sadness.

Spews didn't wait around for proof that Richter was squeaky clean. Later that month, a large block of Internet addresses, including those used by SaveRealBig.com and several other Richter sites, showed up on the Spews blacklist. In response, Richter's ISP eventually cut off service to the sites, forcing him to line up new hosting.

After the hassles and the suspicion, Richter vowed he'd never again do online charity fundraising. But even if he didn't reap any big profits from selling over 10,000 flags, he did acquire a fresh list of "opt-in" email addresses. (The privacy policy at SaveRealBig.com made it clear that the company reserved the right to use information collected from customers "for the purpose of targeted marketing opportunities.")

Richter was on his way to building what would soon become a list of over forty-five million addresses, enabling him to send out tens of millions of spams every day. But by 2003, Richter's spamming would earn him a top-three spot on Spamhaus's Rokso and a lawsuit from Microsoft and the State of New York.

But in the wake of 9/11, it was a flurry of messages from Ohio-based spammer Tom Cowles that caused the biggest uproar from anti-spammers. On September 12, hundreds of thousands of the bizarre emails started hitting in-boxes. All bore Internet addresses registered to Cowles's Leverage Communications and carried the provocative subject line, "How you can help WTC victims. (BTW: Anti-spammers Support Bin Laden!)"

The top third of the message listed the addresses of web sites operated by the Red Cross and the Federal Bureau of Investigation. In the bottom third was a collection of already well-publicized phone numbers set up for relatives of potential victims by airlines and other entities involved in the attacks. Sandwiched between the two sections was a single-spaced, 250-word rant against spam opponents.

"Anti-spammers are terrorists at heart and attack websites and email accounts of companies wishing to bring their products and services to the general public via email, an environmentally sound, REMARKABLE medium!" cried out Cowles's message. It also accused anti-spammers of launching denial-of-service attacks against his site, an act which he said was akin to terrorist violence.

"American marketers are under Attack! For apparently using environmentally sound bulk email to deliver products, services and public service messages," said the message. It added that recipients should do their part "to help Freedom and the American way" by requesting to be removed from a marketer's list. "Not," said the message, "by harassing his vendors, dial-up providers or website companies." The section concluded by warning recipients that "when you make yourself known to be an anti-bulkemailer, you align yourself with Hackers, Terrorists and Un-American groups."

Upon seeing the bizarre spams, Steve Linford said it was time to consider placing Cowles's ISP, SprintLink, on the new Spamhaus Block List. Linford also added an entry about the incident to

A photo of Knights of Freedom founder and leader "Bo Decker" (Davis Wolfgang Hawke) was featured on the neo-Nazi group's web site in 1999, which he designed.

Hawke ran the Knights of Freedom from his Wofford College dorm room prior to moving off campus in March 1999.

Photo credit: Spartanburg Herald-Journal/Gerry Pate/Spartanburg, S.C.

Photo credit: Spartanburg Herald-Journal/Gerry Pate/Spartanburg, S.C.

Shown here as a junior at Wofford College, Hawke turned his fascination with Nazi knives and other weapons into a bustling online business when followers abandoned the movement after learning Hawke's father was Jewish.

Still named Andrew Britt Greenbaum at the time, Hawke discovered white-power web sites while surfing the Internet from his childhood home in Westwood, Massachusetts, an affluent suburb of Boston.

After graduating from Westwood High School, where he was a chess standout, Andrew Britt Greenbaum legally changed his name to Davis Wolfgang Hawke in 1996.

A fake driver's license created by Hawke. In 2000, he used spam to advertise booklets about creating fake identification from a site called PrivacyBuff.com.

Former spam king Sanford Wallace behind the nightclub he operated in Rochester, New Hampshire, October 2003.

Andrew Brunner, owner of CyberCreek Software, battled with anti-spammers repeatedly in 1999.

Photo credit: David Fields

Piers "Mad Pierre" Forrest is credited with being the first spam fighter to observe that former neo-Nazi Hawke had become the operator of a spam operation named QuikSilver Enterprises.

Steve Linford, operator of the Spamhaus Project, launched the first comprehensive database of major spammers, the Register of Known Spam Operations (Rokso) in 2000.

Ronnie Scelson, shown here in his Slidell, Louisiana, data center, has been on the Spamhaus Rokso list since its inception.

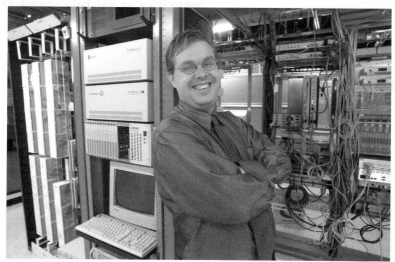

COWLES, THOMAS A

Mug shot of Thomas Cowles taken by the Wood County, Ohio, sheriff after his arrest in 2002 for allegedly stealing computer equipment from former spam partner Eddy Marin.

COWLES, THOMAS A   (W M 04/17/1968)

South Florida spam king Eddy Marin has been ranked one of the Internet's top spammers since 2000.

Brad Bournival at the 2001 U.S. Open chess tournament in Framingham, Massachusetts, where he first learned about spamming from Davis Hawke.

Photo credit: Tony Cortizas, Jr.

Davis Hawke ran QuikSilver Enterprises from his third-floor apartment in this house on Crescent Road in Pawtucket, Rhode Island, from 2002–2003.

Andrew Sledd, great-great grandfather of Davis Hawke, was a civil rights pioneer and the first president of the University of Florida.

Alan "Dr. Fatburn" Moore, the owner of UltimateDiets.com.

Francis Uy, the Maryland anti-spammer who battled with Dr. Fatburn in 2002–2003.

Scott Richter, CEO of OptInRealBig.com LLC, refers to himself as a "high volume email deployer," but Spamhaus says he's one of the biggest spammers in the world.

Photo credit: John Johnston

Scott Richter (L) and anti-spammer Adam Brower outside the Federal Trade Commission headquarters during a 2003 conference on spam.

Atlanta attorney Pete Wellborn has successfully sued several spammers as well as defended anti-spammers from lawsuits.

Photo credit: Tony Cortizas, Jr.

With Hawke as his partner-in-spam, Brad Bournival, shown here in a 2003 photo, made a million dollars selling penis-enlargement pills under the company name Amazing Internet Products.

A web site for Pinacle, the private-label brand of penis-enlargement pills spammed by Hawke and Bournival during 2003.

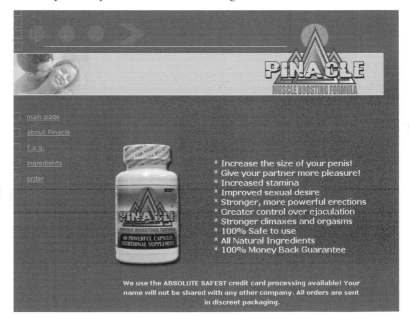

Amazing Internet Products leased a 2,700-square-foot office in this restored mill in Manchester, New Hampshire, from which it sent spam and shipped out orders.

Davis Hawke rented this home on Black Plain Road in North Smithfield, Rhode Island, from 2003–2004.

Davis Hawke, with his Ford Crown Victoria, at his rented house in North Smithfield, Rhode Island, in 2003.

Time-travel spammer Robby Todino lives with his mother in this rented home in Woburn, Massachusetts.

A photograph sent to Robby Todino purportedly depicting a portable time-travel device.

Brad Smith (L), general counsel at Microsoft, and New York State Attorney General Eliot Spitzer announce parallel lawsuits against Scott Richter in 2003.

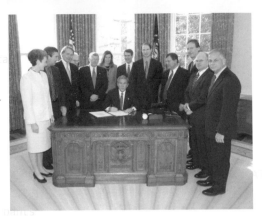

President G.W. Bush at the signing ceremony for the Controlling the Assault of Non-Solicited Pornography and Marketing (CAN-SPAM) Act of 2003.

Davis Hawke leased the top floor of this building on Main Street in Pawtucket, Rhode Island, at the start of 2004. It was the home of Hawke's new cell-phone spam operation, The Phoenix Company.

The Phoenix Company's home page for RaveX, an ephedra product Hawke touted via cell-phone spam in 2004.

Photo credit: Tony Cortizas, Jr.

Brad Bournival at a chess tournament in 2004, after being sued by America Online for spamming.

The home page of Sizer XXX, a penis-enlargement product spammed by Bournival in early 2004.

Attorney Jon Praed of Internet Law Group helped file the 2004 AOL lawsuit against Hawke and Bournival.

Photo credit: Gerald Oskoboiny

Jennifer Archie, partner at Latham & Watkins, worked with AOL on its 2004 litigation against Hawke and Bournival.

Jason Vale, a champion arm wrestler and cancer survivor, was sentenced to sixty-three months in federal prison in June 2004 after ignoring a 2000 court order to stop selling apricot pits as a cancer cure.

Assistant U.S. Attorney Charles Kleinberg prosecuted the government's case against Laetrile spammer Jason Vale.

Cowles's listing on Rokso. "All we can assume is that someone at Empire Towers is in need of some immediate psychiatric attention; this is truly sick," concluded the entry.

For Karen Hoffmann, the Toledo anti-spammer who had been on a mission to track Cowles's every move, the strange 9/11 messages from Empire Towers were her first sighting of Cowles in months. Hoffmann posted a copy of his spam at the web page she had dedicated to Cowles, and, in a message on Nanae, she said she was shocked that he would stoop so low as to use the attacks on America as an occasion to criticize anti-spammers.

Then Hoffmann tried making a direct appeal to Cowles: "Tom, if you're reading this, please contact me via email."

Hawke Tutors Bournival

Hawke belatedly kept his promise to Bournival. In September 2001, an email message arrived from "Johnny Durango" (an alias Hawke was using at the time). Hawke invited him to meet him that Friday night at the Internet Chess Club, a chess site located at ChessClub.com.

ICC was one of the top online chess organizations and had attracted thousands of members since the early 90s. ICC programmers developed software that enabled chess players to compete against other members all over the world. Besides a graphical user interface that allowed players to move chess pieces on their computer screens with a click of a mouse, the program also had a chat feature so members could converse while they watched or played online matches.

Bournival had relied on ICC chat for giving chess lessons, and he felt right at home when Hawke suggested they use the technology to discuss spamming. On the system, Bournival's "handle," or nickname, was FrappeBoy, a name he had chosen because the ice-cream drink was one of his favorites. (On that Friday evening, Hawke used the handle SchoolShooter, in reference to the Columbine high school massacre. He enjoyed choosing online nicknames that threw his opponents off balance.)

After Bournival located Hawke, he sent the system a command instructing it to create a scratch game. Then he sent a message to Hawke to let him know the number of the game board he had created.

Once they both had the board up on their screens, Hawke and Bournival didn't actually play chess. Using the system's "kibitz" command, Hawke told Bournival that he had decided to let him take over his pheromone business in exchange for a 50 percent cut of his sales. To get him started, Hawke said he would send Bournival his ad and a list of 50,000 email addresses he had harvested from eBay. He instructed Bournival to get a copy of Group Mail, a free mailing program from a company called Aureate Media. Hawke said he would wait while Bournival downloaded the program so Hawke could show him how to configure the software's various settings.

As Bournival was navigating to the Aureate web site, the program's console indicated that someone else had joined them. (ICC games were generally open to other members, who could watch the game and trade comments using the kibitz command.) It was Mauricio Ruiz who had wandered in.

"Yo, Johnny. Is this where I learn Spamming 101?" Ruiz asked.[7]

"Pull up a chair, grasshopper. I was just telling Brad how to get started," said Hawke.

A rapid typist, Hawke said they should begin by signing up for Internet access accounts with several low-cost ISPs. A company called StarNet was his personal favorite. Hawke told them to configure Group Mail to send their messages through one of the ISPs' mail servers. That took care of the sending side of the business. To take customer orders, Hawke instructed them to register a couple of web sites with a low-cost hosting service such as ValueWeb. Hawke said he would email them the HTML web page code he used. The code included a link to a form Hawke had created for gathering order data and processing credit card transactions.

"At the end of each month, I'll add up your orders and cash you out," said Hawke. He told each of them to email him a street address to which he should send checks with their earnings.

At that point, Ruiz had grown bored with the tutoring session and suddenly headed out after saying a quick goodbye. Hawke was eager to finish up as well.

"One last thing," Hawke said to Bournival. "You're going to need product."

Hawke said he'd make the trek to New Hampshire in the next week or two and bring Bournival a couple of cases of pheromone concentrate. After Bournival sold those, he could restock directly from the supplier in Wichita, Hawke said. Then he told Bournival he'd be in touch soon and signed off.

Nearly a month went by, and "Johnny" still hadn't delivered the pheromone. Bournival had stopped going to classes at Manchester West High and tried to occupy himself with assembling the other aspects of his new spam business. He bought a book about web site design and created a couple pages for taking pheromone orders based on Hawke's design. As Hawke suggested, he did some small trial runs with Group Mail, sending spams to test addresses he had created, known in spammer parlance as seed accounts. When he ran out of things to do, Bournival registered the address NHChess.org and started building a site for the New Hampshire Chess Association, the chess club he had joined soon after discovering the game in 1999.

When Hawke finally showed up at Bournival's apartment, located on a treeless section of Montgomery Street on the western side of Manchester, he and Bournival lugged two large cardboard boxes of pheromone bottles from the trunk of his car up the flight of stairs to the second-floor apartment.

Inside, Hawke looked around the cramped home. Bournival's computer was on a desk in the room he shared with his stepbrother. The dogs were yapping and frantically darting around the apartment.

"When business takes off, you're going to want your own office," Hawke said. In the meantime, he suggested the two of them should get a post office box in the QuikSilver company name. That way, Bournival could keep his home address a secret from customers. Using Hawke's car, they drove the mile and a half into downtown Manchester to get something to eat and visit the Mail Boxes Etc. branch on Elm Street.

As they were filling out the paperwork for the post office box, the clerk at the Mail Boxes Etc. store said she would need to see identification from each of them. Bournival produced his driver's license, and Hawke slapped his down on the counter as well. As the clerk recorded the information from the two cards, Bournival could make out the word "Massachusetts" across the top of Hawke's license. "Johnny" had told him his grandparents lived outside Boston and that he planned to spend the evening there on his return home to Tennessee. But as Bournival focused more intently on the upside-down card, he was puzzled to see the name Davis Hawke.

Bournival didn't ask "Johnny" about the name on the license, figuring it was just part of his effort to protect QuikSilver Enterprises from sabotage. (Bournival considered QuikSilver, with its connotation of mercurial speed and trickery, the perfect name for an Internet marketing company.) But that evening, after Hawke said goodbye and headed for Route Three to Boston, Bournival went online and typed "Davis Hawke" into the Google search engine.

At the top of the search results were a handful of news articles about Hawke's neo-Nazi days, along with several pages devoted to him at the web site of the Southern Poverty Law Center, which tracked hate groups. Bournival read each of the articles carefully as the recognition sunk in. Hawke didn't use aliases such as "Johnny Durango" or "Walter Smith" simply because anonymity made life as a spammer easier. Hawke did it because he was also hiding from his past.

cH@pTer
§e√en

Shiksaa Meets Scott Richter

Shiksaa was a big believer in *spammus interruptus*. When new junk emailers appeared on her radar screen—by sending her spam or getting mentioned in anti-spam newsgroups—she made a point of paying them a preemptive online visit. If the spammer had an America Online account, she would add the screen name to her buddy list and wait to be notified that he or she was online. Then Shiksaa would gently let the newbie know that anti-spammers like her would be hounding them every step of the way. She wanted to divest them of any illusions that junk emailing was an easy way to make a buck. Better to nip a chickenboner in the bud than to try to reform a full-blown, Rokso-grade spam operation.

But it didn't work out quite that way with Scott Richter, president of Colorado-based SaveRealBig, Inc. In July 2001, months before Richter gained the attention of other anti-spammers for his post-9/11 U.S.A. flag ads, Shiksaa added his AOL screen name to her buddy list. When Richter signed on one Saturday evening, she was all over him.

"Hey Scott. I hear you're spamming. Why?"[1]

Richter responded that she must have confused him with Chris Smith, a Minnesota spammer who used the nickname Rizler. But Shiksaa refused to back down.

"Help me out here Scott. One of my friends said you spammed him. I was simply asking if that was true."

"Not that I know of," said Richter.

To help jog his memory, Shiksaa sent Richter the Internet address of several newsgroup postings where copies of his spams had appeared. The messages advertised pagers from a company controlled by Richter. At least one of the spam runs had apparently been relayed through a mail server in Russia.

A couple of minutes went by, and Richter still hadn't responded. Shiksaa assumed he was reading the newsgroup link she had sent. While she was waiting, the AOL "You've Got Mail" voice sounded, so she checked her in-box. Waiting for her there was a message from one of America Online's administrators; it was a notice that the company had just received a report that she was violating AOL's terms of service. The message cited an excerpt from her conversation with Richter.

Before Shiksaa had a chance to explain, AOL's Member Services department suspended her account for spamming.

Shiksaa managed to straighten out AOL over the phone and convinced the company to reinstate her account. But the incident taught her an important lesson about Richter: he knew how to work the system.

Shiksaa would later learn that Richter was the son of a certified public accountant and tax lawyer in San Diego, California. Richter saw less of his dad, Steven S. Richter, after age eleven, when his parents divorced and his dad moved out. But Richter had acquired his father's interest in making and holding onto money.

Unlike his father, Scott didn't go to college and get a business degree. Instead, he spent his time after high school running RAM Amusement Investments, Inc., a vending-machine business he incorporated in 1991 with his mother as corporate secretary. That business frequently took him into bars and restaurants, and he eventually opened his own chain of 50s-style restaurants around Denver known as Great Scott's Eatery, as well as a nightspot called the Colorado Sports Café.

Spending so much time around good food did a number on Richter's weight. At one point the six-foot-one Richter pushed the scales at nearly 300 pounds. So when the Internet beckoned Richter to try his hand at online entrepreneurship in late 2000, spamming diet pills seemed a natural choice. He even featured himself in a before-and-after photo at a web site for Inferno, the ephedra-based supplement he was selling.

Deep in debt at the time as the result of stock market losses, Richter initially could afford to hire only small-time spammers to deliver his Inferno ads, which listed the Colorado Sports Café's street address as SaveRealBig's corporate headquarters. But as the cash flow picked up, Richter turned to MindShare's Postmaster General system for most of his mailing.

Shiksaa had noticed complaints on Nanae about SaveRealBig spams emanating from MindShare's service. In late August, she posted a note on the newsgroup observing that Richter apparently was using "dirty" mailing lists—containing addresses of people who hadn't opted in to receive them—and that Postmaster General didn't seem to be aware of the problem.

In early November 2001, more glaring proof appeared that Richter's lists weren't of the highest quality. Using the Postmaster General system, SaveRealBig had emailed ads for six-dollar cellphone booster antennas to an Internet discussion list dedicated to the Debian computer operating system. The ads carried the subject line "Vital Emergency Strategy" and played on fears that new terrorist attacks would bring the sorts of communications breakdowns that plagued World Trade Center rescue efforts: "Worried that you or your loved ones won't be able to summon help in a crisis? The Amazing ezBooster is the solution!"

By the end of the month, Richter's ads had caught the attention of America Online. The big online service warned MindShare that, due to member complaints, it intended to remove SaveRealBig from the "white list" of bulk emailers allowed to send messages to AOL members. In response, MindShare's abuse manager (and former MAPS employee) Kelly Molloy Thompson contacted Richter by email with an ultimatum: "You, as a list owner, will need to submit documentation that the AOL addresses on your list were in fact collected through an opt-in process."[2]

According to Thompson, Richter's documentation minimally needed to include the date and time the user opted in, as well as his or her Internet protocol address. Failure to produce such evidence within three days, she said, would result in SaveRealBig's messages "being silently discarded" by AOL's spam filters.

Richter was unable to produce the proof by AOL's deadline. Like many email marketers, he had built his mailing lists, which had grown to over ten million addresses at the time, largely through what are known as coregistration deals. Under such arrangements, operators of web services sell or trade their customer lists to other marketers. In some cases, customers haven't actually given permission for their information to be shared, yet unscrupulous marketers nonetheless pass off their lists as "opt in." In other instances, sites hungry for sales leads essentially trick visitors into granting permission through confusing fine print and numerous checkboxes. Then there are the lists sold as "co-reg" leads which actually contain a blend of data, some of it harvested from the Internet. Not surprisingly, spam complaints from coregistration lists can be common.

(Under pressure from ISPs such as AOL for complete documentation of coregistration data, some fraudulent bulk emailers turned to software programs that could dummy up "proof" that their addresses were not harvested from the Internet or otherwise obtained without the permission of customers.)

Cut off from mailing to AOL through Postmaster General, Richter began focusing his ads on general Internet addresses. But even then, his mailing lists continued to get him—and MindShare—

into trouble. In early December, spam from Richter arrived in the email in-box of anti-spammer Morely Dotes. The message was sent through the PostMaster General service and carried the subject line, "Why should men have all the fun?" It promoted a product called Vigel, which it claimed was "a topical gel that increases feminine sexual pleasure and excitement." According to the SaveRealBig web page advertised in the spam, Vigel contained menthol and the amino acid L-arganine and was "guaranteed to improve your sex-life or your money back!"

Morely Dotes forwarded a copy of the spam to MindShare's Internet service provider with a recommendation that it block all traffic from the company, which he called "a spam-for-hire outfit, with no legitimate users."

At the time, Richter publicly relished the bad-boy image he was gaining among anti-spammers. When several of Richter's SaveRealBig sites were kicked off San Francisco ISP Hurricane Electric in December 2001, Richter posted a note to Nanae that celebrated the action.

"The more attention we get the more money we make. We are going to be big. REALBIG, the name we use says it all … we are legit and getting stronger by the day. The more people talk about us the more companies find us. COMPLAINERS=$$$$$$," wrote Richter.

A few days later, as spam fighters were discussing Richter's listing on the Spews.org blacklist, he jumped into the fray: "I love the public's eye and the attention. Keep chatting; I LOVE EVERY MINUTE OF IT. MAKE ME FAMOUS."

But contrary to his public posturing, Richter was privately seething over the attention his spams had generated. In early January 2002, he phoned management at Peer 1 Network, an ISP based in British Columbia. Rob Mitzel, the ISP's abuse coordinator, had posted what Richter considered defamatory comments on Nanae about SaveRealBig. When Richter threatened to sue the company, Mitzel published a public apology on Nanae.

"On behalf of Peer 1 Network and myself, I would like to apologize to Scott Richter, Richter Enterprises, and his various SaveRealBig. com domains, for any slight I may have caused him," began Mitzel's mea culpa. (He concluded with a postscript that stated, "I am not doing this on my own volition. This is being required of me by my company.")

The incident followed a similar lawsuit threat from Richter against Communitech, a Missouri ISP that found itself on the Spews blacklist in September 2001 for hosting Richter's sites. In December 2001, Richter targeted Communitech employee Randy Rostie after he announced the ISP had kicked Richter off its service.

"I will take pleasure in suing you personally RANDY for all your remarks you made about us," said Richter in a newsgroup message. "I hope your company is ready to stand behind you. They will lose a lot more than your remarks will ever profit you," he added.

Meanwhile, Richter continued his public shenanigans aimed at getting under the skin of anti-spammers. In January, Shiksaa noticed that Richter had somehow managed to get himself listed at an online gallery of top spam fighters. Richter had apparently duped the site's operator into including his photograph among those of scores of anti-spammers.

"Paging Snotty Scotty Richter," wrote Shiksaa in a message to Nanae, "you're a spamming slime ball and not an anti-spammer."

By February 2002, Richter's SaveRealBig was in big trouble, thanks to smothering blacklists and a shortage of ISPs willing to carry his web sites. In a change of strategy, Richter decided to try a more conciliatory tone with anti-spammers in general and Shiksaa in particular. He announced in a message to Nanae that his company was going to "reconfirm" its list of thirteen million email addresses as part of an effort to clean up its practices.

Richter said the process would involve sending a message to the entire list asking recipients to confirm their interest in future mailings from his new company, OptinRealBig. To give the reconfirmation effort legitimacy, Richter said he wanted to retain the services of "a reputable person to oversee this process...so that there are no questions about us doing anything wrong."

A few days later, Richter followed up with a message specifically addressed to Shiksaa, pleading with her to put the past behind her.

"I hope that you will not chase around our new sites, as we are doing what you have wanted us to do for some time...life is much too short for games and I would much rather work with the Anti Spam groups than against them," he wrote.[3]

But Shiksaa wasn't buying. She pointed out that he had recently registered the domain Spam-Stopper.org under his father's name.

"Here's a novel way to stop spam, Snotty...stop spamming!" Shiksaa said.

Then she posted the Internet address of Goodman & Richter, the San Diego law firm where Richter's father was a partner. Shiksaa noted that, according to a profile at the site, Steven Richter had one son.

"Poor Mr. Richter only had one loser son. That must really rankle," she wrote.

"I am old enough to never make fun of your family, but I could stoop to your level if you want me to," was Richter's reply. "Let me know if you want to be professional or not. I can play with you either way."

Shiksaa backed off at that point. Then a few days later, she received an instant message from a stranger using the screen name EZBulkMail4U.[4]

"Leave Richter alone. He's trying to do the RIGHT THING."

"Go to hell, spammer," she replied.

"You people don't know who ur messin with."

"And who might you be?" asked Shiksaa.

"I won't tell you that, sorry. But I'd be careful if I was you. That's a warning."

"Careful of what, pray tell?" she asked.

"Someone will get in trouble over this thing," said EZBulkMail4U, and then he signed off.

Shiksaa wasn't intimidated by the warning from EZBulkMail4U and went right back to tangling with Richter on Nanae. One day in the middle of March, newsgroup regulars were treated to some especially heated banter between the two. At the time, spam fighters had been discussing the belated announcement by MindShare that it had hired Kelly Molloy Thompson as well as another former MAPS director named Peter Popovich to enforce its anti-spam policies. Some anti-spammers argued that the continuing flow of spam from MindShare's Postmaster General service proved that the former MAPS employees had been co-opted.

Suddenly, Richter piped up with an offer to hire Shiksaa as his company's email abuse officer.

"I would give you what ever you wanted to run our AUP [acceptable use policy] and would give you full control. I just think you're too scared to take the challenge," said Richter.[5]

Shiksaa suggested he save himself the money and download the AUP templates available for free from Spamhaus.org.

"I'm sure there are people who are willing to help you as long as you pay their price," Shiksaa said. "I don't like you, Snotty, and my life is far too busy to waste a second on someone whom I know first-hand is a liar and a vicious little worm."

Richter simply replied, " I love you, Shika Poo."

Shiksaa contemplated his comment for a moment.

"Sad thing is, Snotty, you're telling the truth. You want me, but I always promised my dad I'd never date outside my species."

Hawke Goes Home to Rhode Island

Frigid air cascaded through the open windows of Davis Hawke's new apartment in Pawtucket, Rhode Island. The temperature outside that night in January 2002 dipped into the low twenties. It was only marginally warmer inside the unheated bedroom on the top floor of the triple-decker at 40 Crescent Road. But Hawke slept soundly on a mattress on the floor, covered by just a thin blanket.

Since leaving the South that fall, Hawke had become obsessed with his health. He was a strict vegan, eating no animal products whatsoever and relying primarily on edamame soybeans for his protein. He consumed no refined sugar and completely abstained from alcohol, cigarettes, and recreational drugs. Sleeping in a well-ventilated bedroom was part of that regimen. Unfortunately, Pawtucket, a mill town just outside Providence, had some of the worst air Hawke had breathed in years. Ozone levels in Rhode Island regularly exceeded limits set by the Environmental Protection Agency, and the state was vexed with one of the nation's highest rates of childhood asthma.

But the cold night air was good preparation for a goal Hawke had of spending a week without a tent or other equipment on Mount Washington, the highest peak in the Northeast, renowned for its brutal weather. To harden himself for the challenge, he had been reading about a boot camp run by the U.S. Air Force called SERE, which stood for Survival, Evasion, Resistance, and Escape. SERE taught students how to survive in all types of weather conditions and captivity situations, and many went on to become members of elite forces such as the Army's Special Operations group.

Aside from the mattress and a table with his computer, there were few furnishings in Hawke's new apartment. He had unloaded most of his belongings the previous autumn in northern Vermont. When he and Patricia decided to get out of Tennessee, they had picked Vermont for its rugged terrain and its concealed-carry gun law. (The state allowed citizens to own and carry guns without a permit.) On a reconnaissance trip to Vermont, they had found a nice cabin to rent in the hills outside Lyndonville. The woods and hiking trails were perfect for raising their wolves, and yet the town was right on I-91.

But after a few months, Hawke became restless. He had been living with Patricia for nearly three years. When they first met he had liked that she was a loner and wasn't preoccupied with her appearance. But lately she had become too antisocial for him and was putting on weight. The whole thing just started to feel way too much like marriage. So, Hawke left Patricia behind when he moved to Rhode Island. He intended to continue supporting her and to visit her regularly in Vermont, but he needed his freedom.

Hawke chose Pawtucket because of Mauricio Ruiz. He lived with his parents just ten minutes away in North Providence and was commuting to classes at nearby Bryant College in North Smithfield. The clincher was when Hawke made a few calls about rentals the following winter and found the apartment on Crescent Road, which was not only cheap but didn't require a credit check.

Moving to Pawtucket was a homecoming in many ways. Hawke was now just thirty miles from his birthplace in Newport and equidistant from Lakeville, Massachusetts, where he spent his early childhood, and Westwood, Massachusetts, the home of his 80-year-old grandparents. Unbeknownst to them, he had used his laptop computer and their phone line to mail several batches of spam for diet pills and Banned CDs. On Christmas Eve 2001, he even spammed some ads for Ginsu knives from their house. (Hawke also kept one of his money stashes in a hollowed out book he hid on a bookshelf in their house.)[6]

The bonus in Pawtucket was Paola Castaneda, his old high school girlfriend. They had lost contact during college, but in Tennessee he found out she was still single and living in Pawtucket. He looked her up during a visit to the area in the summer of 2001, and they hit it off again.

And Hawke's apprentice, Brad Bournival, was now just a couple hours away in southern New Hampshire. Since their initial tutoring session, Hawke and Bournival had been in frequent contact by email and telephone. Then, in early February 2002 they decided to hang out together at a chess tournament in Lowell, Massachusetts.

With his 2200 USCF rating, Bournival played in the tournament's open division, while Hawke swallowed his pride and entered the Under-2100 group using his pseudonym Walter Smith. Bournival managed a draw with Paschall in the first round and then drew again in his next pairing. After Hawke split his two matches, both he and Bournival decided to withdraw from the tournament. It would have been a relatively unmemorable competition, except for something Hawke did the first night.

From his room in a Lowell hotel, Hawke sent off a batch of spam, forging the routing headers on the messages so they appeared to come from the operators of the Internet Chess Club site. (He listed Webmaster@chessclub.com in the From and Return-Path headers of the spams.) Earlier that week, Hawke had been kicked off the ICC after the club received several complaints that he had developed a tendency to cheat and verbally abuse other players, especially when losing. When Hawke didn't heed warnings, the club's webmaster permanently banned him from the service. As a result, the club would have to deal with the thousands of error messages and complaints generated by Hawke's spam.[7]

It was Hawke's maiden run for an herbal Viagra alternative called V-Force. He wasn't convinced V-Force would sell well, but he decided it was the perfect product to embarrass the prudish operators of the ICC. His ads said that the thirty-dollar bottle of pills would "turbo-boost" a man's sex drive. The yohimbe, zinc, and other ingredients in V-Force were guaranteed to counter impotency, dramatically increase the user's "staying power," magnify his orgasms, "and even add some extra length and girth" to his penis.

Hawke didn't hide the fact that QuikSilver was responsible for the Joe-job. At the bottom of each spam was listed the Manchester, New Hampshire post office box he and Bournival had opened the previous October. But the ICC simply shrugged off the Joe-job and was content just to have Hawke off its membership roll.

Hawke's experiment with V-Force produced some sales, but he never followed up with repeat mailings. He was distracted at the time by some infrastructure work he was doing for QuikSilver. By the spring of 2002, Hawke's Pawtucket apartment remained austere, but he had furnished it with a T1 line from AT&T. The high-speed connection enabled him to set up several computers in his parlor, each with its own zippy link to the Internet. That way, he could split his mailing list into several chunks and let different computers simultaneously churn away at it. Meanwhile, there would still be plenty of network bandwidth to carry out other tasks such as uploading files to his web sites or just surfing the Internet. (To prevent anti-spammers from discovering his T1 and the twenty-five IP addresses that AT&T had allocated to him, Hawke always used Send-Safe, which concealed the true origin of his spams.)

But Hawke's Crescent Road apartment wasn't all business. It also became the site of numerous poker games involving Ruiz and Michael Clark, a high school kid from Pawtucket who was one of the top scholastic chess players in the state. After Hawke discovered the tennis courts in Slater Park, he befriended several tennis players, including a Lebanese immigrant named Loay Samhoun. Ruiz's girl-friend Liliana also often hung out with them and became pals with Paola. And Ruiz's cousin, Mike Torres, was a regular member of Hawke's poker posse as well.

After six lonely years living in the South, Hawke suddenly found himself at the center of an active social circle. It didn't strike him as especially ironic that so many of his new cadre were non-white or that he had picked up their rap-music-inspired slang.

Hawke had always taken a philosophical view of race. To him, the races were not equal; each had its strengths and weaknesses, with whites ending up with the balance in their favor. But that didn't mean Hawke couldn't allow that, for example, a black might be brilliant—or a poor athlete for that matter.

Bottom line: Hawke no longer cared about which race would survive. All that mattered was how *he* would survive.[8]

Hawke's views on race had been tempered by 2002, but they still hadn't caught up with those held by his great, great grandfather one hundred years before. Both Hawke (Andrew Britt Greenbaum) and his father (Hyman Andrew Greenbaum) had been named after ancestor Andrew Sledd, who was a civil-rights advocate at the turn of the century.

As a professor of Latin at Emory University in Georgia, Sledd published a controversial 1902 magazine article in the *Atlantic Monthly* entitled "The Negro: Another View."[9] The 32-year-old Sledd had written the piece after a train on which he was traveling stopped en route so that passengers could observe a lynching that was taking place beside the tracks.

Sledd's article described how the crowd, "mad with the terrible blood lust that wild beasts know," strung up a black man named Sam Hose and delighted in "the indescribable and sickening torture and writhing of a fellow human being." Sledd's article denounced lynching and said that while blacks may not be equal, that was merely the result of segregation and slavery and could be undone "by process of development."

After the article appeared, Sledd was branded a race traitor. An effigy of him was burned in the streets of Covington, the Georgia town where the lynching took place. The board of Emory soon demanded his resignation and for decades did its best to hush up what came to be known as the "Sledd Affair."[10]

Sledd was eventually celebrated in the North as a courageous prophet against prejudice, and he triumphantly returned to Emory a dozen years later as a professor of theology. But budget problems at the University led to severe faculty salary cuts, forcing him to live his final years close to poverty. Sledd died destitute at the age of sixty-nine, with his family forced to sell his furniture and books to pay off his debts.

For Davis Hawke, the ending of Sledd's story would have pained him the most. But for some reason, Hawke's parents never told him of his namesake ancestor's civil-rights activism.

Hoffman Catches Tom Cowles

After a brief stakeout, the Ohio Bureau of Criminal Investigations finally decided to make its move. In the late morning of Thursday, March 7, 2002, five unmarked cars pulled up outside 1133 Corporate Drive, a low-slung white building in an upscale corporate park in suburban Toledo. A dozen agents from the BCI and Federal Bureau of Investigation piled out, some with guns drawn. They were looking for Thomas Carlton Cowles, president of Empire Towers Corporation.

Karen Hoffmann watched it all go down from her car across the street. She couldn't clearly make out what was happening, but she snapped a few photographs anyway as the BCI agents swarmed the building's front entrance. Earlier that morning the officer in charge had called to give her a heads-up that the raid was scheduled for eleven. It was her reward for assisting law enforcement in investigating and locating Cowles.

Hoffmann was the one who first discovered that Cowles had moved into the 1133 Corporate Drive location. A few months back she had spotted the address in some Internet domains registered to Cowles. She visited the building several times to take photographs, which she posted at "As the Spamhaus Turns," her web site dedicated to Cowles and his spam operation. One of the photos showed the front door of the office, which had a paper sign taped to it that read "Leverage Communications," the name of one of Cowles's companies. In subsequent reconnaissance trips, she had also spotted a dark green convertible parked out front. Hoffmann had been on the lookout for the vehicle after a former Empire Towers employee described Cowles's car to her.

Hoffman first got involved in the case in December, on an invitation from the Wood County (Ohio) sheriff's department. A deputy there had been assigned the task of serving Cowles with the court order from authorities in Broward County, Florida, where Cowles was charged for the August 2001 third-degree grand theft of approximately $16,000 worth of computer equipment allegedly owned by his former business partner, Eddy Marin.

During a search for clues on Tom Cowles's whereabouts, the sheriff's deputy ran across Hoffmann's site dedicated to the man and his spamming operation. At the time, Hoffmann had recently updated the site with a series of photos she had taken of Cowles's residence in the woods beside a river in rural Bowling Green. She had also created separate sections dedicated to his relatives, including 24-year-old sister Shannon; his father, Thomas Herman Cowles; and his brother, Alfred, who was serving time in an Ohio prison for rape.

Even with the detailed dossier Hoffmann had compiled, the Wood County sheriff's office couldn't get its hands on Cowles to serve him with the court papers. So it bumped the matter up to the fugitive task force run by the state's Bureau of Criminal Investigations. In reviewing the case, BCI investigators suspected Cowles might also be involved in something bigger, perhaps an international crime syndicate that trafficked in stolen computers. Undercover agents watched the building at 1133 Corporate Drive for signs of shipments coming or going, but nothing suspicious had happened. Even Cowles's convertible seldom left the lot.

Cowles blamed Hoffmann and her web site for galvanizing anti-spammers into attacking him. Besides the usual hate mail and annoying phone calls, he was subject to particularly bizarre telephone messages from a kook who phoned nearly every day, threatening to kill him. Cowles's 20-year-old wife Dasha was so freaked out by the calls that she refused to be in the house alone when he worked late, which was most nights. So Dasha had begun spending evenings with him in the office, and Cowles had put in a futon so they could crash there if necessary.

That Thursday morning, Cowles was awakened by knocking on the interior door to his personal office. His sister Shannon, who was Empire Towers's secretary, stuck her head in the doorway.

"Tom, the FBI is here!"[11]

"O.K., hold on," he groaned.

Cowles clambered out of bed and grabbed his pants off a nearby file cabinet. Dasha sat up in bed, pulling the covers up to her neck.

"Tom, what are you going to do?" she asked.

"Don't worry. I'll deal with them."

Cowles put on his shirt and then sat down on the floor to pull on his socks and shoes. Suddenly, the door opened again, and a team of BCI agents barged in. Dasha screamed as three officers shoved Cowles to the floor and handcuffed him while others stood by, guns drawn.

Outside, Karen Hoffmann was waiting impatiently in her car for the culmination of more than a year of researching Empire Towers: the sight of Cowles being led out of his office in handcuffs. Instead, she saw a lone BCI agent leave the building and head toward her. After she rolled down her vehicle's window, the agent in charge asked whether she had a list of the computer equipment allegedly stolen by Cowles from Marin.

"There's a couple truck loads of computer gear in there," the agent said.

Amazingly, the BCI had neglected to obtain an inventory from prosecutors in Broward County prior to the raid; such a tally would be necessary in procuring a search warrant. The agent asked Hoffmann, whom the BCI considered the expert on Thomas Cowles, if she could contact Marin and get him to fax over a list of the stolen gear pronto.

"Right now?" asked Hoffmann.

"Right now," he replied.

Hoffmann reluctantly left the scene and raced home. From her office computer, she fired off emails to Kim and Eddy Marin. (Eddy had been released from prison in January 2002.) To her relief, moments later she received a fax from the Marins with a list of their missing equipment. Hoffmann sped back to Corporate Drive, only to find that Cowles had already been transported to the Wood County jail. A few BCI agents were still milling about, waiting to execute the search warrant when it arrived. When one of them invited Hoffmann to BCI's downtown Toledo headquarters to help write up the warrant, Hoffmann was happy to oblige.

After she got the news from Hoffmann, Kim Marin sent an instant message to Shiksaa.

"Guess who just got arrested," she asked.

Shiksaa was away from her computer at the time and didn't respond, so Marin left her a note.

"They nailed the piece of shit and they are waiting for a search warrant for the pig's warehouse to try and recover my property. Talk to you later. Karen can give you more scoop since she is there," said Marin.

That evening, Hoffmann wrote up an account of the day's events and posted it to her web site. She reported that authorities said they found Cowles "crouched behind a file cabinet," and that the "mattress" in the room suggested Cowles had been "camping out in the office" in order to elude arrest.[12]

At the top of her web page about the arrest, Hoffmann posted a copy of the booking photo taken of Cowles that afternoon by the Wood County Sheriff. Cowles was wearing prison garb; he was unshaved and his shoulder-length hair was unkempt. Cowles's eyes looked red and swollen, prompting Hoffmann to compose this description of her feelings about the events of the day:

Yeah...I'm sad. Sad because there are still so many unanswered questions. Sad because his eyes are so sad. Sad because take away the crime, and he's just a normal computer geek with incredible skills that could have been put to good use. And, sad because his arrest doesn't give me any closure. Why does such a charming local boy turn to a life of crime when he has such a brilliant mind?

Cowles was hashing out an entirely different set of questions in his cell at the Wood County Justice Center. He was astounded that state attorneys in Florida had decided to file criminal charges against him. As he saw it, the case was a simple civil dispute between former business partners over the ownership of five computers. Why were prosecutors in both Florida and Ohio dedicating thousands of dollars to such a silly case? And why were they doing it all on behalf of a convicted money launderer and cocaine dealer?

Cowles partly blamed Hoffmann for his situation. He believed she had cajoled authorities into pursuing the charges against him, probably under the pretense that it was a great way to incapacitate one of the Internet's biggest spammers. But most of all, he blamed Marin.

Cowles ended up spending four nights in the pokey, thanks to a bureaucratic screw up that delayed his arraignment until Monday morning. So as not to miss the event, Hoffmann and a friend arrived at the Bowling Green Municipal Courthouse twenty minutes early. Hoffmann had learned that prisoners didn't appear in person and instead were arraigned over closed-circuit television, so she took a seat in the courtroom's third row near the TV.

While they waited for the start of the hearing, Hoffmann and her friend noticed a young woman walk into the courtroom and head right toward them. Hoffmann hadn't seen the woman before, but she immediately knew it was Cowles's Russian wife, Dasha.

Dasha strode to the front row, turned around to face Hoffmann, and pulled something out of her purse. There was a flash of light as she snapped Hoffmann's photo with a disposable camera.

"You have to leave," ordered Dasha.[13]

Hoffmann was stunned. "No, we don't. We have a right to be here," she replied, looking around for the bailiff or anyone else in authority who could back her up. But the courtroom was empty.

Her pretty face contorted with anger, Dasha pointed at Hoffmann. "We are filing a stalking complaint against you. And trespassing. You can't harass us like this."

In researching Cowles, Hoffmann had learned that Dasha kept a tank of eight piranhas in her house. Seeing Dasha in person for the first time, Hoffmann understood the younger woman's taste in pets.

"I'm not stalking anybody, and I'm staying right here," Hoffmann replied.

Dasha scowled at Hoffmann before turning away and walking briskly out of the courtroom. Moments later, she returned with a half-dozen people, including Cowles's attorney, father, and sister. Without making eye contact with Hoffmann, they filed into the row ahead of her on the other side of the aisle and took their seats.

The hearing lasted only a few minutes. Cowles appeared on the TV monitor, wearing his prison uniform and looking nearly as disheveled as he had in his arrest photo.

After brief statements by Cowles's attorney and the county prosecutor, the judge set the bond at $5,000 and ordered Cowles to deal with the grand theft charges in Florida before March 29, when the judge would conduct Cowles's extradition hearing.

As Cowles's entourage left the courtroom and gathered in a conference room outside, Hoffmann and her friend remained behind for a few minutes, hoping to avoid another confrontation. Once safely back home, she wrote up an account of the hearing and published it on her web site, along with a photograph she had taken outside the Wood County jail. (Cowles posted bond and was released from the jail later that day.)

Hoffmann heard nothing more regarding the threatened stalking complaint. The only hint she had that Cowles was back in action came a few days later, when Shiksaa announced on Nanae an unusual discovery. According to Shiksaa, Cowles had recently assigned some very familiar names to two of his computer servers. The machines now bore the names Shiksaa.leveragecomm.com and Karen.leveragecomm.com.

Despite this virtual nod to her, Cowles didn't even glance at Hoffmann during his next court appearance. At the March 29 extradition hearing, Hoffmann and her friend decided to keep a lower profile and sat in the back of the courtroom. Cowles entered with Dasha and his attorney, and they all took seats a few rows up. Cowles, dressed in a suit, looked frighteningly thin to Hoffmann. His skin had an unhealthy pallor, and his long hair desperately needed washing.

When Cowles's case was called, he and his lawyer rose and stood before the judge, who demanded to know why Cowles hadn't been to Florida to face the charges there. Cowles's attorney assured the judge that his client fully intended to resolve the matter but had run into obstacles lining up legal representation in Florida. The attorney asked the court to grant a continuance to allow Cowles to continue working to resolve the Broward County charges.

The judge was visibly annoyed by the request. He turned directly to Cowles.

"You knew what the ground rules were. If you had been to Florida, this would have gone away," said the judge. Then he summarily announced that he was denying the request for a continuance and revoking Cowles's bond.[14]

"Bailiff, please take Mr. Cowles into custody," he ordered.

Astounded by the sudden turn of events, Hoffmann watched as Cowles emptied his pockets at the bailiff's desk. She was caught further off guard when Dasha stood up and started snapping photos of Hoffmann and her friend. Dasha's camera flashed repeatedly, causing Hoffmann's friend to call out, "Lady, stop taking my picture!"

The commotion caught the attention of everyone in the packed courtroom. Embarrassed at the spectacle Dasha was creating, Hoffmann and her friend rose and quickly made their way out of the building, with Dasha snapping a few final shots in the hallway for good measure. Hoffmann contemplated getting her own camera from her car and returning to exchange fire with Dasha, but she abstained. To date, Hoffman had restricted herself to taking photographs of Cowles's property but not of him or his relatives. She considered it rude to photograph someone without permission. But Dasha, evidencing what Hoffmann considered a typical spammer's mentality, wouldn't take no for an answer.

In an update to her web site that evening, Hoffmann described the bizarre hearing. She reported that Cowles was probably facing an extended stay in the Wood County jail unless Broward County authorities expedited his case.

"Stay tuned for the next exciting episode, when Florida's plans for Tommy are revealed," she wrote in concluding her account of the events.

As it turned out, Cowles spent four more nights in jail before being released April 2. His attorney arranged a hearing for him the next morning in Florida's Broward County Courthouse. He pled not guilty, posted a one-thousand-dollar cash bond, and took the red-eye back to Ohio. Then he began what would eventually become a two-year wait for trial.

With Cowles finally in the grip of the long arm of the law, Hoffmann lost some of her inspiration. She continued to be Nanae's expert on Empire Towers and kept a watchful eye on the company and its leader, but Hoffmann didn't provide the promised updates to her site. In fact, she didn't touch it again until early August of 2002, when an Associated Press story about spam appeared in newspapers and on Internet news sites all over the world.

The article, the second in a three-part series on spam, discussed how "relentless anti-spam vigilantes" were hounding Cowles and other bulk emailers. According to the AP, Cowles admitted to counter measures such as obfuscating the addresses of his web sites. For years, Hoffmann had been trying to get the media interested in exposing Cowles, and finally it seemed that her little web site had paid off. But then the article abruptly shifted gears:

> But Cowles is also the target of a stalker who has created a Web site larded with pictures of his home, his driving record and a pair of police mug shots from non-spam-related arrests.
>
> "We had to go to a prosecutor to stop this woman from following my wife and taking pictures of her," Cowles said.

The article didn't mention Hoffmann by name, but anyone who plugged "Tom Cowles" into a search engine could easily figure it out. (Her site appeared near the top of search results.)

Hoffmann was enraged. The article made her look like a nutcase. She had never followed Dasha or Cowles or threatened them in any way, with the exception of exposing their spam operation. Nor had anyone in law enforcement ever contacted her about any stalking complaints. In fact, state and local authorities had turned to her for assistance in tracking down and arresting Cowles. Why, she wondered, hadn't the AP mentioned that crucial fact?

Hoffmann emailed a detailed critique to the AP reporter and posted a copy on her site and on Nanae. She noted that he hadn't given her a chance to defend herself. (The reporter had attempted to contact her by email prior to publishing the article. But when she replied three days later with her phone number, the reporter emailed her back to say he was "pretty much done with the story," and he never phoned her for an interview.)

Anti-spammers on Nanae sympathized with Hoffmann, but the consensus was that she had no legal recourse. Hoffmann contented herself with knowing that the article had indirectly caused Cowles's true nature to be revealed. In a note to Nanae, she reported that traffic to her site had suddenly gone through the roof, the result of web surfers searching for more information about Cowles.

Hoffmann's note also drew a reply from Scott Richter, who had been following the Nanae discussion. In June, Richter's spamming had earned him a place on the Spamhaus Register of Known Spam Operations. But he wasn't mentioned in the AP story.

"I was wondering if you sell banner space for advertising on your site?" Richter joked with Hoffmann.

"LOL. Yes," she replied. "Send cheesecake."

CHAPTER *eight*

Amazing Internet Products

Brad Bournival might have been precocious at chess, but his first attempt at spamming was downright pitiful. In October 2001, he mailed ads for an herbal energy pill to a list of 50,000 email addresses. Hawke said he had bought the list from Alan "Dr. Fatburn" Moore, who had harvested them from eBay. The addresses usually gave Hawke a good response rate—nearly two-tenths of a percent—so Bournival braced himself for a deluge of around one hundred orders worth several thousand dollars.

A week went by, and he mysteriously still hadn't received a single order.

Bournival stuck with it, though. After some additional coaching from Hawke, the 17-year-old was soon pulling down nearly one thousand dollars each week as a spammer, mostly from sales of pheromone cologne and ink-jet refill kits. The money was proof that he had made the right decision to drop out of school. Young relatives and friends still in school had no money or were working minimum-wage jobs, jealous of his new career as an Internet entrepreneur.

On Hawke's suggestion, Bournival plowed some of his spamming profits back into the business. He bought a couple of new computers and had a DSL line installed in his mother's apartment on Montgomery Street in Manchester. The phone company didn't do inside wiring, so Bournival had to snake the wire from the network interface box at the back of the building up the siding and into a window on the second floor. Inside, he used duct tape to secure the wire to the floor so no one would trip on it. But that didn't stop the pit bull owned by his mother's boyfriend from chewing through the wire one day and temporarily downing his Internet connection.

Bournival's web sites were held together with the digital equivalent of duct tape and were prone to similar problems. In March of 2002, anti-spammers discovered that his pheromone-labs.com site, which he shared with Hawke, was insecure and allowed anyone to browse the customer order data, including credit card numbers. Someone posted a note to Nanae about the discovery and published the domain registration record for the site, which included Bournival's name, address, email, and home phone number. It was just six months into his spamming career, and Bournival had already been outed on Nanae.

When Shiksaa heard the news about the open directory, she surfed to pheromone-labs.com and took a look around for herself. The ordering page caught her eye—it listed QuikSilver Enterprises and a post office box in Montpelier, Vermont. She posted a message on Nanae reminding anti-spammers that QuikSilver was run by Davis Wolfgang Hawke, who was prone to using numerous aliases. She assumed Braden Bournival was one of them.

When an anti-spammer named Terry announced he had sent an email to Bournival to warn him about the security problem, Shiksaa fired off a quick reply.

"Why? He's a longtime spammer," she wrote.

Terry, obviously in awe of her, apologized. "One day I will learn…" he said.

Soon after the incident, pheromone-labs.com was added to the Spews.org spam blacklist. Because Bournival's domain was actually hosted on a web server operated by Dr. Fatburn, Spews listed the site as part of Fatburn's record. Since early 2002, Hawke and Bournival had been using the Maryland spammer to host some of their sites. They also arranged to use landing pages at Dr. Fatburn's 2002marketing.com site. It was all part of an uneasy truce worked out between Hawke and Fatburn in late 2001. Hawke had agreed to stop ripping off Fatburn's diet pill ads and instead to start sending out spams for Extreme Power Plus (EPP). Hawke's sales of EPP earned Fatburn a commission from Dutch International.

But the commingling of QuikSilver and Maryland Internet Marketing on Spews meant Dr. Fatburn would often be blamed for Bournival and Hawke's spams for months to come.

Occasional setbacks didn't dampen Bournival's desire to ratchet up his spam income. He experimented with a variety of different products, quickly dropping those that didn't sell well, such as Quick-Bust, a "breast enhancer." But in time he began to resent the revenue split he had agreed to with Hawke. It seemed increasingly like a tax for being allowed to use Hawke's merchant account. Bournival was able to convince Hawke to lower his cut of Bournival's sales to just 20 percent. But the younger spammer wanted even more for himself.

When Bournival turned eighteen in April 2002, he celebrated by registering his own trade name—Basic Internet Marketing Services—with the New Hampshire Secretary of State. Then he signed up for his own credit card merchant account. Now he was able to capture all of the profits from any spam he sent, without Hawke knowing. To prevent his mentor from becoming suspicious, Bournival continued to do the occasional mailing for Hawke and even began handling some of his order fulfillment—packing up and shipping out bottles of diet pills and other products. That way, Hawke would continue to provide him with mailing lists and other benefits.

Bournival had an explanation ready if Hawke ever discovered he was being double-crossed: *You're the one who preaches that a person's first concern should be himself. I'm only doing what you taught me, or what you would have done yourself in my shoes.*[1]

During his visits to Pawtucket, Bournival had seen how Hawke was capable of manipulating the people around him. Michael Clark, the Rhode Island high school chess star, was totally under Hawke's spell, even mimicking his mannerisms. Hawke had also gotten Mauricio Ruiz under his thumb by paying Ruiz's rent and otherwise helping him out financially. Even when he was socializing with people, Hawke was always in charge, with everyone else just along for the ride. Bournival promised himself he would never let Hawke control him in that way.

That June of 2002, Bournival discovered what would become his breakout product. Certified Natural Laboratories (formerly Internet Product Distributors), the Kansas firm that had been supplying him with pheromones, informed him that it had developed a new supplement. The primary ingredient of Maxaman was the aphrodisiac and stimulant yohimbe, but Certified wasn't going to market the product like previous herbal Viagra alternatives. Instead, Certified would position Maxaman as a penis-enlargement pill.

Certified Natural provided Bournival with sample ad copy that claimed Maxaman could increase a man's penis size by 25 percent. The pills accomplished this, according to the ad, by boosting blood flow to the penis, "thus expanding the sponge-like erectile tissue in the penis, leading to size gains in both length and thickness." Maxaman worked its magic fairly quickly, according to Certified. After taking Maxaman for three to eight weeks, "you should be able to notice an increase in thickness in both erect and flaccid states, as well as an overall increase in length." Noting that "a recent survey showed that 68% of women are unsatisfied with the size of their partner's penis," the ad included a helpful chart that depicted "the most recent data on penis size. See how you measure up!"

None of this information appeared at Certified Natural's web site about Maxaman. The site simply described the product as a "male-muscle boosting system" and delicately suggested Maxaman enabled men to "enhance their anatomy without dangerous surgery."

The site made no specific promises about size gains, nor did it include instructions that appeared in the ad about "how to measure your penis size correctly."

Bournival wasn't bothered by the discrepancies, which suggested Certified Natural was wary of making fraudulent claims but didn't mind if its spammers did. Bournival was just happy to add a new product to his mix, and he began spamming for Maxaman using Certified Natural's ad copy. Bournival added hyperlinks in the messages to send traffic to special landing pages he rented at Dr. Fatburn's 2002marketing.com site and at a couple other sites Bournival and Hawke had previously set up with an ISP in China. Bournival paid around five dollars per bottle and sold them for twenty-five dollars each, plus a hefty seven-dollar shipping charge.

Since the Certified Natural ad was in HTML format, the language used to render web pages, it was relatively big, so some recipients might not be able to view it properly in their email. So Bournival decided he needed a plain-text version as well. He had always admired Hawke's copywriting skills, and in July he asked his mentor to pen a new Maxaman ad.

At the time, Hawke was on cruise control. Through much of 2002 he had been lackadaisically spamming diet pills and the Banned CD and coasting off the commissions from Bournival's pheromone sales. The two had long ago agreed not to encroach on each other's product lines, and Hawke considered Bournival's move into penis pills a minor violation of that deal. Hawke had abandoned V-Force after a couple mailings in February 2002 and had sporadically spammed Pro-Erex, another herbal Viagra product, for a few months after that. Nonetheless, he was flattered by the request and ended up producing a gem of an ad for Bournival. Hawke's ad opened with the provocative line, "Sex is like fixing your '69 Corvette...":

> ...You better use the right tool for the job or it'll be a disaster! The genetic lottery determines your penis size the instant you're conceived—*POOF* that's all you're getting! But that's all about to change, thanks to

modern science! Finally, a real formula has been designed to make IT bigger…FOREVER! No painful pumps or exercises are required! Just take a "Maxaman" pill with meals and watch it grow to amazing dimensions!

Hawke's ad for Maxaman promised full refunds to users who didn't see two inches of growth. He also wrote some bogus testimonials, such as one from "Lauren from Newark NJ," who said that her boyfriend had started taking Maxaman when she was away on vacation. "When I got back a week and a half later, he told me he had a surprise for me. And boy what a surprise it was!"

Hawke concluded the ad by inviting men to give their mates a similar treat: "Think about how you'll feel when she cries out your name during sex, or after it's over and she hugs you like she's never hugged you before. So place your order now! She will love you for it."

Spammers had been hawking penis pills for several years before Bournival discovered the niche. But he found that the marketplace was nowhere near saturation. Orders for Maxaman started pouring in, with response rates running near three per thousand emails delivered. Bournival decided to hit hard, and he mailed run after run of both the HTML and plain-text ads.

By the end of the summer, he could barely fill the orders fast enough, and nearly every inch of floor space in his mother's apartment was occupied with cartons of pills and packing material. He hired his 26-year-old stepsister to help him with shipping and paid her seventy-five cents for each order she packed. It worked out to about twenty dollars per hour. Sometimes his mother pitched in as well.

In October 2002, Bournival added a third Maxaman ad to his spam runs. He stole the ad copy—which opened with the question, "Want a big penis?"—from a message that arrived in his in-box from a spammer advertising Vig-RX, a competing penis-enlargement product from Leading Edge Marketing, a firm based in the Bahamas that also did business as Albion Medical.

The ad featured some of the most audacious language of any spam he'd seen. It described Vig-RX as a "doctor-approved pill" that provided "up to three full inches" of penis growth. "You'll radiate confidence and success whenever you enter a locker room, and other men will look at you with real envy," promised the Vig-RX ad. The spam then graphically detailed how women enjoy large penises, but concluded with this warning: "Remember, a penis larger than 9" may be too large for most women. But if for some reason you need even more, it is possible for you to safely continue taking Vig-Rx. The choice is up to you..."

In his haste to try out the Vig-RX ad copy in his own Maxaman spams, Bournival neglected to replace all occurrences of the word "Vig-RX" and even left in place a hyperlink to the Vig-RX spammer's web site.

But it hardly mattered. Orders for Maxaman continued to roll in. With his penis-pill profits, Bournival upgraded his network connection, adding a T1 line to the apartment, which enabled him to pump out ads even faster. He also bought his first car, a used Dodge Intrepid that he paid for with $5,000 in cash. For years he had been addicted to car-racing video games, and he finally had his own wheels. The Intrepid would be the first of a collection of muscle cars Bournival would buy with his spam income.

Meanwhile, Hawke devoted a good chunk of time during the summer of 2002 to updating the *The Spambook*, which he renamed *The Bulkbook* and sold for thirty dollars. The revised edition included a new section, "The Mindset," that described the temperament required to be a successful spammer:

> *If you are bothered by complaints or easily swayed, then you should stop reading this immediately and find another plan for making money. You will encounter a large number of unpleasant responses to your emails and hostile consumers who are not at all happy about finding junk email in their Inbox on Sunday morning. But you must rise above these complaints and remember that spamming is essentially GOOD for the consumer.*

*Dealing with the negative reaction to your emails will be much easier if you
are confident about the product you are selling. As long as you are offering
a quality product at a fair price, there is nothing to feel guilty about, no
matter what the reaction to your emails.*

According to *The Bulkbook*, losing a site due to spamming complaints was the biggest problem facing bulkers:

*Let's say you send a million emails on Sunday night and Monday
morning your site is shut down for spamming. Uh oh! Your customers click
on the order link in your email and get a message like this: "The webpage
you are attempting to access is unavailable. The owners of this website
have violated our terms of service and their account is terminated." This
screams "fraud" to your customers. They certainly can't place an order
online, and they won't be too eager to place a telephone order or send cash
if they see a message like that. Your goal must be to maximize the life of
your website. It's not easy, but I know some tricks of the trade.*

Hawke then provided a detailed description of "The Switcheroo," a
technique he claimed to have developed for avoiding lost sales from
web site downtime. The trick, also known as "domain floating,"
required lining up more than one ISP to host a spammed domain.
When the primary hosting firm canceled Hawke's account after
receiving complaints, he went online and modified the DNS-delega-
tion information on file at his domain registrar, so that the domain
now directed users to the new hosting firm's server.

Assuming spammers had adopted his technique of sending ads
on Friday evenings, Hawke described how the Switcheroo would
work:

*Since you can expect your website to be nullified on Monday
morning, you need to...point your domain to your secondary webhost on
Sunday night. It will take 12-24 hours for the change to take effect, and
this will be your only downtime all week. As soon as the delegation details
are updated - presto! You're back online again, and your customers will*

never know you switched from one webhost to another on Monday...and
yes, it works every time.

Hawke might have written the book on bulk emailing, but his spam-related income was dwarfed by Bournival's in late 2002. Bournival was clearing up to fifteen thousand dollars each week, but in the middle of December, his joyride with Maxaman came to an end.

Certified Natural notified him that it had been receiving too many complaints about his Maxaman spams. The company loved the money he was bringing in, but it did not like the heat generated by his ads. So Certified proposed a new "private label" agreement. It would package the pills under a new name, "Pinacle," but without any identification linked to Certified Natural. It would also provide Bournival with professionally designed web pages incorporating the new Pinacle product identity. No other Certified customers would be allowed to sell pills under the Pinacle name.

Bournival wasn't happy about killing his golden goose. Maxaman had made him one of the wealthiest teenagers around. It would take some effort to update his ad copy and rebuild his web sites with the new pages. But it could be a plus to market an exclusive product. Bournival agreed to the new plan, and a few days before Christmas 2002, he started mailing out his first ads for Pinacle.

To his relief, the orders came in more strongly than ever. But that just underscored another problem he'd been having: bumping into the $30,000 combined monthly limit on his Basic Internet Marketing Services merchant accounts. To give himself more headroom, he had arranged to open an account in his grandfather's name as well. But for the past couple of months, Bournival had been forced to halt mailing before the end of the month because he had exceeded the sales limit on his accounts. It was aggravating to know that he was leaving money on the table like that.

A possible solution presented itself when Bournival was playing chess one day with a local chess star. Kevin Cotreau, a 41-year-old former New Hampshire state chess champion, ran a small computer consulting business. The holder of a USCF rating of over 2200, Cotreau was fascinated by Bournival's story of becoming a victim of his own spam success. As they talked, Bournival asked Cotreau if he'd be interested in getting in on the lucrative penis-pill business without having to send a single spam message. All he had to do was use his solid credit rating to sign up for a merchant account with a high monthly limit, say $250,000. Then Bournival would send his Pinacle orders to Cotreau, who would submit them to the bank for processing. Bournival would pay Cotreau a 5-percent cut on all orders he processed through the account.

The two sealed the deal in January 2003 by jointly incorporating Secure Internet Marketing LLC.

Anticipating a huge surge in sales, Bournival decided it was time to move his business out of the apartment and into a proper office space. After shopping around a bit, he found a 2,700-square-foot space in a refurbished mill building in downtown Manchester. The previous tenant had been the failed U.S. Senate campaign of former New Hampshire governor Jeanne Shaheen. Now Bournival would use it to house dozens of computers, work areas for packing and shipping, and row upon row of penis pills in cartons.

Bournival also hired a lawyer to create another company, Amazing Internet Products, LLC. As a limited liability corporation, the new company would potentially shield Bournival to some extent from legal problems arising from the business. Or so he was told.

Bournival was finally ready to bust loose, but weeks went by and Cotreau failed to locate a financial services firm willing to give him an unlimited merchant account. That's when Hawke waltzed into Bournival's office with an enticing but mysterious offer.

Hawke said he had been talking with a guy who made millions of dollars during the dot-com boom years. This person had helped found some sort of online payment-processing firm along the lines of PayPal but had cashed out before the company went bust. According to Hawke, the fellow, who was in his forties, had numerous connections in the banking industry and was willing to broker a deal with Hawke for a limitless merchant account—in exchange for a 10-percent cut, 2.5 percent of which would go to the bank.

"Does he realize you are a spammer?" Bournival asked, incredulous.[2]

"Correctomundo," said Hawke. "He has no problem whatsoever with spam."

Then Hawke laid his cards on the table.

"I could let you process your orders through me and my contact," he suggested, and then added, "but I have a better idea."

Hawke said he and Bournival should start a new spamming company as equal partners. They would continue to sell Pinacle, but Bournival would primarily handle order fulfillment and customer service, while Hawke would do most of the spamming. In addition, Hawke would create an affiliate system, orchestrating a team of spammers who would send out ads for Pinacle and earn a commission—something along the lines of what Dr. Fatburn was doing with his diet pill and anti-virus software business. Finally, of course, Hawke would handle the crucial merchant-account relationship.

Bournival said the idea sounded interesting, but he had doubts about the key element: the mystery financier. Next thing Bournival knew, Hawke was on his cell phone, setting up a meeting with the man, who was based in the Midwest. A few days later, Bournival and Hawke, dressed in suits and trying their hardest to impress, were taking the financier on a tour of the new headquarters of Amazing Internet Products LLC. That evening, they closed the deal over dinner in the Bedford Village Inn, a luxury restaurant and guesthouse built on the site of a nineteenth-century farm in the woods outside Manchester.

In the nearly eighteen months since Hawke first tutored Bournival, the two spammers had never really combined forces. But in March of 2003, armed with their unlimited merchant account, together they unleashed a torrent of Pinacle spam on the Internet.

As Amazing Internet Products, they sent millions of ads that month, with Bournival pumping them out from his T1 in Manchester and Hawke doing the same with his in Pawtucket. Hawke also enlisted some of his Rhode Island gang to join up as the first Pinacle Affiliates. He set up Mauricio Ruiz, Loay Samhoun, and the two Mikes—Clark and Torres—with software, mailing lists, and Pinacle ad copy and promised them a twenty-dollar commission for every fifty-dollar bottle of pills they sold. (Amazing Internet paid Certified just five dollars per bottle, leaving plenty of room for profit after affiliate commissions.)

The group stuck primarily with the ads Bournival had ripped off from Vig-RX, using a rotating collection of message subject lines, including:

Size DOES Matter. Enlarge your penis NOW!

Transform your rod into a monster

Want a king-size PENIS in one week?

Grow your PENIS 2 inches in 2 days!

Add to your manhood

Bournival began using the site he maintained for the New Hampshire Chess Association as a staging area for Amazing Internet Products's web sites. He would upload files to a special directory at NHChess.org, after which Hawke would download and distribute them to the company's handful of web servers scattered throughout the world.

With the launch of Amazing Internet Products, Hawke and Bournival debuted a new technique for keeping their spammed sites online. In the past, they had registered only a few sites, choosing relatively memorable names such as producthaven.com, never-paymore.com, and 2003marketing.net. When a site came under attack from anti-spammers, they would use Hawke's Switcheroo technique and modify the domain record so it pointed to a different ISP's web server, preserving the domain for use in future spams.

The new method, by contrast, treated domains as expendable. The spammers registered scores of addresses with nonsensical names such as jesitack.com, soothling.com, scorping.com, and kohrah.com. Each pointed to one of several web servers, usually located in China or controlled by a Rokso-listed South American spam-hosting company called Super Zonda. If a domain got blacklisted after a spam run, Hawke and Bournival would drop it completely and begin using one of the other warehoused domains in subsequent spams.

When registering domains for Amazing Internet, Hawke and Bournival usually listed a bogus name ("George Baldwan" and "Clell Miller" were two early favorites), along with the address of their MailBoxes Etc. box in Manchester and Bournival's phone number and Yahoo! email account.

But for a brief period, either Hawke or Bournival—neither admitted to being responsible—also put Alan "Dr. Fatburn" Moore's name on some of their numerous domain registrations. When Dr. Fatburn found out, he assumed Hawke did it to shunt onto Fatburn some of the complaints and harassment about spams from QuikSilver and Amazing Internet.

Dr. Fatburn was doubly furious a few weeks later, when Hawke abruptly stopped selling EPP diet pills so he could work full-time on Amazing Internet's Pinacle campaign. Hawke had been sending his orders for EPP to Dutch International, which processed them and paid Dr. Fatburn a commission on each sale for having signed up Hawke as a distributor. A few weeks after Hawke cashed out, Dutch International received several thousand dollars of customer product returns and charge-backs on Hawke's account. The company sent Hawke a bill for the balance he owed, which Hawke simply ignored, as he was prone to do with many of his debts. As a result, Dutch International ended up taking some of the money out of Dr. Fatburn's subsequent commission checks.

Although Amazing Internet Products was just a few weeks old at the time, the groundwork for its eventual demise was already being laid.

Fighting Dr. Fatburn

Aside from Davis Hawke, Dr. Fatburn had few major problems with his downline distributors or sales affiliates. In 2002, their spams—for diet pills, colon cleanser, and herbal Viagra—helped make him a wealthy man. As proof, Dr. Fatburn posted scans of his commission checks at his web site, ultimatediets.com, showing he had made up to $14,000 in a single month. (That was just the tip of the iceberg. Fatburn would later make nearly that much daily selling counterfeit anti-virus software.)

He boasted that his income enabled him to purchase, without a mortgage, "a new 2,400-square-foot home in a very nice area of Maryland." In less than twelve months, Fatburn had gone from being a chickenboner to being quoted in mainstream press articles about email advertising. In December 2002, his photograph even graced the pages of a *Newsweek* article about spam.

The beauty of it was that Dr. Fatburn had stopped pushing the send button himself around August 2002. He paid marketing affiliates a commission of nearly 60 percent to do that dirty work, but the hefty fee was worth it to insulate him from the hassles of drumming up sales. Unfortunately, his web sites remained under constant attack from anti-spammers and had been listed on blacklists such as Spews for months. But that didn't stop him from publishing his name, home address, and telephone numbers in big print on his sites. His mindset remained the same as it had when he put his name on his first spams in 2001: he was an honest, ethical businessman who had nothing to hide.

Dr. Fatburn's decision to leave the spamming to others came shortly after his first online encounter with Shiksaa. One morning in late July of 2002, she contacted him over AOL Instant Messenger (AIM).[3]

"Hey, Dr. Fatburn. How's the bulletproof hosting going?"

"Going great. Why do you ask?" he replied, and then asked who she was.

"I'm an anti-spammer, Dr F."

"Oh, that's a cool job I guess," said Dr. Fatburn.

She tried to get him to talk about the "bulk friendly" hosting he had advertised at the Bulk Barn and his ads for herbal Viagra. But Fatburn wasn't taking the bait.

"Glad to know you are around...Why don't you get a real job?" he asked.

"I have a real job, hon."

Then Shiksaa cut and pasted the domain registration for his site Bulkherbal.com, which included his contact information in Maryland.

"That is you, no?" she asked.

"The funny thing about this whole thing is I don't send out anything. I have hundreds of affiliates marketing my products and one or two guys spam. Yet you lump my entire business as a spam operation. It's quite comical."

"Yes, I saw your info from the Bulk Barn, soliciting spammers," she replied.

"Actually Bulk Barn, for those who do not actually read all the posts, is a great place to find opt-in lists of retail buyers. Bet you didn't know that, did you?"

Shiksaa nearly spat her morning coffee onto her keyboard.

"Opt-in? LOL!" she typed, and for good measure added "hahahaha."

Later that summer, others took notice of Dr. Fatburn's expanding junk email operation. Symantec, the big California-based software firm, was ramping up efforts to block sales of unauthorized ("counterfeit") copies of its popular Norton SystemWorks anti-virus and computer utility software. Symantec's anti-piracy division had learned that Dr. Fatburn had begun marketing CD-ROMs of Norton SystemWorks, without manuals or retail packaging. In a September 2002 *BusinessWeek* article about software scams on the Internet, Symantec's director of security said the company was investigating several suspected counterfeiters, including Dr. Fatburn.

Dr. Fatburn denied that there was anything illegal about his sales of Symantec products. The article quoted him as saying he got the software from wholesalers and that Symantec had originally intended the CD-ROMs for distribution by PC manufacturers.

"Nothing we sell has ever been pirated, bogus, or advertised as anything but what the customer ordered," Dr. Fatburn told the magazine.

Despite Symantec's saber rattling, weeks went by, and Dr. Fatburn heard nothing directly from the company. Then, in late November 2002, ads touting anti-virus software from one of Dr. Fatburn's affiliates landed in the personal email inbox of Francis Uy, a computer technician and tutor at Johns Hopkins University in Baltimore, Maryland. The 33-year-old Uy (pronounced Wee) had been a spam opponent and Nanae participant for years, but he was glad to see this particular message.

A month before, the State of Maryland had enacted a spam law governing junk emails sent by or to citizens of the state. Under the law, residents could sue in small claims court for up to $500 for every offending spam they received. Uy considered the law flawed, because it contained a "knowledge clause" that required the recipient to prove that the spammer should have known the recipient was a Maryland resident. But Uy hoped the law would help pressure spammers who operated in the state. And Linthicum, Maryland–based Dr. Fatburn provided Uy with the perfect test case.

From his office at Johns Hopkins, Uy dug up Dr. Fatburn's phone number and called him. Uy wanted to verify that the spam wasn't the result of a Joe-job. A prickly Fatburn answered and admitted the message was probably legit, but claimed it had been sent by an affiliate and that he was not responsible. Uy hung up without identifying himself.

That evening, Uy added a new page to his personal home page at the Tripod home page service. He gave it the title "Frankie Say No Spam," below which he created a section called "Maryland's Most Wanted Spammers." There, he listed several of Fatburn's phone numbers, email accounts, and mailing addresses. The page also offered links to articles that mentioned the spammer, along with information about the Maryland spam law. Uy also added the line "Don't crap in my back yard!" at the top of the page.

For weeks, Dr. Fatburn was unaware of Uy's site. But in December, he suspected something was amiss when he began to receive more than the usual number of harassing phone calls from anti-spammers. One called his cell phone in the middle of the night while he and his fiancée were sleeping. "We're watching you..." the male caller kept repeating. Others phoned on his toll-free number and sang him the "Spam, spam, spam, spam" line from the Monty Python skit.

The surge of attention from anti-spammers forced a change in tactics from Dr. Fatburn. He started fudging the contact information in his Internet domain registrations, replacing his real name and street address with the pseudonym "John Smitherine" and a post office box. Fatburn also made arrangements to have a security system installed at his house and contacted the telephone company to discuss tracing his calls.

The wave of harassment had already made Dr. Fatburn rather testy when Shiksaa contacted him over AIM one December afternoon and began to needle him about his company's spam.

"Shut your mouth," he snarled. "Hit delete if you do not like what affiliates mail you. We help the economy and people save money. You do nothing but bitch!"[4]

A few days later, after Shiksaa continued to pester him about his business, Dr. Fatburn lashed out at her again. He called her a "crazy woman" and ordered her to leave him alone.

"I am too busy making thousands of dollars to worry about talking to a lunatic anymore, so we will part company as of now," he said. Shiksaa honored Dr. Fatburn's request and didn't chat with him again, even when he tried several times to initiate contact with her via instant message later that month.

But other anti-spammers continued to hound him by telephone. In January 2003, after someone phoned to harass him, Dr. Fatburn asked the caller how he had gotten his phone number. The man told him the information was published on the Internet at a site called "Frankie Say No Spam."

Dr. Fatburn typed the words into a search engine and moments later was staring at Uy's web site. A furious Fatburn scoured the site for information about its author. On one page he found a link to what appeared to be the home page of the author's wife, as well as a mention of his daughter. After a little sleuth work, Fatburn was on the phone to Uy's home. An answering machine picked up, so Fatburn left a brief message including his phone number and a request that Uy return his call.

A few days passed, and Dr. Fatburn still hadn't heard back from Uy. He might have pursued Uy harder if a public-relations disaster hadn't suddenly exploded in his face. On January 15, 2003, Internet-News.com published an article about a security flaw at Fatburn's Salesscape.com web site. The hole enabled web surfers to view hundreds of customer orders for Norton SystemWorks, including names, addresses, phone numbers, and email addresses—but not credit card numbers. The reporter was unable to reach Dr. Fatburn for a comment. But a Symantec spokesperson told InternetNews that Fatburn's company, Maryland Internet Marketing, was selling pirated software and that Symantec had warned him to cease and desist.

"He is not the kind of guy to listen the first or second time around," said the spokesperson, adding that Symantec was proceeding legally.

When Dr. Fatburn heard about the security problem, he moved quickly to protect his customer-order directory with a password. But a few weeks after the article appeared, Dr. Fatburn was added to the Spamhaus Register of Known Spam Operations (Rokso). Soon thereafter, Shiksaa broke a long hiatus and contacted Dr. Fatburn over AIM.

"Georgie, have you been sued yet?"[5]

"No, and I wont be," was his curt reply. "We don't break any laws."

"You're selling pirated Symantec products," she said.

"Symantec knows where I live and knows what we sell is their software. It's not pirated, never was," he replied, adding, "Believe what you want, anti. You guys have so many things screwed up."

"Alan, you know you spam. I know you spam. The entire world knows you spam," said Shiksaa.

"If I was breaking the law, they would have did something," insisted Fatburn.

"Uh huh. I feel sorry for you. You're a pathetic loser."

"Believe what you want. I truly do not care. You are nothing to me. Never was, never will be," he said.

"You dig me. All my spammers do."

Dr. Fatburn wasn't sure what Shiksaa meant by that.

"I am making more money in one week then you will see in your lifetime. Who is pathetic now?" he asked.

"You are, Alan."

"Say what you want. I couldn't care less. Just don't say it to me via email, or IM. You have been warned," he said.

Then Fatburn pulled out the heavy artillery.

"Note that my attorney has been in the process of digging up all your libelous posts and will use it against you in our suit. See what's it like being sued by someone who has the means to bring you to justice for your words."

"Yeah, whatever," Shiksaa typed in reply.

"We may have freedom of speech in this country, but you cannot make wild claims about a corporation and think we are not going to take legal action. You will be my project this year," he threatened.

"Yeah, whatever," she repeated.

"Get ready, Susan, because I know more about you than you know."

While Shiksaa was mulling over that statement, Dr. Fatburn went on to say that he was also in the process of getting the Nanae newsgroup shut down.

"You guys will have to find another place to hang together and talk about your pathetic lives," he said.

Shiksaa had intended to keep quiet at that point, but she couldn't hold her tongue after seeing this last threat.

"LOL!" she blurted out. Since Nanae was a part of the Usenet system and was distributed on computers all over the world, it would be both legally and technically impossible for anyone to eradicate the newsgroup.

But Dr. Fatburn wasn't finished with her yet.

"Your actions are going to be the end of all you stand for," he predicted. "Have a great night and sleep tight knowing that tomorrow, when you return to your boring job, I will be here loving every second of my so-called pathetic life."

Many spam fighters on Nanae hadn't paid much attention to Dr. Fatburn prior to that day in late February 2003. But when Shiksaa published the log file of the conversation, and anti-spammers saw Fatburn's threats to silence her and the newsgroup, many went scurrying to search engines to dig up information on him. Some discovered Francis Uy's web site and the various phone numbers published there. That set off a new wave of harassing phone calls to Dr. Fatburn, including a chilling one that warned him to be careful when he started his car.

Dr. Fatburn had had enough. One Saturday afternoon in early March, he reached Uy at his home by telephone. Fatburn insisted that Uy take down his web site within twenty-four hours or face a lawsuit.

"Why? It's all public information," said a startled Uy. He pointed out that the site contained only data that had been published on the Internet. He told Fatburn that he had lifted Fatburn's contact information directly from his own sites.

Dr. Fatburn told him that wasn't the point.

"You're inciting people to harass me. I've got people calling me in the middle of the night with death threats. They're signing me up for magazine subscriptions and books. It's all because of your web site," Fatburn insisted.

Uy was surprised to learn that some anti-spammers had gone too far. But he stood his ground. "I'm not the one harassing you," he said.

Frustrated with Uy's stubbornness, Dr. Fatburn vowed to take any action necessary to get the site shut down.

"You've got a family. You've got a daughter. Is that worth one little page? You don't realize the repercussions of your actions," he said.

Dr. Fatburn had touched a nerve. Uy's wife, a doctor, had always tolerated Uy's spam fighting, but she didn't like it intruding on their personal lives. Still, Uy held his ground with Fatburn and refused to take down his site.

After the phone call ended in a stalemate, Uy contacted his lawyer for advice. Uy was certain the First Amendment protected his site, but he wanted to be sure.

Lycos, which operated the Tripod home page service, wasn't going to wait around for legal lightning to strike. Responding to a complaint from Dr. Fatburn, on March 5, 2003, Lycos disconnected

Uy's site. According to the company, Uy had violated Tripod's Terms and Conditions of Use, which gave Lycos the ability to terminate any site "for any reason or for no reason at all, in Lycos's sole discretion, without prior notice."

Uy submitted an official request to Tripod appealing the shutdown, and then he posted a message to Nanae.

"Dr. Fatburn knocked down my Tripod site," he announced. "Looks like he's got at least three or four neurons in his little head. Anyone have an inside contact at Tripod who could restore my site?"

Uy never managed to convince Tripod to reinstate his service. But as often happens when Internet users encounter censorship, several mirror copies of Uy's site suddenly appeared on other domains. Uy also set up his own mirror at the Geocities home page service, which Dr. Fatburn was unable to get shut down. As a result, while the world was preoccupied with the U.S. military invasion of Iraq, Fatburn was forced to ratchet up his threats against Uy.

On March 26, Uy received a phone call from the Computer Crimes Unit of the Maryland Police. An officer informed him that Dr. Fatburn was leaning on police to charge him as an accomplice to harassment. The officer suggested that a State Attorney might take up the case if Uy didn't remove his site.

Uy's lawyer had advised him that Fatburn's case was weak and would be deemed frivolous by any court. But Uy didn't cherish the idea of being led off in handcuffs. Ten years ago, before he was a family man, he might have stoically allowed himself to become a martyr over spam. But, as Uy posted in a message that evening to Suespammers, an Internet mailing list, his wife had made clear that her reaction would be chilly if he got himself arrested.

"We have a nice couch, but I'd rather not sleep on it," he wrote.

Uy made a call to the State Attorney's office and managed to convince prosecutors to hold off filing criminal charges against him. But he didn't realize that Dr. Fatburn was also pursuing a civil case against him. As Uy was eating dinner with his family on the evening of March 31, a deputy from the local sheriff's office knocked on the door. The deputy handed Uy a Petition of Peace order and a notice to appear in an Anne Arundel County district court a week later. Normally used to restrain spouse abusers, the order prohibited Uy from going near Moore or his property. But it did not require him to take down his web site.

On the morning of April 7, Uy met his attorney, Jon Biedron, at the Glen Burnie courthouse. Although they were confident of their legal position, Uy and Biedron had some doubts. Typically, the district courthouse was a venue for adjudicating things like driving violations or family disputes, with cases usually lasting less than ten minutes. How would a judge in one of the lowest courts in the land handle a First Amendment case involving the Internet?

Judge Robert Wilcox began by questioning Dr. Fatburn about why he filed the complaint against Uy. After showing the judge a printout of Uy's web site, Fatburn argued that the posting of his personal contact information might look harmless, but it was inciting others to harass him.[6]

"The whole idea behind that web site is that I am a company that people in his anti-spam community should take notice of and take action against," said Fatburn. He then held up a stack of invoices and said anti-spammers were responsible for signing him up for subscriptions to book clubs and dozens of magazines.

"As a direct result of this guy over here's actions," said Fatburn, gesturing to Uy, "we actually fear for our lives."

After listening to Dr. Fatburn for about ten minutes, Judge Wilcox seemed ready to issue his ruling.

"I don't need to hear [Uy's] counsel. I know what he's going to say. Doesn't [Uy] have a Constitutional right here? You're asking me to stop him from posting stuff on the Internet," said the judge. He noted that the harassment Dr. Fatburn was experiencing was potentially illegal, "but to say that [Uy] is doing it, simply by providing identifying information…that's where I'm having the trouble."

Fatburn's attorney, Cheryl Asensio, sought to shift the momentum of the conversation. She asserted that Uy had personally made harassing telephone calls and sent packages to her client. But when the judge asked whether she had proof of those claims, she admitted she didn't.

"Then how can I pass an order?" asked Judge Wilcox. "Isn't the burden on you to provide clear and convincing evidence? If you tell me you don't know who did it, we don't even get to first base," he said.

"I didn't get him to admit on the stand that he's done it, but it's certainly in his statements," argued Asensio.

"Do you want to call him as a witness?" offered the judge.

Asensio hesitated briefly. "May I call my client first?" she asked.

"Sure," answered the judge.

Until this point, twenty-five minutes into the hearing, Uy and his attorney felt they had a slum-dunk case going. But now it looked as though Dr. Fatburn was going to milk his day in court for all it was worth.

Indeed, for nearly an hour, Asensio questioned Dr. Fatburn in detail about the harassment he had undergone and Uy's alleged role in it. Her questions to Fatburn frequently caused objections from Biedron that were sustained by the judge. The whole proceeding, taking place before a nearly empty courtroom, had the air of a law school mock trial.

Finally, it was Biedron's turn to cross-examine Fatburn. He began by asking Fatburn whether he recalled posting his name, address, cell phone number, and photograph at one of his business web sites.

"It's contact information for my customers," answered Fatburn.

"So, that's a yes?"

"That's a yes."

When Biedron was through questioning Dr. Fatburn a few minutes later, Asensio called Uy to testify. She began by asking why Uy had contacted the *Washington Post*, which the day before had published an article about his dispute with Dr. Fatburn.

"I wanted people to know about the case," said Uy.

"Do you want Mr. Moore's business to stop?"

"I'd like him to do business differently," he replied.

At one point, Asensio tried to bolster her claim that Uy was directly involved in harassing Dr. Fatburn. She asked Uy, who was under oath, whether he ever ordered magazine subscriptions over the Internet for anyone else.

"I've sent people some gifts," said Uy.

"Any to Mr. Moore?" asked Asensio.

"No."

"Have you ever ordered books on tape?"

"No."

As Asensio concluded her twenty-minute interrogation of Uy, Judge Wilcox said he had a question.

"How did you get [Moore's] unlisted phone number?"

"As far as I know, it wasn't unlisted. He's got it published on a couple of his web sites," answered Uy.

"All the numbers that you listed were discoverable by the public?" asked the judge.

"Yeah, I just went on the web and looked them up and there it was," said Uy.

Judge Wilcox had heard enough. As the hearing approached the two-hour mark, he said he was ready to rule on the case.

"What we have here is a petitioner who is aggrieved, and rightly so," said the judge. "But I think he has the wrong target. Clearly, if we could identify the persons ordering these magazines or making these phone calls, this court would have little hesitation granting the requested relief or enforcing any sanctions. But I cannot find from the evidence that Mr. Uy did anything wrong. He did something that Mr. Moore doesn't like, but that's not the same thing. So I will deny the petition for the domestic order."

With that, the hearing was over. Uy and Dr. Fatburn separately left the courtroom without so much as a nod of the head toward the other. That afternoon, Uy celebrated the decision by posting a note at Slashdot.org, a popular discussion site that refers to itself as "News for nerds." Uy briefly recounted the court hearing and concluded with a note about Dr. Fatburn:

> [He] tried to send me a message, and wanted to make an example of me. Instead, I had a message for him: every time you try to mess with me, I will post it on the 'net, and more people will learn about you. I don't encourage harassment against you, and I don't need to. The facts speak quite loudly enough. Your best option is to crawl back under a rock and suck it up, or move to some state other than the one I live in.

Dr. Fatburn returned to his home office determined to appeal the court's ruling. To him, the case strongly paralleled a recent one involving the operators of a web site that encouraged attacks on operators of abortion clinics. In Dr. Fatburn's case, Uy had made no obvious appeals for antis to attack him. But Dr. Fatburn believed the proof was out there somewhere.

Still smarting from his courtroom defeat, Dr. Fatburn was hit with much bigger legal troubles a week later. On April 15, 2003, Symantec filed a lawsuit against Dr. Fatburn in a federal district court for Central California. In its complaint, Symantec accused Dr. Fatburn of trademark and copyright infringement, unfair competition, and false advertising, among other charges. The software firm asked the court to stop Fatburn from marketing any products bearing Symantec trademarks and to force him to pay compensatory and punitive damages.

The same day, America Online filed a separate suit against Dr. Fatburn. AOL's lawsuit, filed by the firm's outside counsel Jon Praed, focused on the spams sent by Fatburn and his affiliates, which included numerous unidentified "John Doe" defendants. AOL accused Dr. Fatburn and his henchmen of violating Virginia business and computer crime statutes when they sent its members millions of fraudulent ads for everything from diet pills and herbal Viagra to anti-virus software. AOL claimed the messages typically listed false information in their headers in order to conceal their senders' true addresses. AOL's complaint asked a federal court in Virginia to prohibit Dr. Fatburn and his affiliates from sending ads to AOL subscribers and to compel him to pay damages.

As soon as he found out about the double-barreled lawsuits against him, Dr. Fatburn knew his days as an email marketer were over. And when they read about the lawsuits against their former business partner, Davis Hawke and Brad Bournival realized their days were probably numbered as well.

cHapter
nine

The Shiksaa Shakedown

A ringing telephone roused Shiksaa from her sleep one night in late December 2002. According to her bedside clock, it was four in the morning. But she fumbled for the phone and answered, worried that it might wake her 80-year-old father who lived with her and was quite frail.

"Hello?" she mumbled into the phone.[1]

"Is this Susan?" asked the unfamiliar male voice on the other end.

"Yes, it is," she replied, at once relieved and annoyed.

"Hey, it's Bill Waggoner."

Shiksaa's grogginess instantly disappeared. "How the hell did you get this number?" she demanded. It was an unlisted number that she gave out to very few people, none of whom were spammers.

"Someone just IM'ed it to me. I wanted to see if it really was your number," replied Waggoner, a Las Vegas–based junk emailer who had been on the Spamhaus Register of Known Spam Operations (Rokso) since it began in 2000.

Shiksaa sat up in bed. "You idiot. Do you realize it's four in the morning? Don't ever call this number again, or I'll call the police," she snarled. Then she hung up. She tried to get back to sleep, but she was struggling to understand how the unlisted number had gotten into circulation. Only one explanation made sense. She had recently phoned Scott Richter, head of OptInRealBig LLC, using the line. He must have captured the number with caller ID.

The next day, Shiksaa contacted SBC and got a new unlisted phone number. A customer service representative recommended that she file a police report about the call. Later, she tracked down Waggoner over AIM and confronted him.

"I know who gave you my phone number. Scott Richter himself," she said.

"Yeah, so what's that have to do with anything?" replied Waggoner. "So I called your ass at four a.m. So?"[2]

Shiksaa had been double-crossed. Since early 2002, she and Richter had conversed frequently over AIM. At one point, Richter became her underground informant, passing along dirt he had discovered about other spammers. In May 2002, he even gave her the login information to his account at the Bulk Barn spammers club. ("Merry Christmas" he said in handing her his username and password.) In exchange, Shiksaa invited him to hang out in the #Spews Internet relay chat (IRC) channel, where she and other anti-spammers conversed about their battles with junk email.

Despite her new rapport with Richter, Shiksaa remained cautious. While he seemed truly interested in going legit, Richter still had one foot on the dark side of spamming. In July 2002, Shiksaa discovered that Richter was in cahoots with Florida junk emailer Eddy Marin, whom she considered one of the most egregious spammers on Rokso. Richter hadn't disclosed the deal to Shiksaa. Instead, it came out after anti-spammers stumbled upon an open directory on a web server operated by Marin's company, OptIn Services. The server exposed several megabytes of confidential business information, including invoices and correspondence.

In quickly shuffling through some of Marin's files, Shiksaa found email from Dustin Parker, the 16-year-old head of technology for Richter's Colorado-based OptInRealBig.com. In the message, Parker was making arrangements with Marin's brother, Denny, to host Bodyimprover.com, one of Richter's diet pill sites.

When she confronted him about it, Richter had explained to Shiksaa that he was forced to make deals with the likes of Eddy Marin because no other Internet service providers would do business with him. Richter blamed Spews and Spamhaus blacklists for his inability to line up other providers.

A month later, in August of 2002, Richter posted the latest in a series of requests to be delisted from Spews. In a conciliatory message to anti-spammers on Nanae, Richter said that his history as a junk emailer might make it hard for him to get off spam blacklists.

"I consider using the Internet a privilege and do not take it for granted," wrote Richter. He added a tip of the hat to Shiksaa for helping him clean up his act.

"Susan has been very generous in giving me her time and assistance. Even though she doesn't have to, she does all of this as a volunteer to me," he said.

Shiksaa acknowledged Richter's comment by saying she was always happy to try to help someone who was trying to help himself.

"Good luck, Scott," she concluded.

Later that August, Richter had tipped off Shiksaa that Bill Waggoner was trying to figure out her true identity. After getting a promise from Shiksaa that she wouldn't divulge the information, Richter cut and pasted portions of an AIM conversation he was having at the same time with Waggoner.

"I found out something about Shiksaa. Really interesting," Waggoner told Richter. According to Waggoner, he had discovered that Shiksaa worked as a reporter for CNN.

"Got her social security number," Waggoner boasted.

"Want me to ask him any thing else, before I pass out laughing?" Richter asked Shiksaa.

"Yes," she replied. "Ask him if he has a thing for me like you do," she said, inserting a smiley-face emoticon to show she was only kidding.

"I'm trying to be serious about this," said Richter. Then he pasted another snippet of the log of his simultaneous conversation with Waggoner.

"If I sue, they are going to come here. Even Linford. I can sue him even if he's in Finland," Waggoner had told Richter, referring to Spamhaus's London-based director Steve Linford, whom Waggoner appeared to believe was living in Finland.

Like a lot of the spammer intel Richter relayed to Shiksaa, the information about Waggoner was nothing she hadn't heard before. Earlier that summer, Waggoner had contacted her over AIM and threatened to sue her if she didn't remove his record from Rokso.

"I am researching you and all of the guys who run that right now, and I am close to finding out the goods on everyone. Before I take you guys down hard, I am trying to be polite," Waggoner had said.

"Don't threaten me, ass-wipe," replied Shiksaa.

"It's not a threat. I've already got investigators on your scene, finding your assets, etc."

"You couldn't find your ass if you had a search warrant, flashlight, and a road map," said Shiksaa.

"You really think you're dealing with a moron here, eh?" he asked. "Lady, this can be easy or hard."

"Go away, Billy Bob," was her response.

But Waggoner continued to press the issue.

"I am going to be driving your car, owning your house," he said. "Shiksaa, take my record down and everything will be fine for you."

Although she disliked having to cut off the lines of communication with spammers, Shiksaa had used AIM's "block" feature to prevent Waggoner from contacting her further. Weeks went by, and he still didn't deliver on his threat to sue her.

Meanwhile, Richter had some legal problems of his own. Unknown to anti-spammers, in August 2002 Richter had been charged by the Colorado attorney general with eight counts of theft.

The charges resulted after Richter bought large supplies of stolen cigarettes and other hot items from a Denver undercover policeman between December 1999 and July 2001. Detectives believed that Richter and a business associate were involved in a fencing operation. Richter, who was still running the Colorado Sports Café at the time, claimed he intended to use the cigarettes in his vending machines. He made several trips into one of Denver's grittiest neighborhoods in his Lexus sport-utility vehicle to make the buys.

On January 2, 2003, Richter pled guilty in Adam County District Court to a single count of conspiring to commit theft. He was sentenced to pay nearly $40,000 in restitution and was placed on probation for two years. The court also ordered Richter to perform forty hours of community service. The settlement went unpublicized at the time, but in an article that appeared in Denver's *Westword* newspaper a year later, a detective with the city's antifencing unit called Richter "one of the best crooks I know." Richter claimed the episode was a clear case of entrapment.

Despite his legal problems, by the early spring of 2003, Richter appeared close to clawing his way out of spammer purgatory. It had been nearly six months since Richter's email ads landed in spam traps set up by Spamhaus and many other junk email opponents. Under the guidelines for Rosko, Richter and OptInRealBig had almost been spam-free long enough to qualify for removal from the blacklist.

"We have seen nothing implicating your outfit directly in many months," conceded spam fighter Adam Brower in a late-February 2003 posting to Nanae in response to Richter's request that a block of his company's Internet addresses be removed from the Spews blacklist.

"You've done a great job of restructuring your entire business model," chimed Karen Hoffmann, referring to Richter's efforts to send ads only to people who agreed to receive them. "Hang in there, Scott. Keep up the good work," she added.

But Richter's public plea on Nanae failed to convince the mysterious operators of Spews to take him off their blacklist. So Richter turned his attention to pressuring Shiksaa privately to change or expunge his Spamhaus Rokso record. Richter was especially incensed that his mother's contact information had been added to his Rokso listing.

Shiksaa explained that Spamhaus avoided listing relatives unless they were involved in the spammer's business. Shiksaa pointed out that the name and address of Richter's mother had appeared in a couple of Richter's corporate registrations, making her fair game. Junk emailers often listed relatives in their corporate documents and domain registrations to avoid detection when signing up for web hosting and other services.

Richter had all along denied that he was responsible for Waggoner getting her unlisted phone number. But in early March 2003, Richter proved he was willing to use her personal information as leverage. One evening he sent Shiksaa a teaser of an email. It arrived with the subject line "Quick Question" and appeared to be seeking her advice as an Internet sleuth:

> *Sorry to bother you. I know your busy but wanted to know if you had a link for searching for addresses in California. Wanted to find out info about an Address. Think its residential and in the Stanton area. Thanks Scott.*

Half an hour later, a follow-up message arrived from Richter. This one simply said, "All I have to go on is this," and then listed the street address of her condominium in Stanton, California. Richter signed the message, "Thanks for assisting."

In the nearly four years that Shiksaa had been a spam fighter, she had always tried to protect her address from all but the most trusted spam fighters. She had made arrangements to list Adam Brower's contact information, not her own, in the registration record for her Chickenboner.com site. (She had originally used bogus contact information when she registered the site in 2000 but was forced to list valid information after spammers complained to the company hosting the site.) Similarly, in her Nanae postings, Shiksaa had never revealed so much as the town she lived in, although she made no secret of the fact that she was in southern California and even sometimes mentioned that she resided in Orange County.

The thought that Richter and other potentially vindictive spammers now had her home address was chilling. Fending off kooks by email, IM, and even telephone was something she had become quite adept at. But having them physically stalking her was not something she was prepared to face. Southern California was home to several notorious junk emailers, including some known for making threats of physical harm against anti-spammers. One of them, Rokso denizen Saied "Sam Al" Alzalzalah, lived about an hour north in Beverly Hills. Sam Al had repeatedly emailed violent threats to Spamhaus director Steve Linford. Once, Linford's girlfriend had answered the phone when Sam Al called, and the spammer told her to get out of the house because he was coming to shoot her. Linford shrugged off the threats, but he was a guy living in England, thousands of miles away from Sam Al.

Adding to Shiksaa's worries was her father, who was hospitalized in late January after fainting on a golf course. He was taken to a hospital emergency room, where doctors discovered he had an infection that required immediate treatment. He was home again after his hospital stay, but Shiksaa did not want him worrying about her safety. And yet she knew she should warn him to be extra vigilant now that their address was potentially in the hands of her enemies.

Shiksaa saw only one way out. On the morning of March 6, 2003, she contacted Richter over AIM.[3]

"Scotty, you up?" she asked.

"Yes," came his immediate response.

"My dad is still ill and he does not need to worry about me. I am composing a letter to Steve [Linford] and resigning. Not just Spamhaus, but spam fighting in general," said Shiksaa.

At that moment, she was ready to hang up her LART if it would protect her father from harassment. But even as she typed the words to Richter, she knew he probably saw it as a bluff. Could she really walk away so suddenly from Nanae, Spamhaus, and the last four years of her life?

"If you believe in what you do, you should continue your fight," said Richter. But, he added, if she truly intended to resign, she should first remove his mother's personal information from Rokso.

"You can take that up with Steve," she replied. Then she continued, "It's ironic, since I really wanted to help you and Bill [Waggoner]. So, you won."

Richter advised her to "only do what is right" in deciding whether to quit spam fighting and whether to leave his family information posted on Rokso.

Shiksaa repeated that she was not responsible for his Rokso record.

"Anyway," she said, "I never wished you any ill will. But my dad is sick and I can't have him upset."

Richter became philosophical. "Susan, when you are on your death bed, you have two choices…" he began. Then Richter switched gears somewhat. "I believe in karma. You can fix a lot of the damage you have been associated with. I would hope your dad wants you to do that and make him proud," he said.

"You may not believe this, but I really was on your side," Shiksaa admitted. "I wanted to help you go the right way. I never hated you or anything like that."

Richter ignored her olive branch. "Then you have the power [to remove] what I asked on my record," he insisted.

Shiksaa fired right back. "You have the power to tell me where my info came from. I gave you my word that I would not tell a soul," she said.

Richter bristled. "I haven't posted your family info all over Nanae. That says a lot for me having class," he said. "[But] it doesn't stop you from blasting the world with my info...my damn mom's info for Christ's sake. You're worried about your info—imagine your dad's info all over Nanae for the trolls to use."

Shiksaa read that as a veiled threat, but she tried to remain calm. "I'm sorry it came to this, Scott," she said.

Then Richter said something that puzzled her. "Leave it there," he said, suddenly feigning nonchalance about his Rokso record. "I'd rather make a site of antis' info and run it, maybe like a hobby for me. I need some thing to do," he added.

Shiksaa was startled by Richter's reply. She broke off the conversation at that point, after criticizing him for his decision to "cop an attitude."

The next morning, Richter sought her out over AIM. He revealed that he had gotten her street address from Steve Hardigree, head of Boca Raton–based Internet Media Group, Inc. Hardigree had been in the bulk email business since around 1996 and had been listed on Rokso from day one. Shiksaa knew Hardigree frequently did deals with Eddy Marin and other south Florida spam kings.[4]

"They're serving you for some crap...I'm sure that soon enough you will know what their suit is for," said Richter.

"Serving me for what?" asked Shiksaa. "Calling them spammers? They are spammers."

Richter said Hardigree had revealed his lawsuit plans on a secret Internet mailing list for an elite group of spammers. For years, spammers everywhere had been driven crazy with desire to unmask the mysterious operators of the Spews blacklist. Hardigree and his Boca Raton spamming buddies seemed to believe that she, Shiksaa, was behind Spews. Richter said he was planning to travel to south

Florida later that month to meet with some of the men, and he'd try to get the details of their lawsuit plans.

"Can I see the letter? Please send me a copy," she asked.

"I would be killed for that in this industry," Richter replied. He added that he would continue to feed her information gleaned from the list.

"Why are you associating with a secret spammer cabal if you're cleaning up?" she asked.

"Because, thanks to Spamhaus and Spews, I'm forced to host with them and pay high rates not to get shut down."

Shiksaa paused before replying. "I have nothing to do with Spews, Scott, and anyone who thinks so is insane," she said.

"I know you're not Spews," said Richter. "I'm also confident that who is Spews and associated with it will be well known shortly."

The idea of being sued by spammers seemed ludicrous to Shiksaa. But while the threat of a lawsuit in and of itself didn't bother her, she did worry about the attention it would bring.

"I have had threats made against me, Scott," she told Richter.

"Yes, in Nanae maybe," he replied. "You cannot call someone every name in the book and not expect them to call it back."

"I have never advocated anyone doing anything abusive to a spammer," said Shiksaa.

"Ruining someone's life could be taken to heart I guess," he replied.

"Ruining? How the hell did I ruin anything? I posted information that is publicly available," said Shiksaa.

Richter contemplated her question a moment. "Let me ask you this," he said. "If someone hid and posted bad things about your dad's realty company, would you be pissed if he lost his license over it and had no business left?"

"That's apples and oranges, Scott. If he was violating a law or something, then he would deserve it," she replied.

Rather than continuing to debate the point, Richter returned to the subject of his Rokso record. He asked Shiksaa who was responsible for compiling it.

"I need to know. Whoever does it is obsessed with me. I'm worried that they're watching me like Karen [Hoffmann] used to do to [Thomas] Cowles. I mean, whoever is in charge of me has gone overboard," said Richter.

"Yeah, I feel the same way about me," she replied.

When their conversation was through, Shiksaa contacted the other members of the Spamhaus team. After explaining the situation, she was able to persuade them to remove references to Richter's mother from his Rokso listing. It would have been the perfect opportunity to announce to the group her plans to retire from spam fighting. But Shiksaa held back.

Instead, a few days later, Shiksaa announced on Nanae that rumor had it she would be the target of a lawsuit aimed at revealing her role in Spews. Shiksaa said she was flattered that Steve Hardigree thought she possessed the knowledge to run the blacklist. "Alas, I am not Spews," she wrote. Then Shiksaa added a comment directed at the Boca spammers.

"Gentlemen, wrap the tinfoil more tightly, please, because you are all becoming far too paranoid." (In Internet culture, those who act paranoid are often derided as believing that a tinfoil hat can ward off mind-control rays.)

Two weeks passed, and no news on the legal front for Shiksaa. But then a strange note appeared partway into a Nanae discussion about Spamhaus. The "From" line said the posting was from "Susan Gunn" at email address *spambusta1@aol.com*. To the few anti-spammers who recognized her legal name, the message's content clearly wasn't from Shiksaa.

"The fun has started," said the note. "The fallout will be long and hard. Iraq may not be the main stage any longer. Antispews.org will dominate soon!"

The anonymous "Spambusta1" appeared again later, posting another message on Nanae using an AOL account. Again, the "From" line listed Shiksaa's real name, Susan Gunn. The post's subject line read "Shiksaa Tells All about Spamhaus to BB." The acronym at the end apparently referred to Bulk Barn, the spammer site.

In the message body, the author wrote, "To all the ones who have suffered damage from Spamhaus and Spews, this is your information that you paid for by joining BB." Then Spambusta1 listed Shiksaa's real name, along with the street address of her condo in Stanton. The message also included information copied from the State of California Department of Real Estate site. It was her father's broker license, listing their condominium complex's street address as his main office, along with other data about his realty companies. Below that, Spambusta1 offered this explanation:

> Susan was very easy, and others who participate in Spews have even been easier. We will release that information shortly so that all may file for damages against them. Please use this information correctly; we only list it for research purposes about anti-spammers as Spamhaus does about spammers. All we feel is that the playing field should be played evenly now.

Shiksaa was mortified to see her father's name on Nanae. He didn't even own a computer, let alone work as an anti-spammer. She wasn't sure what Spambusta1 hoped to accomplish by posting her dad's real estate broker information. There was nothing embarrassing about the record, contrary to what Richter had implied in their recent chat.

Spambusta1 may have hoped the posting would finally drive Shiksaa out of the ranks of anti-spammers. But it had the opposite effect. After reading and rereading the message, she was more determined than ever to fight back. She hadn't wanted to dignify Spambusta1's posting with a response, but she couldn't resist. Around noon on March 30, she posted a reply:

> *I happen to be very proud of my father. Not only was he his sole sup-*
> *port by the time he was ten, he served his country at a great sacrifice to*
> *himself. He and his crew were shot down, and my dad refused to bail out*
> *until his whole crew was safely out of the aircraft. He also spent nearly two*
> *years in different POW camps, suffering numerous injuries. And he's pres-*
> *ently recovering from major surgery...so if any one of you motherfuckers*
> *disturbs him in any way whatsoever, you will be answering to me and the*
> *police.*

Spambusta1's original message drew more than 400 replies over the course of several days. Most were from anti-spammers ridiculing the author's investigative skills. (Spamhaus's Steve Linford said—incorrectly—that the home address posted for Shiksaa was actually an office building.) But a couple responses also appeared from people cheering Spambusta1's work. "It's about time someone outed this cunt," wrote an anonymous person who used a Yahoo! return address. The message, from someone listing his name as "Give Us An Out," continued:

> *It is only the beginning. It would not surprise me at all if cunt*
> *Shiksaa begins to suffer some incredible bad luck. She has done a lot of*
> *aggressive shit to some people. Some of those people may wish to return the*
> *favor in their own special way. As far as her Dad goes...Fuck'em!!!*
> *Having a daughter like Shiksaa is worth killing yourself over.*

Spambusta1 was back the next day, ready to rebut Linford with threats to publish photographs of Shiksaa's condominium. "It is a very nice Condo. Nice dead end street. Did any one notice the brown van? We moved it today per direct orders as we are staking out a member of Spews currently and will begin with the posting of information on who is behind them next," he wrote.

Shiksaa and her supporters tried to determine who was behind the postings. Short of getting a subpoena for AOL, there was no way to unmask Spambusta1 directly from the Internet protocol address listed in his messages. Studying the language of the messages for telltale characteristics was unproductive as well. Shiksaa knew it probably was the work of Hardigree, Marin, or the group of south Florida spammers she began to refer to as The Gang That Can't Shoot Straight. But it could just as well have been any of the dozens of spammers she had tangled with over the years.

Richter tried to distance himself from the postings. In a note on Nanae, he admitted that at times he "might not see eye-to-eye with Susan, but I try and have some class." Richter claimed that people close to him knew he wasn't a violent person. Then he added a note addressed to what he called "high-deployment mailers," chiding them not to resort to the same tactics anti-spammers used to harm them. Richter concluded his posting by saying he hoped Spambusta1 wasn't somebody he knew.

That Friday evening, Spambusta1 was back on Nanae with news that he had created a site at the Tripod home page service. The site was entitled "Shiksaa Shakedown" and included three photographs of the outside of her condominium. One showed the gray gatehouse, with its locked, eight-foot fence, at the entrance to the complex. Another was taken a few steps from her garage door. The third was shot from the ground just below the deck outside her second-story bedroom window. Someone had doctored each of the photos with digital image-editing software. The picture of the condominium complex entrance included the words, "The Gates of Hell?" The shot of her garage was altered so the white door appeared to be covered with graffiti, above which were the words "Does this say Shiksa?" On the photograph of her deck, someone had circled some drink cans on the railing and a table, and added the word, "Beer?"

But what bothered Shiksaa the most about the Shakedown site weren't the photos. It was the publication of her latest unlisted phone number. Since Bill Waggoner had called her in December on her old unpublished number, she had been extremely circumspect about the new one. She knew someone must have tricked or paid off an employee at the phone company to get the number. She downloaded a copy of the Shakedown site to her computer for use in the police report she would file Monday.

But the online attacks on Shiksaa continued that weekend. An unidentified person began pumping out emails to people all over the Internet in an effort to Joe-job her. The messages were spoofed to appear as though she had forwarded them from her AOL account. They carried the subject line, "How to Boycott America, the Global Bully" and encouraged support for a boycott organized by activists running a site called AdBusters.org. The boycott was aimed at undercutting America's role in the world by weakening its major corporations.

The bottom of the note included instructions on how to be removed from the boycott's mailing list. "Please contact Susan Wilson, Islamic Peace Activist" it stated, followed by Shiksaa's street address, with her country of residence listed as "United States of Aggression." (The use of Shiksaa's married name, which she had accidentally published in the alt.test newsgroup in 1999, suggested the Joe-jobbers were not affiliated with Spambusta1.)

As Shiksaa mulled over the events of the past few weeks, she realized this was not the time to quit spam fighting. It didn't matter how tired she was of battling vindictive spammers. If they thought they could drive her out, they had very badly underestimated her. If anything, they made her more determined than ever to get in their faces.[5]

Shiksaa increasingly came to place the ultimate blame for her troubles at the feet of Scott Richter. He had painted himself as her confidant and defender against The Gang That Can't Shoot Straight. Yet he had also taunted her with her confidential information weeks ago, and he did nothing to stop its dissemination by others. Shiksaa decided it was time to abandon her naïve allegiance to Richter and her other spammer sources.

On April 8, Shiksaa assembled a small collection of AIM log files from her conversations with Richter, Waggoner, and a handful of other junk emailers. She sanitized the logs somewhat by replacing the spammers' true screen names with generics such as "CO Spammer" for Richter and "702 AC Spammer" for Waggoner. Shiksaa then published the log files at Chickenboner.com and announced the project, which she called "The Bulk Barn Diaries," on Nanae.

"I've decided to post my memoirs relating to the spam wars, including instant messages from a number of spammers. Kind of a spammer-undercover type thing," she wrote.

The move agitated the junk emailers involved, and they immediately sent Shiksaa frothing complaints. But she ignored them. She really didn't care if she burned any bridges. Not after what they had done to her.

It was almost an anticlimax when, a week later, the long-threatened lawsuit from Florida arrived.

Mark Felstein, the personal lawyer for Florida spam king Eddy Marin, filed the lawsuit against Shiksaa and eight other anti-spammers in a Federal court for Florida's southern district. In his complaint, Felstein listed as his client and plaintiff EmarketersAmerica.org, a Florida nonprofit. Besides Shiksaa, the individual defendants named in the complaint were Steve Linford and his brother Julian, Alan Murphy, Steven Sobol, Clifton Sharp, Richard Tietjens (a.k.a. Morely Dotes), Adam Brower, and Joe Jared. Also named as defendants were Spews.org and Spamhaus.org, along with their domain registration service, Joker.com.

According to the complaint, members of EmarketersAmerica.org included unnamed "email marketers, Internet service providers, and other related businesses." The complaint alleged that the eight defendants were all officers of both Spews and Spamhaus and accused them of libel, invasion of privacy, business interference, and other charges. The complaint requested punitive and compensatory damages from the defendants.

State of Florida records showed that Felstein had incorporated EmarketersAmerica.org just over a month before, naming himself as a director. In an interview with a Florida business magazine, Felstein claimed that EmarketersAmerica.org had approximately fifty members, forty of which had paid $3,000 in annual dues. He refused to name the members, citing fear of reprisals from anti-spammers.[6]

But Shiksaa and the other codefendants (who came to be known as "The Nanae Nine") were fairly certain that Marin and his gang were behind the lawsuit. It wasn't clear to the anti-spammers why they had been chosen as targets for the suit. They saw it as a thinly veiled attempt to make them roll over and disclose the true operators of the Spews blacklist. They were determined to make Felstein regret the lawsuit. They made arrangements to enlist the services of Pete Wellborn, the Georgia attorney who had earned the nickname "The Spammer Hammer" from successful litigations against high-profile spammers, including Sanford Wallace.

Meanwhile, Scott Richter was watching the legal proceedings from a safe distance. As U.S. troops took control of Baghdad that week, he began to mail millions of email ads with the subject line "Get the Iraq Most Wanted Deck of Cards." The spams promoted "the one true collector's item from Operation Iraqi Freedom"—replicas of the playing cards given by the Pentagon to coalition soldiers. The cards featured photos and brief descriptions of the fifty-five most-wanted leaders of Saddam Hussein's regime, with Saddam himself depicted on the ace of diamonds.

The spam campaign turned out to be even more successful than Richter's post-9/11 U.S. flags project. Although he hadn't even received his stock yet from the supplier, within a week of sending out the first spams, he had already taken 40,000 orders for the playing cards.

This time, Richter wasn't giving the money to charity.

Patricia's Graveyard Gambit

Just outside St. Johnsbury, Vermont, the tire on Davis Hawke's Ford Crown Victoria blew. It was barely six o'clock on a chilly morning in late April 2003. Brad Bournival had been dozing in the passenger seat, when Hawke cursed loudly and pulled over to the shoulder on I-93. They had been on the road for about four hours, after spending the evening at Foxwoods Casino in southeastern Connecticut. In recent weeks, Hawke and Bournival had regularly taken some of their profits from penis pills to the casino's seventy-six-table poker room. And tonight, like most nights, the spammers came away a bit richer.

But Hawke had seemed distracted when they cashed out around two a.m. As soon as they got outside, he was on his cell phone, trying to reach Patricia. Since moving to Rhode Island that winter, Hawke had been back to Vermont only a couple of times. That left Patricia mostly alone, except for their wolves. She had been taking classes at Lyndonville College, and Hawke usually phoned her every few days. But he'd been unable to reach her for a week, and she wasn't responding to the messages he left on the answering machine.[7]

When they got to Hawke's car in the casino parking lot, Hawke said he had decided to head up to Vermont and check on Patricia. Bournival had never been to Lyndonville, so he agreed to go along. He would regret it later when, by the side of the freeway that morning, Hawke revealed that the car had no spare tire. (Although Hawke had hundreds of thousands of dollars stashed away, he insisted on driving beat-up used cars. He was particularly fond of old Crown Vics, especially if they had been police cars in a former life.)

Hawke tried phoning Patricia again, in hopes that she would drive down to pick them up. No answer. Fortunately, Bournival had a AAA card and arranged a tow into St. Johnsbury. As they waited for the tire shop to open at eight, the young men grabbed breakfast at a bagel shop and were back on the road by 9:30.

Such temporary diversions were nothing extraordinary for the co-owners of Amazing Internet Products. They had encountered several problems at the start, most notably when AOL suddenly cranked up the effectiveness of its spam filters. But after switching to a new proxy-based mailing program, Super Mailer, they were able to get their messages through. Soon, business was humming along again nicely. With their new no-limit merchant account, both Hawke and Bournival often pulled down over a thousand dollars per day. Pinacle penis-enhancement pills remained their cash cow, but the partners also experimented with spamming for products such as human growth hormone and CD-ROMs containing information about government grants. They also mailed the occasional run of ads for Power Diet Plus pills and the Banned CD.

As Hawke eased the Crown Vic into the cabin's empty driveway, Bournival noticed the building's front door was wide open. Hawke cut the engine, jumped out of the car, and ran to the cabin. Bournival trailed right behind, half expecting to find Patricia's lifeless body on the floor.

Inside, the cabin appeared to have been ransacked. Books had been knocked off the shelves onto the floor of the living room. Couch cushions were flung about the room. Dishes, some of them with dried-on food, had apparently been hurled onto the floor. Hawke yelled Patricia's name as he moved quickly through the small house. Her clothes were gone from the bedroom closet. So was a thick roll of hundred-dollar bills he had stashed behind the wall paneling.

"Fuck," was all Hawke said as he circled back to the open front door. On the front step, Hawke cupped his hands to his mouth and howled loudly. Then he began walking around the back of the cabin, howling. He was hoping to call in Dreighton from the woods somewhere. At the edge of the clearing, Hawke suddenly dropped to his hands and knees on the ground. "Fuck!" he shouted again, as he realized a large stash of cash he had buried there was gone.

Bournival watched Hawke get up and walk slowly back toward the cabin. He stopped just outside the front door and stared down at the ground, as if unwilling to face the scene inside again.

Bournival took a step toward him. "What do you think happened?" he asked.

Hawke didn't answer. He just shrugged, his eyes glassy with tears. He seemed afraid to speak, in case his voice might crack. Hawke pushed past Bournival and headed back inside.

Bournival remained outside. He'd never seen much emotion from Hawke, and he wasn't sure how to deal with this unusual display. Bournival's instincts told him Patricia had grown tired of being Hawke's squaw and had run out. Bournival surmised that she had probably taken what she considered her half of Hawke's money. He wondered whether she would also try to plunder the Swiss bank account Hawke had sometimes mentioned.

When Hawke came back outside a few minutes later, Bournival suggested they visit the college and ask around about Patricia.

"Yeah, that's a good idea," Hawke said. It was the first time Bournival could recall being the one to set their agenda.

After persuading college officials to track down one of Patricia's professors, Hawke learned that she had missed several meetings of her biology class. But he was unable to find anyone who could provide information about her current whereabouts. After a brief stop back at the cabin, during which Hawke gathered up some of his belongings, the two young men hit the road heading south. Hawke dropped Bournival at his place in Manchester and returned to Pawtucket alone.

At that point, Hawke tried the only lifeline he had left. He sent Patricia an email.

To his surprise, she wrote back a couple of days later. She revealed that she was somewhere in Michigan and had both wolves with her. She also admitted that she had used some of the cash she took to buy a new pickup truck. Hawke persuaded her to email him her phone number. When they finally spoke, he pleaded with her to come home. She refused, saying she was starting over. She had cut her hair short and dyed it blonde as part of an identity change. Taking a page from Hawke's old PrivacyBuff.com site, she used a technique called the "graveyard gambit" to sign up for a social security number in the name of a girl who had died in infancy.

Hawke offered her a deal. If she came back with all his money, he'd find a nice, big house where they could live. He promised he'd spend more time with her. He'd pay for her to take classes at a college in Rhode Island. He'd even buy her a fur coat.

Patricia told him she'd think about it.

The next day, she was on her way to Pawtucket. A few weeks later, they moved into a new three-bedroom house together in North Smithfield, a few miles outside Pawtucket. The place had a two-car garage and a large, sunny yard with an in-ground swimming pool, flowerbeds, and ornamental trees. It was the sort of tidy suburban home where young, professional couples might start a family.

But once Patricia returned all of Hawke's money—aside from the cash she'd spent on her truck—he was done dabbling in domesticity. Patricia had been his lodestone for the past five years. But he didn't want a wife, and he sure as hell didn't want children. He didn't want to wake up one day attached to a ball and chain, no longer free to bang young women or hang out in casinos or hike up mountains in the middle of the night. His ten-year plan was to be living on a tropical island somewhere, ideally with a little tropical girl by his side.[8]

Creampie Productions

By June 2003, America Online boasted around thirty-seven million customer accounts, making it by far the biggest Internet service provider in the world. Since each of these subscribers was entitled to register up to seven different screen names, AOL actually maintained some ninety-two million email addresses on its system.

Davis Hawke and Brad Bournival owned a list of all of them.

They had bought the list for $52,000 in late May 2003 from a fellow spammer. The man, who said his name was Sean, told them he had a copy of the complete AOL member database, including customer names, street addresses, and telephone numbers. Sean said he bought the list from an AOL software engineer who had stolen it from the big ISP's customer-data warehouse.

Neither Hawke nor Bournival gave much thought to the fact that buying the stolen list from Sean might make them coconspirators in a crime, namely a violation of the U.S. Computer Fraud and Abuse Act. To them, the AOL screen names would be a gold mine. (Hawke and Bournival had no immediate use for the AOL subscribers' physical addresses and telephone numbers.) Amazing Internet previously used a list of around twenty million AOL addresses that Hawke had assembled from a variety of sources, including web page harvesting. But the old list contained a large percentage of undeliverable addresses. That often caused AOL's mail servers to automatically drop connections from Amazing's spamware programs in the middle of a run, since AOL had tuned its servers to recognize potential spam attacks.

Earlier that spring, Bournival had tried to solve this problem by signing up for Massive F/X, a web-driven bulk-email system marketed by Tom Cowles of Empire Towers. The company charged around $3,000 per month for a package that allowed spammers to send emails using a proprietary system Cowles had developed.

When Bournival talked to Cowles by phone, the Ohio spammer boasted that Massive F/X, if used properly, was capable of getting through any spam filter, including those deployed by AOL. But after Bournival wired Empire Towers the first month's fee, Cowles never sent him his account login information. Bournival bugged Cowles by phone nearly every day for a week, and Cowles kept promising to set him up the next day. But in the end, Cowles never delivered and stopped taking Bournival's calls.

Although it was pricey, AOL's stolen customer database gave Amazing Internet a huge surge in sales in June. The list contained only real, deliverable email addresses, so the response rate was much better than other lists. Plus, Hawke knew he could easily turn around and sell the addresses to other spammers to recoup his investment. He had already made some quick money that spring selling his lists of eBay and AOL addresses for hundreds of dollars.[9]

As customer orders for Pinacle pills flowed in that June, Hawke began to rethink his past reluctance to spamming for pornography. Amazing Internet had accumulated a verified list of well over 100,000 people who wanted bigger penises. It would be a no-brainer to cross-market porn to that list.

One night, Hawke and Mauricio brainstormed a possible plan. They could produce their own amateur videos, a popular segment of the Internet porn business. To save money, they could film the whole thing in Colombia, where Mauricio and his girlfriend Liliana had family. They'd develop a new niche, XXX-rated videos with amateur young women from all over South America.[10]

Neither Hawke nor Ruiz knew anything about videography, but they knew Bournival had played around with video editing on his computer. Hawke brought Bournival in on his plan, and Creampie Productions, their new company, was born.

Soon, Liliana was helping Hawke make arrangements with a firm in Bogotá that could do the filming. Then, with Hawke and Bournival fronting their expenses, Liliana and Mauricio flew to Colombia. They had no script to work with or even any specific directions for the video. They simply rounded up a handful of girls and a couple dozen guys and paid them to perform sex in front of the camera. A week later, Mauricio returned home with DVD-ROMs containing ten hours of raw video and a huge grin on his face.

Bournival took on the job of editing the video down to marketable segments. But after previewing parts of the film, his excitement about Creampie Productions waned. The young women weren't especially attractive, and the quality of both the audio and video was mediocre. At the time, Bournival was swamped with running Amazing Internet Products, so the DVDs remained on a shelf in his apartment. (Bournival nonetheless changed his profile at chessclub.com to include the line, "I am a video producer of amateur pornos.")

Hawke, however, was fascinated by Mauricio's tales of his adventures with women in Colombia. The stories revived Hawke's dissatisfaction with monogamy. He'd seen Internet sites that offered to match up American men with young Latinas from South America. But Hawke had a more direct plan in mind. He bought Ruiz another plane ticket, this time to Bolivia, and gave him instructions to bring home for Hawke an attractive teenaged woman willing to prostitute herself.

But even though Hawke authorized Mauricio to offer up to $2,000 per week for the woman's services, he returned empty-handed. A determined Hawke then sent Liliana down to Colombia with the same mission. Always more reliable than Mauricio, she quickly lined up a few prospects and emailed photos of the girls to Hawke. After he made his selection, Liliana ran into troubles getting a green card for the young woman. But soon she brought home to Hawke a pretty 19-year-old named Margie.

Hawke took no pleasure from food—his regimen of tofu, vegetables, and rice was simply a way to sustain his body. Even money was no longer a powerful driving force. All Hawke really cared about that summer was getting laid.[11] And now, he had his very own live-in prostitute.

Hawke had recently convinced Patricia it was a good time to find her new digs closer to Dartmouth, Massachusetts, where she would begin graduate-level coursework in microbiology at the University of Massachusetts campus there. Hawke paid Patricia's rent at the new place, which was thirty miles from Pawtucket.

At first, Hawke didn't tell Patricia about his plans for the prostitute. But when he finally revealed the arrangement, she tried to shrug it off. *He's just a guy,* Patricia told herself. She knew he didn't love the whore.[12]

(H@pTer
+en

The Pinacle Partnership Program

Margie spoke hardly any English, and Hawke had only a rudimentary command of Spanish. But he wasn't paying her $2,000 a week for her conversation skills. In the first month after Margie arrived in Pawtucket, Hawke made sure he got his money's worth of sex. Even when he was working at his computer, she was on duty. Theirs was a purely professional arrangement; neither was under any illusion that they would fall in love or that Margie would become Hawke's Colombian bride.

At the time, summer 2003, Hawke was doing relatively little spamming. Instead, he spent most of his time recruiting and directing other spammers to sell Pinacle on commission for Amazing Internet. Using a new alias, "Dave Bridger," he posted want ads at BulkersClub.com and other spamming forums. He also mailed the recruiting ad to a list of several thousand addresses he had harvested from spam sites. The ads invited "real bulkers" to join him in peddling penis-enlargement pills.[1]

"You'll market a product called Pinacle, an herbal penis enlarger that sells like water in the desert. Everyone wants this stuff; guys buy it for themselves, girls buy it for their guys," said one ad. Hawke claimed some members of his affiliate program were earning $20,000 in commissions each week. "This product pulls a massive amount of sales...All you do is MAIL, MAIL, MAIL. And collect your commission check," promised a later version of the ad.

Hawke's recruiting ads included the address of a web site, product-zone.com, which offered more information about spamming for Pinacle. The Pinacle Partnership Program site included a demonstration of how affiliates tracked order statistics and commission payments. There was also a greeting from Dave Bridger:

> My goal is simple; to help you make as much money as possible, as fast as possible. The most important thing you can do is mail, mail, mail. The more mail you send, the more sales you will make, which puts more cash in your pocket. I will help you along the way...You will find this is the most profitable, fastest-paying and most reliable sponsorship program for bulk mailers.

Soon, over 150 people had signed up to become Pinacle sales affiliates. Many appeared to be amateurs or chickenboners, such as the affiliate named Bill whose email address revealed that he operated an ostrich farm. A half dozen Pinacle affiliates were women, including one who called herself "Miss Daisy" and who earned a $1,000 bonus from Hawke for her spamming.[2]

Some big-league bulkers signed on with "Dave Bridger" as well. Tony Banks mailed for Hawke as Affiliate #31. Banks was listed on the Spamhaus Rokso list as a "criminal spammer" who had been in the business since 1997, but he never managed to pull in many orders for Pinacle. Bruce Connolly, who was on Rokso as a business associate of Louisiana spammer Ronnie Scelson, joined the Pinacle program too. Connolly produced no orders at all, leading Hawke to think he was just doing reconnaissance on Amazing Internet's business.[3]

But most of Amazing Internet's sales were being generated by the handful of Rhode Islanders whom Hawke had personally recruited. Hawke's Pawtucket tennis buddy, Loay Samhoun, was the company's top affiliate for several weeks running. Mauricio Ruiz spammed in fits and starts, pulling lots of orders when he put his mind to it. Mike Torres and Mike Clark blasted out Pinacle ads in droves as well. And Bournival, who was also handling all the shipping and customer service, kept a steady stream of ads flowing from Amazing's offices in New Hampshire.

Throughout the summer of 2003, thousands of computer users from all walks of life decided to give Pinacle pills a try. They didn't seem to care that Amazing's sites contained no phone number, mailing address, or even an email address for contacting the company. Or that the Pinacle order form didn't protect customers' data using industry-standard encryption technology. Nor had shoppers apparently bothered to check the FDA web site, which said there was no medical evidence that yohimbe, the active ingredient in Pinacle, actually made penises bigger. (In fact, the FDA warned that yohimbe could be dangerous to people with heart disease and could potentially cause renal failure, seizures, and death.)

Despite these red flags, most of Amazing's customers ordered two bottles of Pinacle at $49.95 each. (A bottle contained sixty capsules, approximately a month's supply at the recommended dosage of two pills per day.) Among the users of Pinacle was the manager of a $6 billion mutual fund, who asked that his order be shipped to his Park Avenue, New York, office. The president of a California firm that sold airplane parts, who was active in his local rotary club, gave out his American Express card to pay for six bottles, or $300 worth, of Pinacle. A restaurateur in Boulder, Colorado, asked for four bottles. The coach of an elementary school lacrosse club in Pennsylvania also requested four bottles. The president of a credit repair firm wanted three bottles. A soldier in Texas who was a frequent user of bodybuilding products ordered from muscle magazines requested two bottles of Pinacle.[4]

As orders rolled in, Amazing Internet was soon grossing over $500,000 monthly from Pinacle sales alone. Most of it was profit, since the spammers paid just five dollars per bottle to their wholesaler, Certified Natural, and gave affiliates twenty dollars per order.

The company's monthly shipping tab was a couple thousand dollars—more than what Hawke and Bournival had been *earning* at the start of their spamming careers. And Amazing's rent ($1,600), telecommunications ($7,000), and web-hosting ($1,000) costs only ran about $10,000 per month.

With his new wealth, Bournival walked into the Hummer dealer in Manchester that summer, picked out a yellow, four-door H2, and paid for it with $54,000 in cash. (He had totaled his Dodge Intrepid in May while drag racing with Mike Clark. Bournival hit a tree outside Goffstown, New Hampshire, going fifty miles per hour but walked away without serious injury.)

Bournival also moved out of the Montgomery Street apartment and rented his own expansive bachelor pad. The newly built, 5,300-square-foot custom home, located in an upscale suburban neighborhood in Manchester, cost Bournival $3,000 per month in rent.

But as the summer stretched on, Amazing Internet hit a few snags. Someone in Washington State used the state's consumer-friendly anti-spam law to file a lawsuit against the company. When Bournival agreed to pay $1,500 to settle the case, Hawke ridiculed him, saying he was encouraging other anti-spammers to try to bleed them dry. But Bournival shrugged off the criticism. He and Hawke were in synch on many business matters, but Bournival didn't share his partner's views on dealing with financial obligations. Hawke bragged that he avoided paying bills whenever he could. Despite his enormous stashes of cash, Hawke routinely missed rent payments and was often overdue on phone and other utility bills. Hawke would even walk out of a restaurant without paying the tab—as long as it wasn't a vegetarian place he planned to frequent.

Other problems arose that summer when articles appeared on the Internet about Amazing Internet Products and about how its colorful owners were making a small fortune selling penis-enlargement pills.[5] Hawke blamed Bournival for the unwanted publicity. Bournival had carelessly listed his Manchester address and phone number in some of the company's domain registrations. What's more, one of Bournival's old high school friends, whom Bournival had briefly hired as a marketing consultant, spilled the beans to a reporter about Amazing Internet's business practices.[6]

As a result of the media exposure, an assistant New Hampshire attorney general called Bournival into her office in August for a discussion. But the state took no action against Amazing Internet Products, other than ordering the company to provide refunds to a couple customers who had complained.[7]

Still, Hawke warned Bournival that he was generally being too flashy. Even the license plate on his Hummer, which said "Cashola," cried out for attention. But Hawke had created his own set of problems for the partnership. Mostly through laziness rather than his tendency to stiff creditors, Hawke sometimes fell behind in paying sales affiliates. He also made some enemies in the spam underground when he began selling lists of email addresses and open proxies, with customer satisfaction well short of ideal. Hawke also angered the developers of two spamware programs when he began marketing "cracked," or unauthorized, copies of the software to other spammers.

In his private emails to affiliates and other spammers, Hawke usually didn't go through the trouble of routing his messages through a proxy. As a result, the Internet protocol address of his cable modem was easily discernable in the email message's headers. At one point during the summer, someone remotely hacked into one of his computers. Fortunately, the PC contained little more than software, mailing lists, and some personal photos.[8]

By December of 2003, sales of Pinacle began to stall rapidly. Hawke and Bournival assumed it was partly due to consumers losing interest in the product. So they scrambled to line up new items to sell, such as a portable lie detector they marketed under the name "Truster."

But the spammers realized their biggest problem was the increasingly impenetrable filters used by AOL and other ISPs, as well as by individual computer users. Amazing Internet's messages simply weren't getting through.

Rise of the Spam Zombies

One Saturday night in mid-June of 2003, Spamhaus.org was staggered by unusually heavy visitor traffic. But this was no weekend rush by Internet users to review the latest Rokso listings. When Spamhaus director Steve Linford checked the site's log files from his control center in London, he discovered that hundreds of computers from all over the Internet were simultaneously bombarding one of Spamhaus's web servers with bogus requests for data. Spamhaus was under what computer experts call a distributed denial-of-service (DDOS) attack. Using special DDOS programs, attackers were trying to cripple Spamhaus with packets of data, rendering the site unusable by legitimate visitors.

Linford quickly fended off the attackers by adjusting the firewall that guarded the edge of Spamhaus's network. Spamhaus had been victimized by DDOS attacks in the past, and Linford might have headed off to bed without giving the matter further thought. But as he scanned the list of Internet protocol (IP) addresses of the computers trying to "packet" Spamhaus, he noticed something odd. Almost all of them were home PCs connected to the Internet via broadband Internet service providers such as Verizon, Comcast, Cox Communications, and Bell South.

For Linford, one of his worst fears was coming true. Since January, computer security experts had been tracking the gradual spread of SoBig, a new breed of computer virus. Once installed on a PC with a cable modem or DSL line, the software had two malicious purposes. SoBig was designed to turn the infected computer into a remotely controlled "zombie" participant in DDOS attacks. SoBig's other purpose was to allow the PC to serve as a spam-sending proxy, through which a spammer could send junk emails with anonymity. In nearly all cases, the owners of the infected systems would have no idea their computers were being used by the virus.

It wasn't clear whether spammers were responsible for the creation of SoBig. But they certainly stood to benefit from it. With an ever expanding network of thousands of hijacked proxies for sending spam, junk emailers could evade anti-spammers and the operators of spam-blocking services. Meanwhile, SoBig's DDOS feature could be used to mire the blocklist sites with bogus network traffic.

Throughout the summer of 2003, Spamhaus and other anti-spam sites, including Spews and the SpamCop spam-reporting service, were repeatedly hit by DDOS attacks from zombies infected with SoBig or related viruses, including one named Fizzer. Meanwhile, the percentage of spam originating from virus-infected computers was soaring. According to spam-tracking services, nearly 70 percent of junk email was entering the Internet through broadband PCs compromised by SoBig and similar malicious software.

To Linford and other veteran Internet technicians, the rise of spam zombies was part of a distressing trend: the acceptance by hackers of spamming as a lucrative profession.

"Once upon a time, hackers hated spammers," wrote Linford in an August 2003 posting to Nanae. "All the real hackers detest spam and the losers who send it. But lately things have changed…hackers now see spamming and scamming as 'kewl,'" he wrote. As an example, Linford pointed to "Styro" and "Foam," the hacker aliases of two New Orleans teenagers. In their member profiles at SpamSoft.biz, an online forum for spammers, the teens listed as their interests "spamming, scamming, and cracking" (the latter is slang for breaking into web sites without authorization). While an earlier generation of hackers had altruistically used their technical skills to help drive scam artists and spammers out of business, this new breed of computer whiz seemed to Linford both mercenary and morally challenged.

Some unidentified anti-spammers decided to fight back against the hacker-spammers by releasing a Trojan horse program of their own. Starting in August of 2003, junk emailers began receiving messages forged to appear as if they were from a spammer known for selling college diplomas. The messages offered a free technique for removing "honey pots" (otherwise known as spam traps) from spam mailing lists. Interested spammers were invited to view an online multimedia demonstration of the software. But the web page listed for the video was actually booby-trapped. If viewed using a not fully updated version of Microsoft's Internet Explorer, the page would silently install a program named honey2.exe on the victim's computer. The code contained a variant of SubSeven, an infamous program designed to allow the target PC to be remotely controlled by an attacker.[9]

It wasn't clear whether any junk emailers fell for the trick. Some quickly recognized the Trojan horse video for what it was and published warnings in SpecialHam.com, a new online forum for spammers. But what was obvious was that the war between spammers and antis had escalated.[10]

Meanwhile, the army of spam zombies continued to grow. As viruses claimed increasing numbers of home computers, spammers discovered a new way to put the infected systems to work. Instead of simply deploying them to send junk email or launch attacks against blacklist sites, spammers were using the compromised PCs to host their web sites. In September, ads for "invisible, bullet-proof" hosting began to appear at SpecialHam.com and other spam sites. For $1,500 per month, one Poland-based group was offering to protect sites from the network-sleuthing tools spam opponents used to identify the Internet protocol address of a site. The group claimed to control nearly half a million "Trojaned" computers, most of them home PCs connected to cable modems or DSL lines. The hacked systems contained special software developed by the Poles that routed traffic between Internet users and customers' web sites via thousands of the hijacked computers. The constantly rotating intermediary systems confounded tools such as traceroute (a utility used to track the path between a user's computer and a remote system), effectively masking the true location of the web site.

By September, incessant DDOS attacks on two smaller blacklist sites, Monkeys.com and Osirusoft.com, forced their operators to announce the permanent shutdown of their services. The Spews site was also frequently unreachable due to the DDOS attacks. But the service continued to function, thanks to Internet users who independently published mirror copies of the Spews "zone files" containing the list of blacklisted IP addresses.

Desperate to identify the source of the attacks, Linford tried to cajole spammers into ratting out the perpetrators. In exchange for information, he offered a form of probation to several junk emailers listed on Rokso. If they turned over evidence that led to the arrest of the attackers, Linford was willing to loosen the rules for the spammers' removal from Rokso.

But some junk emailers misinterpreted Linford's offer. In September, an anonymous person posted a message to Nanae, accusing Linford of trying to blackmail spammers. According to the author, Linford had threatened to keep him on Rokso permanently if he didn't give up information about a suspected source of the attacks. The unidentified spammer included in his note an excerpt of email from Linford.

"You forget who's holding the cards here," Linford had written to the spammer. "We will keep you blocked for years."

In a reply on Nanae, Linford pointed out that the anonymous newsgroup message had been posted from an account owned by Bernie Johnson, a Michigan bulk emailer with connections to spam king Alan Ralsky. Linford revealed that he had been discussing the attacks with Johnson and confirmed that he had offered a deal in exchange for information.

"I've given the same deal to a number of former spammers who today run legitimate hosting businesses and have never been heard of spamming or hosting spammers again. It's called parole for good behavior, a concept enforcement authorities the world over use every day," said Linford.

But Linford's efforts failed to unmask the attackers. And in November, a new virus, specifically designed to knock Spamhaus off the Internet, was spotted. Known as Mimail E, the virus contained code that automatically caused an infected PC to begin attacking Spamhaus.org in order to make it unreachable. But it had no effect on the Spamhaus Block List (SBL), which was actually hosted on over thirty servers located around the world.

A successor virus that appeared in December 2003 had a more significant impact. Mimail F targeted several anti-spam sites, including Spamhaus.org and Spews.org, with a denial-of-service attack. The new code also orchestrated a massive Joe-job on the blocklist services. PCs infected with Mimail F sent a flood of emails that were forged to appear as though they were from Spamhaus.org. The messages informed recipients that Spamhaus.org would be charging their credit cards $22.95 "on a weekly basis," and that a "free pack of child porn CDs is already on the way to your billing address." The spoofed emails also invited Internet users to visit Spamhaus.org, Spews.org, SpamCop.net, and a few other sites to view "all types of underage porn."

For days, irate users swamped Spamhaus with complaints about the spam. Linford did his best to explain that a virus, and not Spamhaus, had generated the messages. He referred the annoyed spam recipients to the web sites of anti-virus software companies, where they could find more information about Mimail. Still, the gripes continued to pour in.

Some gullible recipients even took to posting messages on Usenet newsgroups, warning others not to visit Spamhaus.org or the other sites listed in the solicitation.

"What on earth can we do about these people?" wrote one apparently confused Internet user, referring to Spamhaus. "They're probably just harvesting for email addresses, but who knows? Any ideas as to how to rid the Internet of these types would be appreciated."

To rid the Internet of spam zombies, many spam opponents called upon cable and DSL providers to be more proactive and to take steps such as removing infected customer PCs from their networks. Some ISPs, such as Cox, earned the approval of anti-spammers when they began blocking their users from sending email through mail servers outside the ISP's network. But Comcast, the biggest cable-Internet provider in the U.S., seemed paralyzed by the zombie problem and delayed taking action that would have stopped zombie PCs from sending spam through third-party mail servers. This led some anti-spammers to call for the blacklisting of millions of addresses assigned to Comcast.

As a stopgap measure, in December 2003, Linford began making plans to create a new Spamhaus blacklist. The Exploits Block List (XBL) would contain a constantly updated database of "proxy" computers that had been hacked, infected, or otherwise misconfigured to allow spammers to commandeer them. Spamhaus would gather the data from two existing third-party blacklists and make the XBL available for free to mail server operators.

Linford knew the XBL wouldn't eliminate the problem of spam zombies. But he felt it was spam opponents' best defense against the constantly growing arsenal controlled by spammer-hackers.

Jason Vale Held in Contempt

In the criminal contempt case of *U.S. v. Jason Vale*, defense attorney Jason Vale called his first and only witness: himself.

After being sworn in that morning of July 17, 2003, the former Laetrile spammer took the stand and began telling jurors the amazing story of how he had beaten cancer by eating apricot seeds.

Vale started by explaining how, at the age of fifteen, he had felt something growing in his back.[11]

Judge John Gleeson of New York's Eastern District Court stopped Vale right there. The judge instructed the jury that the case before them was not about the benefits or disadvantages of cancer treatments. What was at issue, he said, was whether Vale had violated the April 2000 injunction prohibiting him from selling any form of Laetrile, also known as B_{17}.

"It doesn't matter to the charge of criminal contempt whether B_{17} is a good thing or a bad thing. A person has to comply with the injunction," said Judge Gleeson.

Vale cautiously returned to his story. He told about how in 1996 he started selling apricot seeds and a video called "All About Cancer" over the Internet. And then he discovered how to send spam.

"I emailed to the whole world. I said the answer to cancer is 'no,' and I kept emailing out," he told the courtroom. "But then some people who got the spams started to complain. They forwarded the emails to the F.D.A....There is a whole political group out there that doesn't like spamming, but I was on a mission. I didn't care. Plus, I learned the technique of emailing out. It might be annoying to someone to press delete when they get the spamming, but the answer to cancer was 'no.'"

Vale tried to quickly sum up how he had gotten into his current legal predicament. But it was hard to condense several years into a neat, coherent story. He rambled on for a few minutes about the mixed legal advice he had received and about the ambiguity of the law. At one point he apologized for slurring his words and explained that he had broken his teeth as a child.

"You are just talking too fast. You sound fine," said the judge.

A week before the trial, Judge Gleeson had tried to persuade Vale, who had no legal training, not to handle the case "pro se," as his own defense lawyer. In a July 10 hearing, the judge had told Vale such trials almost always result in convictions.

But Vale had lost faith in the expensive lawyers he had retained earlier in the case, so he had dismissed them. Vale arranged to have an attorney advise him in the courtroom. However, Vale's "standby" counsel was not allowed to examine witnesses or make statements to the jury. Also at the defense table with Vale was a lawyer from the Legal Aid office. Vale told the judge he was shocked to learn that she hadn't even heard of the federal DSEA (Dietary Supplement Education Act). How, he wondered, could she possibly be of any assistance?

Judge Gleeson said that the fact that Vale's Legal Aid counsel wasn't familiar with some acronym was a "horrible" reason for him to "expose" himself by representing himself. "But, sir," the judge had said, "if that is your choice, I will let you do it."[12]

At the start of the trial, the government began its case with a review of the facts. Assistant U.S. Attorney Charles Kleinberg told the jury how, after Judge Gleeson had issued the preliminary injunction against Vale in April 2000, Vale hadn't actually stopped selling Laetrile.

"He thought he could pull a fast one…in flagrant disregard of the court order," Kleinberg told the jury.

Vale had, in fact, stopped spamming for apricot seeds and other Laetrile-related products. He stuck primarily to mass-emailing ads for other herbal products, such as willow flower for urination and prostate problems, coral calcium for stronger bones, and noni seed juice for "cellular rejuvenating enzymes." And the ordering page at Vale's ChristianBrothers.com web site no longer listed Laetrile products as of May 2000.

But according to Kleinberg, the top of Vale's web page advised visitors to call a toll-free number "for questions about apricot seeds." When Food and Drug Administration (FDA) undercover investigators phoned the number to inquire about purchasing Laetrile, they were informed that Christian Brothers no longer handled such products.

Potential customers were referred instead to a firm named Praise Distributing based in Phoenix, Arizona.

Kleinberg told the courtroom that records on file with the Arizona Secretary of State showed that Jason Vale was behind Praise Distributing. In December 1999, he had registered the corporate name Christian Nutriments, listing himself as president. A few months later, he had changed the company's name to Praise Distributing and listed his grandmother as president. Digging further, investigators discovered that the address on file for Praise was simply a mailbox service that forwarded to Vale's home in New York. Records showed that Vale had paid for the mailbox with his credit card.

In October 2000, Kleinberg revealed, investigators from the FDA and the U.S. Postal Service decided to crack Vale's shell corporation. Armed with a search warrant, they conducted a surprise inspection of Vale's Queens, New York, home.

"The agents literally caught the defendant with his hand in the apricot seed jar," Kleinberg said to the jury.

In the basement of the house, inspectors found 15,000 Laetrile tablets, enough to treat one person for 200 years. Plastic tubs in the basement also stored over 100,000 apricot seeds, a quantity that would last a single person forty-two years. Investigators also found more than 2,000 vials of injectable B_{17}. Other damning evidence included outgoing packages, all bearing Praise's Arizona return address, as well as invoices from suppliers addressed to Praise. While searching the basement, FDA agents used a cell phone to dial Praise's toll-free number. To no one's surprise, a telephone on the desk in the basement rang when they called.

Armed with the evidence, prosecutors had no trouble convincing Judge Gleeson to make his preliminary injunction against Christian Brothers permanent. In November 2000, he permanently banned Vale from directly or indirectly promoting or selling Laetrile.

Kleinberg took a step toward the jury box. "But did the defendant keep his word this second time around?" he asked, gesturing toward Vale. After a pause, Kleinberg answered his own question. "Not a chance," he said.

Then Kleinberg explained how Vale, with the help of his family, quickly made plans to resume selling Laetrile under a new front, Cyto International. In January 2001, one of Vale's employees phoned Woodland Nut, the California wholesaler that had supplied Christian Brothers with apricot seeds. Vale's employee ordered 500 pounds of the seeds on behalf of Cyto, with instructions for Woodland to ship them to a tire and auto center in Queens. A few days later, once the order was en route, the employee phoned the trucking company and changed the delivery address to the camera shop run by Vale's father in Corona, New York.

"As any fan of dime store novels will tell you," said Kleinberg, "you don't change taxicabs in the middle of a trip unless you want to make sure that you are not being followed."

According to Kleinberg, Vale used the same trick to order even larger shipments of apricot seeds in February and March 2001—all in an effort to throw investigators off his path.

"That, ladies and gentlemen, is a crime. It's called contempt of court," said Kleinberg as he concluded his opening statement.

When it was Vale's turn, Judge Gleeson provided him with plenty of gentle coaching. But Vale still had trouble mounting much of a defense. He seemed lost while cross-examining government witnesses and had no real witnesses of his own. Vale had hoped to get testimony from a friend who had purchased seeds from him in the past. But the friend failed to show up at the court to testify, forcing Vale to rest his defense. The one witness he did call to the stand was a friend from church whom he had spotted in the courtroom. After the surprised acquaintance was sworn in, Vale struggled to come up with questions and soon abandoned his intended character witness.

In his closing argument, Vale was clearly unprepared for the verbal challenge. Using an overhead projector, he attempted to persuade jurors that the language of the court's injunction was ambiguous. But Vale's own bizarre syntax often stood in his way, such as when he tried to criticize the government's inspection of his home and its failure to send him a letter warning that he was in possible violation of the injunction:

> If anyone is in contempt of this agreement, it is not me. I am supposed to follow this impossible-to-understand part, and yet, the plain stuff that is alleged to them is, you know, send a letter, or say you have to stop or do it—an inspection. They don't have to call up. They don't have to give a call and say they are coming; they can just come and show up. All this is…another thing that they never did; they never came over and destroyed the product. I believe…I don't know. They never came over and did this but they never did any of the parts of their injunction.

Vale wound up his summation with a plea to jurors to "decide justice" and to understand that he did not "knowingly and willfully" disobey the law.

"I pray you find me innocent so that I can go back and do the things the right way and continue with my life and not go to jail for fifteen…whatever. Thank you," Vale concluded.

On the morning of July 21, 2003, as the jury was sequestered to begin the second day of its deliberations, Kleinberg informed Judge Gleeson and the other counsel of a startling development. Someone outside the courthouse had been handing out pamphlets claiming that jurors had a Constitutional right to ignore the government's evidence under a process known as jury nullification. The pamphlets implored jurors instead to "vote their conscience."

Judge Gleeson was livid. "Does anybody know anything about this?" he demanded.

Vale immediately piped up. "I didn't do it."

"Do you know who did it?" asked the judge.

"Someone I know did it," Vale admitted. "They handed out First Amendment literature, your honor. It doesn't say my name on it."

Judge Gleeson glared at Vale. "There's nothing First Amendment about it. It's an inappropriate attempt to influence a verdict in a criminal case … if anybody in the courtroom does that, I'm going to direct the marshals to arrest you on the spot. It's an outrage," he said.

At a loss about how to handle the unusual situation, the judge decided to query jury members about whether they had seen the handout. Three jurors admitted they had been given what appeared to be slightly different copies of the pamphlet. The judge reminded them individually of their duty to heed the instructions he gave at the start of the trial, and to decide the facts in accordance with the law.

"It's a bunch of baloney," Judge Gleeson said of the pamphlet to one of the jurors who had a copy in her handbag. "Can you continue to perform your function as a juror?" he asked.

"I suppose I can," she replied.

Apparently satisfied with her answer, the judge sent the juror back to the jury room. Then he turned to Vale's standby counsel.

"Why shouldn't I remand Mr. Vale?" the judge asked.

The attorney replied that he hadn't had an opportunity to gather information about the incident, and he requested more time before the judge made a decision to take Vale into custody. Judge Gleeson agreed to give Vale's standby counsel until 5 p.m. that day to prepare an explanation for what the judge said was "a naked effort to improperly influence a jury."

But the court never got a chance to hear more about Vale's involvement in the leafleting effort. At 4 p.m., the foreperson sent the judge a note saying the jury had reached a verdict. Vale was found guilty on all three counts of criminal contempt.

After the judge dismissed the jury, Vale's attorney requested that Vale be allowed to remain free pending his sentencing, perhaps under some form of house arrest. In response, Kleinberg forcefully argued that Vale should be detained.

According to Kleinberg, "the events of today sort of stand alone. They are in a category beyond anything I've seen. And maybe my experience is limited, but the defendant is responsible for just total and complete disregard for this court's orders...it makes him both a flight risk and a danger to the community."

At that point, Vale's attorney tried a new line of argument: his client was beset by mental problems that affected his conduct during the trial.

"I would be able to come forward with certain psychiatric evidence to show that, in fact, there may have been some aspects of this that were affected by diminished capacity," said the attorney. "There's medical conditions going on here...there's a variety of conditions that would soften what's going on."

"I can't trust you," said the judge to Vale. "This very case is about contempt. It's about a refusal, knowingly and willingly, to abide by a court order." With that, the judge set Vale's sentencing for the third week of October 2003. Then he ordered marshals to take Vale into custody.

Vale was booked into the Brooklyn Metropolitan Detention Center, the same facility that held tickling-fetish spammer David D'Amato in 2001. While awaiting his sentencing, Vale was informed that the court had determined he defrauded the U.S. government by claiming he qualified for Legal Aid. In September 2003, Vale was ordered to reimburse the government $31,590 for the costs of his appointed defense attorney.

Vale's October 2003 sentencing date would come and go. As the result of numerous postponements, Vale would remain behind bars awaiting sentencing for nearly twelve months. It wasn't until June 2004 that he would learn his fate.

The Time-Travel Spammer

In May 2003, millions of Internet users got a refreshing break from the run-of-the-mill spam that routinely invaded their email in-boxes. Instead of hawking mortgages, penis-enlargement pills, or weight-loss products, an email arrived that seemed straight out of a science-fiction novel.[13]

The message offered $5,000 to any vendor capable of promptly delivering a collection of far-fetched gadgets for conducting time travel, including an "Acme 5X24 series time transducing capacitor with built-in temporal displacement" and an "AMD Dimensional Warp Generator module containing the GRC79 induction motor."

Dave Hill, a software programmer in Iowa, normally deleted a couple dozen junk emails every day with hardly a glance. But when he received the time-travel solicitation, he hit the reply button instead. Hill sent the spammer a message saying he could get him what he wanted. With a little deft photo-editing, Hill created a fake online store with all the sci-fi items sought by the would-be time-traveler. In July, Hill even shipped an old hard-drive motor disguised as a "warp generator" to a Massachusetts address provided by the spammer, who said his name was Bob White.

When White gratefully acknowledged receipt of the parts a few days later and earnestly asked for help obtaining others, Hill decided to end the stunt. He had expected White to tell him that it was all a joke. But instead White seemed totally serious about his quest for time travel and in need of psychological help.

Hill was not the first Internet user to be drawn into the strange world of the mysterious man some refer to as the time-travel spammer. Since 2001, people have posed as aliens, time-travel equipment vendors, and intergalactic policemen—anything to feed the imagination of the strange spam's sender. The odd interplay began in November 2001, when someone calling himself Robby sent millions of emails with the subject line, "Time Travelers PLEASE HELP."

The three-page, single-spaced message began, "Here is a brief description of my life," and went on to describe how the author had been drugged and poisoned as a child by Denise, a woman his divorced father had dated.

"I and also my Mom made my dad break up with her...My dad never believed me about her or what she did, or the side effects I had from her poisonings. I am 21 now, and since then my life has been obviously completely tampered with. I believe she is the link," he wrote. Robby's message then described how, one morning after taking a shower, he noticed UFOs in the sky and suddenly saw a flash of white light.

"It seemed as if I rotated slightly with this tremendous force on my body and everything went blank for a second. The air was warm and dry for that quick second. I heard this click which sounded like a camera. And then it was over," he wrote. When Robby went to wake up his mother and tell her what had happened, she pointed out that it was 12:30 in the morning, and he should go back to bed.

"This was all real, which proved beyond a shadow of a doubt that time travel is possible for me. I believe it happened as a sign that I am meant for time travel as an only option to correct what has been done to my life," wrote Robby. He concluded his message with an appeal to readers.

"I believe that God is leading me to a time traveler who can help me with the type of time travel needed. Please I am dying! The sooner we can get started the better," he wrote.

Some Internet users speculated on discussion lists that Robby was actually a sci-fi author in search of material. Others suggested the time-travel messages were just a cunning way for spammers to harvest working email addresses. The more common assumption was that the unidentified author of the emails was just out for fun. To play along, a few pranksters even created fake eBay auctions in response to the messages.

But one person who received Robby's message found something haunting about the strange cry for help. Brendan Milburn, a member of the New York jazz-rock trio GrooveLily, penned a tune about it. "Rewind" was released on the band's 2003 album, *Are We There Yet*. It goes like this:

> *Calling all aliens*
> *And time-traveling superfriends*
> *Secretive scientists with secretive client lists*
> *Calling all aliens*
> *I know you've got this practical invention*
> *To move a human through the fourth dimension*
> *I need to get my hands on the remote control of my life*
> *And press rewind…*

It wasn't until August of 2003 that fans of the time-travel spams learned they were actually the work of a 22-year-old Woburn, Massachusetts, man named James R. Todino.

"Robby," it turned out, was dead serious about his desire to rewind time. He lived at home with his mother, who was divorced from his father, an electrician living in nearby Billerica. Robby's psychological problems—he had been diagnosed with dissociative disorder and mild schizophrenia—prevented him from holding down most jobs, unless they involved working at home on the computer.

His parents had long ago given up trying to argue with Robby about time travel. But they worried that he wasn't very street-smart and was easily manipulated. Some people had tried to take advantage of his gullibility and had sold him phony equipment. Others strung him along with long telephone calls and emails that only exacerbated his torment.

But although Todino's time-travel messages made him appear fragile and unstable, he was a remarkably competent and hard-headed spammer. Years before his first time-travel emails, Todino had been sending out garden-variety spams for everything from "free" government grants to "detective" software. Todino had discovered the junk email business just prior to graduating from Shawsheen Valley Technical High School in 1999, where he studied welding and culinary arts. In March 1999, he mass-emailed a "chain mail" scam that attempted to trick naïve recipients into sending him five dollars. Later that year, Todino registered a handful of web sites under the company name RT Marketing and began spamming for a variety of products.

By November 2000, Todino was on Shiksaa's radar. After his web sites were repeatedly shut down for spamming, he broadcast some emails searching for someone to sell him a "bulk friendly" T1 line. Posing as a potential supplier, Shiksaa contacted him over AOL Instant Messenger.

"You need a T1?" she asked.

"Yes."

"OK, how much can you pay? What is your company? I know a guy, but he'll want to know what you want it for," she said.

"My company is RT Marketing…I am willing to pay triple as much as a regular T1 connection if you can keep me up," said Todino.

"I don't understand. What do you mean?"

"Well, basically, I will not be mailing through my T1 connection. I just need the T1 to make my website accessible to the Internet. It will generate complaints, but they will not violate your terms of service," he explained.

Todino gave Shiksaa his real name and phone number, after which she said her friend "Ronnie" would be in touch.

Less than a year later, in August 2001, officials from the Massachusetts attorney general's office were knocking on Todino's door. In the state's first legal action against a spammer, Todino and his company RT Marketing were accused of sending misleading and deceptive ads. Regulators pointed out that Todino's "grant program" was just a list of grant organizations, and the "detective" software was just a list of informational web sites found on the Internet. The state fined Todino $5,000 and convinced him to sign an "assurance of discontinuance" deal, under which he agreed to stop sending fraudulent bulk emails.

But Todino hardly seemed intimidated by the Massachusetts order. Within weeks, he was spamming again under a new company name, PK Marketing, and using more sophisticated techniques to conceal his identity.

Shortly thereafter, Todino's first wave of time-travel spam hit the Internet. It was as if his run-in with the government had somehow triggered the strange quest. Over time, his messages became increasingly specific about the technology he needed to rewind his life. In February 2002, he sent a flurry of anonymous messages appealing to anyone who was a "time traveler or alien disguised as human." The spams stated that his life had been "severely tampered with" and he needed "temporal reversion" to correct it.

"If you can help me, I will pay for your teleport or trip down here, along with hotel stay, food and all expenses. I will pay top dollar for the equipment. Proof must be provided," stated the messages.

Todino accumulated plenty of evidence that the equipment he needed was out there somewhere. Someone sent him a twenty-five-page manual entitled "Dimensional Warp Generator User's Manual," which was apparently created by cutting and pasting material from computer-hardware documentation. Someone else provided a couple automotive wiring diagrams that had been doctored so that they appeared to be time-travel equipment schematics. Others emailed Todino photos of souped up digital watches, apparently meant to look like portable time machines.

Not everyone wanted to help Todino acquire the technology he desired. In August 2002, he got an email, sent from a Hotmail account, with the subject line "Time Travel." It notified Todino that the author was responsible for monitoring "electronic communications." The email warned him to "stop all forms of communication on this topic" and said Todino would be arrested by an agent and returned after receiving a "cranosistanic reversal." Todino was informed to delete the email after reading it, or else be in violation of "Dimensional Displacement Diversion Act of section 44563b-232 Article 40498.442."

To Todino, the emails, phone calls, and documents were further proof that members of a conspiracy, which he referred to as the Renns, were trying to follow his every move and control his life, including his use of the Internet. The information made him more determined than ever to raise the money he'd need to finance his trip back in time.

PK Marketing's commercial spamming reached a peak in late spring of 2003, when Todino broadcast millions of messages advertising "free cash grants" at his site GrantGiveAwayProgram.com. It was around this time that Todino met Davis Hawke (whom he knew as Dave Bridger) at the BulkersClub.com forum.

At the time, Hawke was looking to make some extra money subletting some of the web hosting he had paid for in South America. In a note at the spammer site, "Dave Bridger" advertised "extremely solid" web hosting and boasted that he'd experienced "about 24 hours of downtime in the last three weeks, and we've been up for about five months with no problems." Bridger said he used "DNS floating and IP rotation via proxies" to completely hide the origin of a server, "so it NEVER gets blacklisted or shut down." The price for Bridger's hosting service was $150 for a trial week and $250 per week after that.

After Todino sent him $150 by PayPal, Bridger set up PK Marketing with access to one of Amazing Internet's domains, Pharycon.com. Todino then modified his ads for "free government grants" to list the domain. Later, Hawke also gave him access to Zakarish.com, a site that Hawke also rented out to some spammers who were selling access to pornographic web cams.

As part of his new effort to hide his identity, Todino often listed other people's email addresses in the "From" line of his spams. In the middle of May 2003, he sent out millions of ads with a forged return address belonging to a web site with information about Cairo, Egypt. When Philippe Simard, one of the operators of the site, egy.com, began receiving bounce notices and complaints, he fought back by convincing PK Marketing's credit card processor to shut down its account.

Simard also put up a page at the site explaining that egy.com was not responsible for the spams. The page included a copy of the domain registration for pharycon.com, leading many people to assume that Hawke and Bournival were responsible for the forged messages. Unfortunately for Dr. Fatburn, it was one of the registrations in which Hawke had also put Alan Moore's name, so some of the heat was directed his way as well.

All the commotion over the Joe-job made it impossible for Todino to hide his secret any longer. In August 2003, inquisitive Internet users and reporters fingered the longtime spammer as the source of the time-travel emails.[14] In response, Spamhaus added Todino to the Rokso list, and his record on Spews was updated with the new information.

Several weeks later, an avalanche of what appeared to be retaliatory messages began hitting three anti-spam web sites that had spotlighted Todino as the author of the time-travel spams. Someone had forged the sites' domains as the return addresses on a recent flurry of junk emails advertising anti-spam software. As a result, the innocent sites were inundated with hundreds of thousands of error messages and complaints about the spam.

The messages, which bore subject lines such as "Stop Spam in Its Tracks" and "Say Goodbye to Junk Email," advertised Quickeasysolution.com as the source of an anti-spam software program.

Among the targets of the Joe-job attack was Interesting-People. org, the home of a mailing list moderated by Carnegie Mellon University computer science professor David Farber. The site was slammed with hundreds of thousands of bounce messages from all over the Internet. Similarly, Inertramblings.com, a blog run by Sean Sosik-Hamor, received over 350,000 of the error messages. The operator of Lindqvist.com, Niklas Lindqvist, who was the third victim, reported receiving 30,000 such messages in six hours.

All three sites had published articles about the time-travel spammer's unmasking. But it wasn't certain that Todino was responsible for the Joe-job. The domain advertised in the spams, QuickEasySolution.com, listed a fictitious Woburn, Massachusetts, street address—the same address Todino had given in previous domain registrations. However, it was possible that Todino himself was the victim of an elaborate Joe-job.

But at least one of the attack victims was confident Todino was to blame. In a message on his site, Sosik-Hamor said he had previously been a fan of the strange messages about time travel. "I've thought that the author was pretty cool. A few fries short of a Happy Meal, but cool…Now I feel almost betrayed by Robert," he wrote.

The next day, Todino broke his silence. He changed the home page of QuickEasySolution.com, replacing the ad for "Email Filter" with a new page. On it, Todino denied being responsible for the Joe-job and apologized to the victims. "There are those wishing to do me greater harm then you can possibly comprehend," he said.

Todino eventually took down the page and went back to hawking anti-spam software and government grants. But he stopped sending time-travel spams.

Karen Hoffmann, Sock Puppet

Around Labor Day 2003, Shiksaa's outrage at The Gang That Couldn't Shoot Straight (Marin, Richter, Waggoner, and company) finally began to fade. She would never forgive them for publishing her and her dad's personal information on the Internet. But it appeared that the spammers' litigation against her and the rest of the Nanae Nine had imploded.

On September 3, the mysterious EMarketersAmerica.org (EMA) voluntarily withdrew its lawsuit after realizing it was about to backfire horribly. The EMA had hoped to sue anti-spammers into unmasking the operators of Spews. But it became clear that the lawsuit would expose EMA members' own operations to the same risk. Pete Wellborn, the attorney representing the defendants, had been crowing that he would use the legal discovery process to thoroughly dissect the companies responsible for the litigation.

The day after Wellborn filed a withering 110-page motion to dismiss, EMA attorney Mark Felstein waved his white flag. It was the second humiliation for Felstein in recent months. In June, the New York Bar Association had denied the Florida lawyer's petition for admittance, citing Felstein's history of substance abuse and criminal record. "We are not satisfied that petitioner presently possesses the character and general fitness requisite for an attorney and counselor-at-law," wrote the state's Supreme Court panel.[15]

But Wellborn and his clients weren't going to be content with a Pyrrhic victory. They wanted to send a clear message to spammers who launch legal attacks: don't start what you can't finish. Wellborn tried to persuade the court to refuse Felstein's withdrawal and instead decide the suit on its merits. Wellborn argued that federal law prohibited a plaintiff from unilaterally withdrawing a lawsuit once the defendant has answered the charges.

Meanwhile, Steve Linford announced on Nanae that the defendants wanted Felstein to pay their legal fees. "We're going after Felstein personally for every penny. He's whining he's broke, but that's not going to wash. He can sell his house," wrote Linford, who then posted a copy of the 1998 sales record for Felstein's condominium, which anti-spammers had apparently located in an online database.

Shiksaa's relatively ebullient mood darkened a few weeks later. The October 2003 issue of Conde Nast's magazine for men, *Details*, published its annual list of the ten most influential and powerful men under thirty-eight. To the dismay of anti-spammers, OptInRealBig.com CEO Scott Richter was number nine on the list, which also included rapper Eminem and actor Ben Affleck.

"Ninth largest spamming scumbag, maybe," wrote Shiksaa in a Nanae discussion of the *Details* list. When someone observed that Richter seemed to be adept at generating publicity, she dismissed the idea. "Most psychopaths are good at self-promotion. If you don't believe that, just Google the name of a certain Florida lawyer," she said. Taking some of the sting away for Shiksaa and the others was a quote about Richter from Linford that made it into the *Details* article: "The only power he has is the power to annoy 100 million people."

Then more bad news for the Nanae Nine arrived. In October, Florida district court judge Donald Middlebrooks granted Felstein's motion to dismiss.[16] The EMA case was closed.

Stuck with thousands of dollars in legal bills and still smarting from Richter's adulation in the mainstream media, Shiksaa and her codefendants got an even more stunning piece of news in late November.

According to a new entry in the Spamhaus Rokso record for Scott Richter, three "former spamfighters" had been discovered on Richter's payroll: former MAPS employees Kelly Molloy (Thompson) and Pete Popovich, as well as Ohio anti-spammer Karen Hoffmann. The Rokso entry, ROK2888, stated that the three were employed by Richter to handle network abuse complaints and to perform "listwashing"—the task of removing angry spam recipients from OptInRealBig.com's mailing lists.

The Rokso entry said Molloy and Popovich had been hired by Richter in January 2003 as part of his "continuing efforts to appear legitimate," which represented "a depressing reversal of ethics" according to the anti-spammers.

"Although their employment by Richter was initially presented as salutory [sic], in that their work would eventually clean up Richter's operation, it has long since become clear that they are complicit in his activities," stated ROK2888. The entry added that Karen Hoffman, "turned away in her pursuit of spammer Thomas Cowles," had also joined Richter's company in an "abuse position." A footnote on the page stated, "in Richter's lexicon, 'abuse personnel' denotes not persons who counteract abuse but those who facilitate it."

Although the author of the Rokso entry was never revealed, news of its publication was first announced on Nanae by Adam Brower, who had recently been added to the Spamhaus team. The announcement set off a flurry of discussion, generating over 400 responses. Some people accused the former anti-spammers of being traitors. One person said Richter's abuse personnel were just as culpable as getaway drivers in a bank robbery. But others rose to defend Molloy and Popovich, and supported their efforts to clean up Richter's operation from the inside. They said the Rokso record was unfairly vindictive and undermined the register's credibility.

A few hours later, ROK2888 was pulled from the Spamhaus site. In a note on Nanae, Linford explained that the record would be placed back online after Molloy and Popovich were removed. Karen Hoffmann, on the other hand, would remain. "The info on our internal list," explained Linford, "says Karen Hoffman is fully and knowingly involved in Richter's spam operations."

The Spamhaus team learned that Hoffmann had been consulting to Richter since at least early 2003 and had apparently taken great pains to conceal the fact. When spam recipients emailed Opt-InRealBig.com to complain, she used a number of pseudonyms in her replies, including the name "Karen Hughes." Hoffmann had also used the name Hughes, which wasn't her maiden name, to register for the annual meeting of a technical association called the American Registry for Internet Numbers (ARIN). Hoffmann traveled to the Chicago meeting in October with Richter's computer whiz kid and head of information technology, Dustin Parker, and had listed WholesaleBandwith, Inc. as her company's name. (Richter had recently acquired WholesaleBandwith from a Rokso spammer in Texas named Paul Boes. The company had been booted off over a half-dozen Internet service providers since 2002.)

When the information about her work for Richter finally became public, Hoffmann didn't deny it. She waded into the turbulent discussion on Nanae with a note stating that she wouldn't discuss the details of her employment. (Richter made it a point to get all employees to sign a nondisclosure agreement upon their hiring.) But she defended Richter's practices, noting that several large Internet service providers had "white-listed" him and were allowing his messages to reach their subscribers.

"I've always believed we need a middle ground. There's got to be a compromise. Give them a set of rules to play by. Make sure they play by the rules. Don't want their email at all? Feel free to block them. They're not going away," she wrote.

Hoffmann pointed out that some anti-spammers had known of her affiliation with Richter long ago. Indeed, she had hinted at her new employment in a May 2003 statement at her personal web site, ToledoCyberCafe.com. In the update to her chronicle of tracking Empire Towers spammer Tom Cowles, Hoffmann revealed she had started to take a broader view about the best way to fight spam.

"I'm working behind the scenes with marketers to help them improve their practices. I'm working with consumers and corporations on utilizing technology to stop the spam from hitting their inboxes...I feel it is in everyone's best interests to work with marketers, consumers, ISPs, and lawmakers alike to keep email a valuable communication tool," she wrote.

But Shiksaa could barely contain her disgust at learning of Hoffmann's association with Richter. When an anonymous person (who later turned out to be a Richter employee) posted a note to Nanae defending Hoffmann and pointing out her work to stop Tom

Cowles, Shiksaa dismissed her former friend's contributions to spam fighting.

"Following Cowles around with a camera and publishing other people's research on her web page didn't stop Cowles, nor did it stop any spam. The only thing she is doing to stop spam is removing spam victims who complain from Richter's spam lists...and the whole while passing herself off in this newsgroup as a person who didn't like spam," wrote Shiksaa.

It was Hoffmann's duplicity that bothered Shiksaa the most. Molloy and Popovich didn't announce their Richter affiliation with a bullhorn either. But at least they didn't try to hide it or resort to using aliases in their work for the spammer. (Molloy and Popovich would resign their posts with Richter soon after the Rosko incident.) Nanae regulars never take kindly to "sock puppets"—pseudonymous participants who jump into the newsgroup to defend spammers. But Shiksaa was especially astonished to learn that several Nanae postings by a person calling herself Natasha Dorenkov were actually the work of Hoffmann.

Identifying herself as an abuse coordinator for the MyEmailWizard bulk emailing service, Dorenkov had posted a note to Nanae that April. She requested that Spews reconsider her company's place on the blacklist. When an anti-spammer asked whether her firm had any affiliation with Scott Richter, Dorenkov replied, "Without checking first with our legal department, I think I can safely say that Mr. Richter is an ex–list owner on our system." Then, after being asked whether that was her real name, she responded, "Dorenkov is my married name, although I am no longer married. My given name is Nataliya Byakov. I've always gone by Natasha."

It was all fabrication. In fact, Natasha Dorenkov was an alias Hoffmann had been using to shield herself while handling abuse complaints for Richter's various properties (MyEmailWizard being one of them). Hoffmann wasn't proud of her dissembling on Nanae. But she was quite satisfied with her achievements in Natasha's name.

To spam victims who emailed Richter's companies asking to get off mailing lists, Natasha was something of a heroine. Many average Internet users had been conditioned not to trust opt-out instructions or communications with "abuse" personnel at spam firms. But dealing with Natasha was different. Hoffmann, as Natasha, was always quick to deal with spam complaints and treated spam victims with sympathy.

Yet after Hoffmann was added to Rokso, and Shiksaa confronted her about using the alias Natasha, Hoffmann at first denied it. That proved to be a mistake on many levels. As proof that Hoffmann had been hiding behind the pseudonym, Shiksaa produced a snippet of an AIM conversation between Hoffmann and another Internet user, whose screen name Shiksaa had redacted. In the brief exchange, "Karen Hughes" jokingly told the unidentified person that she was "Natasha."

When she saw the evidence Shiksaa posted on Nanae, Hoffmann was mortified, and not just because she realized it was incontrovertible. Hoffman recognized the conversation; she had been chatting with Dustin Parker at the time. Clearly, Parker had betrayed Hoffmann and had given Shiksaa a copy of the log file of their chat. Hoffmann wondered what else Parker had shared with Shiksaa.

By December 2003, Hoffmann had her own entry on the Spews blacklist. Spews listing S2938 stated that she was "an anti-spammer gone bad" and called her "spammer Scott Richter's list-washer." Besides ListSupport.net, Spews listing S2938 also included the address of her personal site, ToledoCyberCafe.com. Hoffman's Spews entry even contained the IP address of her cable modem service from Buckeye Express.

Hoffmann thought it petty of Spews to black-hole ToledoCyberCafe.com. But what bothered her most was the mystery of how Spews had gotten the cable modem's IP address. She had been very careful not to disclose it in the headers of her newsgroup and email postings and always used her AOL account to post messages. And, as far as she knew, AOL Instant Messenger wouldn't reveal her cable modem's IP address to others.

Hoffmann ran a search for the IP address in all of the text files on her computer. The only place it showed up was in an AIM chat with Parker, in which she had intentionally sent him the IP number. Obviously, that chat log file was among those Parker had given to Shiksaa. But that still left the question of how Spews had gotten her IP address. Somehow it had gone from Shiksaa's hands to the blacklist operators.

As Hoffmann saw it, there were only two possibilities: either Shiksaa had given it to someone connected to Spews, or Shiksaa herself was directly involved with the blacklist.[17]

Richter Unravels

When Scott Richter tried to reach Dustin Parker on his company cell phone one Saturday in early November 2003, the sultry voice of a sex-chat-service operator answered instead. Assuming he had misdialed the number, Richter hung up and again tried phoning Parker, the head of information technology at OptInRealBig. But the call went through to the sex line the second time as well.[18]

This was not a good thing. Richter and other company personnel routinely gave out Parker's number to major customers who needed after-hours technical support or other customer service. Richter's first impulse was to blame anti-spammers. The previous spring, someone had apparently hacked into OptinRealBig's telephone network switch. The hackers enabled a feature that caused the twenty-four phones in the building to begin ringing all at once. Employees had to unplug their telephones for several hours while the company tried to solve the problem.

But anti-spammers weren't responsible for the latest telephone prank. When Richter finally reached Parker on his private line, the 18-year-old admitted he had set up his company cell phone to forward to the sex line. Parker said he did it as a joke. But Richter soon realized that Parker had a different goal in mind. He wanted customers to think OptInRealBig was going out of business.

After picking up his last paycheck on November 7, Parker had joined a mutiny by six key OptInRealBig employees. Parker, the kid who had been Richter's right hand from the start, and into whose PayPal account the two had dumped their first Internet sales, had walked off the job and apparently taken confidential company information with him. Parker, whose name was listed on many of OptInRealBig's domains and who had even lived in Richter's house at one point, was sabotaging the company he helped build. Parker, the mini-Richter—just five-eight, but checking in at around 200 pounds—had double-crossed his mentor in order to work for a new boss, OptInRealBig's former sales manager, Jeff Perreault.

Perreault, 30, had been with Richter a long time too. Richter had listed him as the company's manager when they incorporated OptInRealBig.com LLC shortly after the 9/11 American flag spams. He even made Perreault a 10-percent owner of the firm. But after several months of missing sales targets, Perreault was fired by Richter in October 2003. Richter offered to keep him on as an independent contractor and gave him $10,000 in severance pay when Perreault accepted the deal in writing a week later.

Richter had no idea Perreault would so blatantly breach the contract. The former sales manager, along with Parker and the four other OptInRealBig employees, had quietly set up Avalanche Denver Internet Marketing, their own spamming operation, soon after leaving Richter's firm. Perreault promised that, unlike OptInRealBig, the new company would distribute its winnings more equitably. But first, they'd need some customers. Working from an office Perreault had set up in Denver, the crew was on the phones to prospects, most of them gleaned from stolen copies of OptInRealBig's customer list. They told prospects that Richter's firm couldn't function without

Parker and was likely going under. Some OptInRealBig customers decided to make the switch.[19]

On their way out the door of OptInRealBig, Parker and his colleagues had grabbed several goodies besides the customer list, including a couple of computer hard drives, the company's financial records, and some proprietary software, including OptInRealBig's program for automatically removing spam recipients from mailing lists, as well as the complete database of email addresses generated by the program.

Richter also had reason to believe that before Parker left the company, he had set up OptInRealBig's mail server to intercept email addressed to Richter or his father, the corporate counsel. Records showed that Parker had also tapped into other email accounts to access confidential information. Then there was the report from Hoffmann that Parker had sent copies of his IM logs to Shiksaa, in a clear breach of his nondisclosure agreement. Richter knew there was no telling what kind of information Parker was feeding the anti-spammers. (In fact, Parker had also revealed to Shiksaa he was the one who had "photoshopped" the images of her condo after Richter had given him the photos.)[20]

Richter contacted his attorney in Denver and began working up a lawsuit against Parker, Perreault, and the others. The plan was to hit them with breach of contract, business interference, trespass to chattels, and a slew of other charges. Richter wanted a court to issue a preliminary injunction that would stop the ex-employees from further sabotaging OptInRealBig's business.

But at the beginning of December, Richter suddenly found himself on the receiving end of a lawsuit. Officials from the New York Attorney General's office wanted to talk with him about several batches of spam that had been sent out from May through July of 2003 using proxies and fake headers. New York State prosecutors said they had traced the sites advertised in the spams to a New York company called Synergy6, which said it had subcontracted the emailing to Richter.

Richter knew New York's Attorney General Eliot Spitzer was on the warpath against spammers. In February of that year, Spitzer had pulled off a successful lawsuit against another self-proclaimed "opt-in" email-marketing company. A federal court judge ruled that Monsterhut, a Niagara Falls, New York–based firm, was deceptively representing its service as "permission based" or "opt-in," when in fact Monsterhut's mailing lists contained millions of email addresses of consumers who had never asked to receive ads. The court permanently banned Monsterhut from engaging in such acts in the future.

In a conference call with Spitzer's office, with Richter's dad on the line in San Diego, Richter explained that OptInRealBig had never directly sent any messages for Synergy6 during the period in question. All the email was the work of one of his affiliates, a Texas company named Delta Seven. Richter explained that OptInRealBig had forwarded to Delta Seven the few complaints his company had received about the messages. He provided investigators with contact information for Delta Seven's owners, Paul Boes and Denny Cole, and hoped that would be the end of his involvement in the matter.

But a week later, a certified letter arrived from New York. It announced that state regulators had commenced litigation against Richter, "among others." The letter accused him of a variety of deceptive business practices, including email header forgery, as well as false advertising. A few days later, Richter got word that Microsoft was teaming up with New York on a parallel lawsuit, on the grounds that its Hotmail service had received potentially millions of the illegal spams.

The whole matter apparently grew out of a complaint filed by a Hotmail user in June 2003. After receiving several unsolicited emails for "free" offers from Synergy6, the Washington resident had reported the spam to Microsoft, with carbon copies to numerous agencies, including the Federal Bureau of Investigation, the Federal Trade Commission, and even the International Criminal Police Organization, or Interpol.

Upon investigating the complaint, officials at Hotmail discovered that spam traps they had set up received over 8,000 copies of the messages advertising Synergy6 web sites between May and June of 2003. (The ads had been sent to unpublished addresses created by the service to track spammers, especially those who claimed recipients had opted to receive the messages.) The Synergy6 spams touted a variety of "free" gifts ranging from donuts and sunglasses to electric toothbrushes and a pornographic video entitled *Girls Gone Wild*.

In order to take advantage of the offers, consumers had to provide personal information at the coregistration sites, including demographic data, and consent to receive future mailings from Synergy6 or its partners. In most cases, consumers also had to make a purchase at one of Synergy6's sites in order to qualify for the "free" gift. (The terms and conditions of Synergy6's offer didn't sugarcoat the fact that consumers who registered would have their information sold to "marketing partners." Yet Synergy6 said it was not responsible for helping consumers get off the mailing lists of those third parties.)

After analyzing hundreds of spam samples, prosecutors determined that Delta Seven had routed the messages through proxy computers all over the world in an effort to protect the company's identity and avoid spam blacklists. Out of the hundreds of proxies used by Delta Seven, scores were hacked or virus-infected computers operated by customers of Comcast and other cable companies.

As Richter awaited the details of the New York and Microsoft lawsuits, he decided to drop the hammer on Parker, Perreault, and the other defectors. On December 11, his attorney filed a sweeping lawsuit in Denver district court, requesting not only injunctive relief against the former employees but also punitive and compensatory damages.

Parker was badly shaken by the news. That day, he was pulled over by police a couple of blocks from Denver's Pepsi Center sports arena and was charged with driving while his ability was impaired.[21] Later, Parker contacted Shiksaa and pleaded with her to sign an affidavit saying he had never given her any AIM logs.

After Shiksaa refused to lie for Parker, the two didn't chat again. But she was surprised to get an instant message from Richter around noon on December 17. He matter-of-factly informed her that the New York Attorney General and Microsoft were going to announce a lawsuit against him the next day.

"Should be good news for you guys to cover, since you all love me so much," he said.

When Shiksaa asked for details, Richter told her Paul Boes of Delta Seven was really the target of the lawsuits. According to Richter, Boes was in trouble primarily for sending mail through proxies. Richter's only involvement, as he explained it, was introducing Synergy6 to Delta Seven.

"No idea why I'm part of it," said Richter, who claimed the lawsuit would actually end up helping him. "More press to show I did nothing wrong and don't use proxies," he said.

Shiksaa told Richter to keep her apprised of the details and then said goodbye. But as she thought over the matter later that afternoon, Shiksaa began to wonder whether Richter's indifference to the lawsuit was justified. She knew that Boes and Richter had been business associates for years. Boes had sold his company, Wholesalebandwidth (WSB), to Richter that fall but had stayed on as a WSB customer. Shiksaa did a quick Usenet search and found a handful of reports from Internet users who had received spam from WSB throughout the summer. All of the reported spams contained bogus headers meant to look as if the messages originated from Hotmail or AOL. Such header forgery was obviously Boes's modus operandi.

Shiksaa confronted Richter over AIM. "Scott, you knew Boes forges headers," she said.[22]

Richter replied that he never really looked closely at Boes's messages. In any case, the spammer hadn't been using Richter's network since May, Richter claimed.

"Your abuse desk has nothing on him?" asked Shiksaa.

Richter said he hadn't received any complaints about Boes. "I do not allow anyone doing illegal things," he added.

Shiksaa cut and pasted some of the WSB spams she had located.

"You said he never forged while he was with you," she told Richter. "I say you either are lying, or you haven't bothered to read your abuse mailbox."

"The last thing in the world I need to do is have someone doing something wrong on net space I'm on, as I know I'll get the blame for it," he said.

Shiksaa pasted a few more examples of WSB spam with forged headers. "Why do you continue to deny it?" she asked.

"I do not run the abuse department," he replied.

"Then they knew it, and it went on for months."

Richter paused a moment. "Susan, let me ask you this, and answer honestly..."

"I'm always honest."

"What incentive do I have to throw anyone off? Spamhaus and Spews would never de-list me, right? As long as someone is not breaking a law, what is the point to get rid of business?" he asked.

Shiksaa couldn't believe Richter's swift about-face. "You are responsible to know what goes on in your company," she said.

"I know how to promote and run a business, not a tech department."

"And what's Karen's excuse?" asked Shiksaa, referring to WSB's abuse department head, Karen Hoffmann. "She can read a header can she not? She was your employee. You are responsible."

Before Richter could reply, Shiksaa came right back at him. "You know what? Just to repay you for publishing my father's information out of spite, I'm going to make sure the attorney general's office knows where to find proof of forgeries," she said.

"Susan, I never forged, and I had nothing to do with your dad."

"You published my father's personal information out of malice. Now I'm going to repay that favor, Scott. Don't contact me again. And I hope you get sued into oblivion."

"Whatever," was Richter's only response.

As Richter predicted, New York Attorney General Eliot Spitzer and Microsoft General Counsel Brad Smith held a joint press conference the next day in New York to announce their lawsuits. Spitzer began by describing the three respondents, referring to Richter as the third-largest spammer in the world. Then Spitzer zeroed in on the subject of header forgery. He noted that Microsoft's spam traps had attracted over 8,000 spams from Scott Richter in a one-month period. All of the messages, according to Spitzer, contained bogus headers designed to evade the spam filters used by ISPs and computer end users.

All told, there were 40,000 "fraudulent statements" in the messages, said Spitzer. Then he announced his office's intent to sue the spammers $500 for each fraudulent statement, or a total of twenty million dollars. The goal, he said, was to make other spammers realize their business was unviable.

"We will drive them into bankruptcy, and therefore others will not come into the marketplace to take their place," he promised.

When Microsoft's top lawyer Brad Smith took his turn at the podium, he announced the company's intent to separately seek damages of eighteen million dollars from the spammers.

"If these people have any money left after the New York Attorney General's lawsuit in New York comes to a close, we will be happy to pursue the remainder," said Smith to laughter from the press corps.

During the question-and-answer period that followed, Spitzer was asked whether investigators had determined the profitability of the spammers' businesses. He responded that Richter was "clearing several million dollars a month in profit," and that the damages sought by Microsoft and New York would be "sufficient to wipe out whatever profit he has made."

But one reporter wanted to know how a strong case could be built against Richter, since OptInRealBig apparently had farmed out the spamming to Delta Seven. Spitzer assured the media that prosecutors would be able to establish liability "up the chain of command...and prove without a doubt that those, including Richter...are liable for the misbehavior of those that actually stand there and push the buttons."

New York prosecutors also released 619 pages of exhibits gathered in support of the complaint filed in New York Supreme Court. The evidence included dozens of email messages between employees of Synergy6 and OptInRealBig. The emails showed Richter deeply involved in the day-to-day operations of the Synergy6 spam campaign. In one exchange, Richter shrugged off Synergy6's chief operating officer's concerns that Delta Seven's messages contained forged header information.

"We send out ten-million-plus emails a day, and you on average send me two complaints per day. I think one complaint per three million is real good," said Richter, apparently unconcerned that the bogus headers in the messages made it extremely difficult for average Internet users to determine to whom they should complain.[23]

New York's exhibits also included hundreds of spam samples. The scores of sample spams from Delta Seven included the characters "wsb," a special tracking code OptInRealBig had assigned to Delta Seven. But none of the message headers contained IP addresses assigned to networks directly operated by OptInRealBig.

After news outlets published an array of articles quoting Spitzer and Smith, Richter belatedly responded with a press release about the lawsuits. The argumentative statement bore little of the polish customarily found in corporate press releases on legal matters. It described the lawsuit as "one of the worst orchestrated smear campaigns against legitimate Internet business interests of recent times," and said prosecutors hadn't produced any evidence linking OptInRealBig to the illegal spams.

"If there were 10,000 false and fraudulent emails sent by Optin, it would be good legal practice if the Attorney General would see fit to attach at least one," read the statement. It also criticized Spitzer's "reliance on Spamhaus" as "a fatal error, because Spamhaus is an offshore, anonymous organization which has no legitimate connection with Internet businesses in the United States." Richter's press release concluded by saying OptInRealBig would vigorously defend itself in court and "prevail as one of the most legitimate Internet marketing institutions in the United States."

Spam fighters reveled in the moment. The man they considered one of the most frustrating spammers in the world had finally met his comeuppance. But nearly everyone, including Shiksaa, was secretly worried about whether the charges against Richter would stick.

CAN-SPAM

"Welcome to the death of email, ladies and gentlemen. Would the last person to leave email please turn out the lights?"

That's how a spam fighter greeted the Nanae crowd on the evening of November 22, 2003. Earlier that day, the U.S. House of Representatives had overwhelmingly approved the "Controlling the Assault of Non-Solicited Pornography and Marketing Act," otherwise known as CAN-SPAM. The measure was expected to sail through the Senate and be signed into law by President George W. Bush. After six years of failure, Washington was about to enact its first federal anti-spam legislation.

So why the dire prediction on Nanae? Many anti-spammers felt the proposed law was in fact legalizing junk email—and, in the process, opening the floodgates to spam.

"I said years ago that government would only screw it up," wrote one spam fighter on Nanae. "Will those who have been calling for Congress to do something, please stand up and slap yourselves up side the head?"

CAN-SPAM had been hatched in April 2003 by Republican Senator Conrad Burns of Montana and Oregon Democrat Ron Wyden. Their Senate bill, S.R. 877, embraced an opt-out policy that put the burden on Internet users to unsubscribe from spammers' lists. That was philosophically backward, according to the Coalition Against Unsolicited Commercial Email. CAUCE and other consumer groups believed that U.S. spam law should be based on an opt-in framework, with advertisers obligated to obtain permission from consumers before sending email solicitations.

But the Senate unanimously passed S.R. 877 in October 2003, thanks in large part to support from the Direct Marketing Association and several large ISPs, including America Online and Microsoft. (Many anti-spammers speculated that the ISPs hoped CAN-SPAM would enable them to more easily sell access to their subscribers by mainstream marketers, otherwise known to spam opponents as "mainsleaze.") After being sent to the House of Representatives, the measure gained a few amendments and was approved by the House 392–5 that November, leading one Nanae participant, only half in jest, to call for the blacklisting of Congress's networks.

"I say, add SBL/Spews listings for the U.S. House and Senate servers, for 'spam support,'" wrote the frustrated anti-spammer.

The passage of CAN-SPAM caught many anti-spammers by surprise, but not Spamhaus leader Steve Linford. He'd been monitoring the bill's progress for months and considered it abysmal compared to spam laws recently passed by Australia and some European countries. (In December 2003, a new opt-in spam law in the United Kingdom would go into effect, prohibiting marketers from sending email ads to consumers who hadn't requested to receive them.)[1]

But when Linford jumped into the Nanae discussion of CAN-SPAM, he noted the bright spots in the proposed U.S. law. For one thing, he said, law enforcement officials would appreciate CAN-SPAM's criminal provisions. Linford pointed out that CAN-SPAM would outlaw the use of spam "zombies" and proxy servers.

"Obviously it's not going to happen overnight, but fairly quickly in 2004 I would expect that ... spammers will either emigrate to China, or do jail time for proxy spamming," said Linford. Without legal access to proxies, he argued, spammers would be flushed out into the open and forced to send their emails from their own networks. That would make them susceptible to blacklists such as the SBL.

Other strong points in CAN-SPAM included a ban on collecting email addresses online using automated harvesting tools. It also prohibited forging message headers, and it required spammers to include a valid "From" address. The proposed law further specified that spammers list a valid physical mailing address in their messages, as well as include a working opt-out mechanism, such as a link to a web page for easy unsubscribing.

But opponents of CAN-SPAM found other aspects of the legislation troubling. Language in the bill empowered the Federal Trade Commission to create a Do Not Email list, patterned after the recently implemented federal Do Not Call list. But Congress had not *required* the FTC to create such an email registry. Without it, the onus would be on consumers to unsubscribe individually from potentially hundreds of spammers' mailing lists—even though many Internet users had been taught that opt-out links were usually a fraud designed to harvest verified email addresses. (There had even been recent reports on Nanae that some spammers were using fake opt-out links in an attempt to install Trojan horse software on the computers of unprotected Internet users.)

Also objectionable to many spam fighters was CAN-SPAM's lack of a "private right of action" clause. The law would give the FTC, state attorneys general, and ISPs the ability to sue spammers who violated CAN-SPAM. But individual spam victims would be denied such recourse. As a result, CAUCE predicted that enforcement of CAN-SPAM would be rare and infrequent. The anti-spam group said regulators and attorneys for ISPs lacked the time and resources to pursue more than a few symbolic legal actions against spammers.

"Unless the FTC is given a massive appropriation to pay for more prosecutors and investigators, giving consumers a right to sue is the only way to get enforcement at a frequency to make spammers think twice," said CAUCE in an October 2003 statement at its web site.

Particularly aggravating for many spam opponents was language in CAN-SPAM dictating that the new federal law trumped several states' stronger junk email laws. Among the state spam laws pre-empted by CAN-SPAM was a strict opt-in spam law in California that would have taken effect on January 1, 2004. The measure would have allowed individuals to sue spammers for up to $1,000 per unwanted email message. Not surprisingly, many bulk emailers were relieved to see the California law gutted by CAN-SPAM.

"We are very excited," OptInRealBig.com CEO Scott Richter told the *New York Times* on the day the U.S. House passed CAN-SPAM. "All of our clients had been worried about the California law. In the last two hours we have been booking a lot of orders for January."[2]

Despite CAN-SPAM's critics, Congress and the White House moved ahead quickly to make it the law of the land. On December 16, 2003, Bush signed the landmark bill. The President had no official comment on the Act, but cosponsor Wyden released a statement, saying that the new law created harsh consequences for "kingpin" spammers.

"Swift and aggressive enforcement will be essential," said Wyden. "I will continue to push the Federal Trade Commission and others to use the tools this law gives them to fight against spam."

With little time to prepare before CAN-SPAM went into effect January 1, 2004, email marketers of all sorts struggled to come to grips with the complex law's requirements. Some in the junk email business worried that federal and state authorities would begin aggressively pursuing spammers in the new year. Attendance at an early-January 2004 Las Vegas trade show for email marketers was reportedly down, because many spammers feared law enforcement officials would use the event to make CAN-SPAM arrests. (They didn't.) Meanwhile, some law firms created new practices dedicated to advising e-marketers on how to comply with the federal anti-spam law.

Shiksaa was delighted to see spammers fretting over CAN-SPAM. One evening in late December, she teased Nevada bulk emailer Bill Waggoner over AIM.

"Getting nervous? Are you worried you're going to jail or to court?" she asked.

"No, of course not," replied Waggoner. "Jesus loves me."

"Keep spamming, and maybe you will get sued too. One can hope," she said.

Shiksaa was especially pleased to learn that CAN-SPAM preserved Internet service providers' right to block any messages they deemed unwelcome—even if the spam was in full compliance with the new law.

"There is nothing you can do to force them to accept it," she called out to spammers in a message on Nanae. "Want to sue? Go ahead and waste your money, boys. It's becoming very expensive to run a spam shop."

Online support groups for spammers were abuzz with discussions of how to avoid trouble under the new law. After members of the Send-Safe forum held a December conference call with an attorney to discuss CAN-SPAM compliance, some junk emailers contemplated pulling out of the business.

"I am sure many of you are as worried as I am. I am really unsure what to do. I am considering shutting down my offices and/or scaling way back," wrote one Send-Safe customer, who said she primarily sent spams on behalf of insurance companies.

But other veteran spammers vowed that CAN-SPAM wouldn't mean the end of spamming.

"Sure, it is tougher and the cards are stacked against us, but WE ALWAYS PULL THROUGH. This time will be no different. WE WILL GET COMPLIANT AND continue to mail for sure.

That is our way," said a Send-Safe employee. Indeed, Send-Safe soon released a new "CAN-SPAM compliant" version of its program that used rented email servers in China, rather than proxies, to anonymously send messages. Other spamware vendors released similar products.

Meanwhile, entrepreneurs began developing other offerings aimed at spammers worried about the law. New services sprang up selling "valid froms"—batches of working email addresses that could be used in the "From" line of spams, as required under the law. Operators of the services manually created accounts at free email providers all over the world and resold those accounts to spammers.

"You could easily spend more time signing up valid froms than you spend mailing. You will also drive yourself nuts doing this tedious and boring job," stated one ad for a valid-from service that charged spammers twenty-five dollars per month for fifty valid from addresses.

Several U.S. companies also launched services offering to set up offshore incorporations and merchant accounts for spammers. The web site of one such service promised that incorporating in the Bahamas could shield businesses from the "litigation explosion" in the U.S. and could "protect their savings, investments and other accumulated assets that may be attractive targets for hungry trial lawyers."[3]

But many spammers seemed unperturbed by the new U.S. spam law. In the SpecialHam.com forum, a spammer using the alias "nukeananti" said CAN-SPAM wouldn't change his business practices.

"Honestly, I don't think this law will be easy to enforce, and it will only result in a small reduction in spam. Already many states have laws against spam, and many of them are more restrictive. They don't have the resources to police email, and I doubt taxpayers would want the FTC spending millions of dollars on this," wrote the spammer.

Bottom line, said Nukeananti, "I am going to keep on mailing."

Shiksaa Hangs Up Her LART

Buried within the dense language of the CAN-SPAM Act was an unusual enforcement provision overlooked by many people. Under the new law, the FTC was required to consider a bounty system for those who tracked down illegal spammers. The authors of CAN-SPAM proposed rewards of "not less than 20 percent of the total civil penalty collected" by the FTC. Lawmakers gave the agency until September 2004 to report back on the plan's feasibility.

The idea of paying monetary rewards to anti-spammers was spawned in September 2002 by Lawrence Lessig, an Internet visionary and professor at Stanford Law School. In an op-ed piece, Lessig suggested that spam would abate if the government required spammers to tag their messages as such and forced spammers who don't label their junk email to pay $10,000 to the first recipient who finds them.

"If we deputized the tens of thousands of qualified people out there who are able to hunt offenders, then a large number of offenders would be identified and caught," he wrote.

Lessig believed so strongly in the concept that he staked his job on it. In January 2003, he publicly stated that he would resign his position at Stanford if a spam-bounty system became federal law and did not substantially reduce the level of spam.

Lessig's stunt worked. Lawmakers slipped the bounty provision into CAN-SPAM at the eleventh hour. With the passage of the bill, capturing a spammer's hide had become a potentially lucrative pastime. Yet few anti-spammers rejoiced at the opportunity. Steve Linford pointed out to journalists that Spamhaus and other organizations already had plenty of information about spammers. The problem, he said, was getting prosecutors to act on it.

Shiksaa didn't give much thought to the prospect of a career as a spam bounty hunter. She had never been driven by financial motives. Instead, she believed that her online activism would be its own reward. Yet as Shiksaa entered her fifth year of spam fighting in 2004, she resolved it would be her last.

Shiksaa would never admit it to the spammers, but the events of the past nine months made it clear she was locked in a losing battle. For all her efforts, the spam problem was getting worse, and it was messing up her life in the process. Back when she was getting started, Shiksaa had thought spammers were simply misguided people who would respond to reason. Put a few on the right path, and the tide of spam would ebb. She knew better now. Spam had become organized online crime. The spammers operated in little cartels, with their private spammer forums and closed mailing lists. They knew what they were doing was unethical, but they were too arrogant and antisocial to care.

And some, like Richter, were also savvy enough to give CAN-SPAM—and maybe even the New York and Microsoft lawsuits—the slip. In essence, CAN-SPAM was a truth-in-sending law; it removed spammers' ability to lie about who sent their email. As such, it would create few problems for Richter, who relied much less on anonymity than other spam kings. As Shiksaa saw it, Richter's business was built around a simple premise. Millions of people on his lists were too busy or too computer illiterate to unsubscribe from—let alone complain about—spam. Richter had built his wealth on the small percentage of people gullible enough to buy whatever junk he was offering.

Shiksaa certainly didn't owe Scott Richter any favors. But in January 2004, Richter's dad asked her whether she'd sign an affidavit regarding Dustin Parker, the young computer expert who had deserted OptInRealBig.com LLC. Steve Richter wanted her to testify in writing that Parker had provided her with proprietary company information. He said it was necessary to his son's lawsuit against the former employees.

Shiksaa replied that Parker had merely given her instant-message logs. But she agreed to sign an affidavit to that effect.

"I'm not doing this for him or for you," she told Steve Richter. "I'm doing it because it's the right thing to do."[4]

As the year 2004 unfolded, Shiksaa kept a much lower profile. She avoided heated confrontations with Richter and other spammers over AIM. She couldn't give up on Nanae altogether, but she went long stretches in "lurk-only" mode, reading but not contributing to the discussion. She continued to hang out on #Lart, the Internet relay chat channel popular with her close anti-spam associates. But spam was no longer a crusade. She had certainly lost the desire to poke spammers with a sharp stick just to see how they'd react.

To that end, Shiksaa removed almost all of the files from Chickenboner.com. She took down pages displaying the various photos parodying Andrew Brunner, Bubba Catts, Rodona Garst, Davis Hawke, Bill Waggoner, and others. Shiksaa also removed the "Bulk Barn Diaries"—her log files of conversations with Richter, Dr. Fatburn, and other spammers. She had begun cleaning house back in the spring of 2003, after Mark Felstein sued her and the rest of the Nanae Nine. But now the site was totally spartan.

About the only thing Shiksaa left on her site was the big "Uncle Sam" cartoon on the home page. Like the World War I recruiting poster, the image at Chickenboner.com showed a gray-haired man dressed in red, white, and blue, pointing at the viewer. But an anti-spammer had doctored the image to give the personification of the U.S. government a wooden mallet in his hand. Beneath Uncle Sam were the words, "The Lumber Cartel Wants You."

The Phoenix Company

Davis Hawke spent Christmas Day 2003 at his parents' home in Medfield, Massachusetts. He and Patricia drove up from Rhode Island in his Crown Victoria with their two wolves in the backseat. (Hawke had brought Patricia along on an invitation from his mother.) He was antsy from the moment he pulled into the Green-baums' long driveway.

Hawke had intermittently been in touch with his father since dropping out of college. But he had only recently mended ways with his mother. They had tacitly agreed not to talk about his neo-Nazi period. But she made it clear she didn't approve of his spamming either. The thought of spending several hours in her home filled him with dread.

To break the ice, Hawke presented his mother with a gag gift soon after he arrived. It was one of the Truster portable lie detectors he had been spamming for a couple months. He explained that the handheld unit worked by measuring the stress levels in a person's voice. Israel's Mossad security service, he told her, used a similar device to interrogate suspected terrorists. Peggy Greenbaum didn't even take the Truster out of its box. But he could tell she was pleased to learn he wasn't just selling penis-enlargement pills.[5]

After lunch, they all took the dogs (his parents had a Husky mix) for a stroll through the woods to a nearby pond. It was unusually mild for December, with temperatures in the fifties. As they scuffed across the remnants of snow on the ground, Hawke's mother posed a question.

"Britt, you say you have such a huge business, but why aren't you on the list of the top spammers?" she asked. Mrs. Greenbaum had recently done an Internet search and found the Spamhaus Rokso page. Aside from Patricia's mink coat, she saw little evidence that her son was as wealthy as he claimed.

"Ah, but that's the mark of my success," Hawke replied, not certain whether she was criticizing or just teasing. He explained that getting blacklisted on Rokso made life very difficult. He said his strategy was to keep a low profile and quietly get rich without attracting attention.

Then Hawke told his parents about how he and Bournival were about to launch a major new project. In the coming weeks, he said, they planned to interview several hundred people up in New Hampshire and build a new customer service center. He couldn't tell them much, except to say it would make millions of dollars.

"They're going to want to interview me on *Larry King Live*," said Hawke. But just to be safe, he told his parents, he would continue to rent rather than buy a house, and he would drive second-hand cars.

"You can't own assets in this business," Hawke said.

That was just fine with the Greenbaums. They would have preferred if their son were a doctor or a lawyer. But their moral objections to his choice of career were softened by his pragmatic approach to the business. In any case, they considered spamming a lot better than what he had been doing previously.

When everyone returned from the walk, Hawke told his parents he needed to head out. He said he wanted to get up to New Hampshire right away, so that he and Bournival could begin what would probably be a two-week process of launching the new operation. It disappointed the Greenbaums to see their son leave so soon, but they were happy he seemed so energized by his work. He promised to send them updates by email.

A few days later, Hawke pulled up with a rental truck at the loading dock outside Amazing Internet Products's office in Manchester. He wasn't there to unload telephone headsets or chairs or desks for the hundred new employees he'd told his parents about. Hawke was just claiming his half of the company's forty-plus computers and inventory of pills.

Hawke didn't want to upset his parents at Christmas by revealing that his new project had actually stalled out a few weeks previously, when he and Bournival decided to dissolve their partnership.

The big plan would have involved sending a new form of spam aimed at mobile phones. Hawke and Bournival had discovered that most major cellular-phone providers in the United States operated Internet gateways for forwarding email to subscribers' phones. Few cellular customers in the U.S. used the feature, known as short message service (SMS). But all the carriers had nonetheless set up millions of email addresses with subscribers' ten-digit cell phone numbers as their account name (e.g., *phonenumber@.gateway.carriername.com*).

At first, both Hawke and Bournival saw an excellent opportunity to target the cell-phone gateways with automated spam attacks. They could configure their spam programs to latch onto a provider's domain and pepper it with area codes, prefixes, and number combinations that might be valid for the particular provider. (To spam Sprint PCS in Dallas, for example, they'd start with 2144170000@messaging.sprintpcs.com, and then hit 2144170001, and incrementally work their way through all the possible phone numbers.)

While SMS spamming was common in Europe and Asia, Hawke believed the U.S. market was still waiting to be pillaged. Very few U.S. spammers knew how to mass-broadcast SMS messages. At the same time, he figured most cell phone carriers in the country had poor safeguards to prevent spamming compared to regular ISPs. Even better, as far as Hawke could tell, the CAN-SPAM laws did not apply to cell phones.

But Bournival came to doubt whether SMS spams would actually produce sales. The technology limited messages to a scant 160 characters. Besides, they couldn't contain clickable hyperlinks, so the spams would need to include a toll-free number or a web site address. Bournival argued that most recipients would be annoyed by the spams, and those who weren't would be too lazy to seek more information.

At the time, Bournival had generally lost patience with Hawke as a partner. Hawke's impulsiveness and sloppiness grated on him. Plus, their 50/50 revenue split seemed unfair given how much more work Bournival was doing. (Having access to Hawke's unlimited merchant account seemed irrelevant when business fell off the previous autumn and they were taking in only a few thousand dollars a month.) After agreeing they could each make more money spamming solo, the two decided to divvy up their computer equipment and inventories and go their separate ways.

Hawke and Bournival stayed in regular contact. But while Bournival started 2004 without any major New Year's business resolutions, Hawke was busy setting up an office to house his new firm, the Phoenix Company. He arranged to rent the top floor of a three-story office building on Main Street in Pawtucket, overlooking the Seekonk River. The office occupied over 5,000 square feet in the modern, brick building. Hawke's new crew consisted of Mauricio Ruiz, Mike Clark as technical guru and spamming affiliate, and Jacob Brown—a young guy he met on the Pawtucket tennis courts who had previously been working as a waiter—as office manager. Hawke also hired several young women—most of them friends of Mauricio's—to handle customer service. At one point, Hawke transferred the registrations of hundreds of Amazing Internet Products domains to the Phoenix Company and listed Ruiz as the owner of the domains.

The Phoenix Company started off spamming some of Hawke's old standbys: the Truster lie detector, the Banned CD, and Pinacle penis pills. Then, in late January, when Hawke heard the FDA had announced a ban on ephedra sales effective April 12, he cooked up an idea for a new spam campaign. Hawke arranged with Certified Natural to private-label ephedra pills under the RaveX brand. The name was a reference to "raves"—high energy, all-night dance parties that feature loud techno music and often involve drugs such as Ecstasy and methamphetamines.

Hawke's RaveX web sites, designed by Certified, featured a pink-and-black illustration of a young woman dancing wildly. Beside her in white type were the words, "Pure Ephedra. Buy It While It's Legal." Despite reports of several deaths linked to ephedra, Hawke's spams touted RaveX as an "all-natural stimulant" and claimed it was safe.

"Over-the-counter medicines such as aspirin and Nyquil are far more dangerous than RaveX," said Hawke's spams.

To increase his odds of getting his spams into AOL, Hawke switched to a new program called Dark Mailer. Developed by Russian programmers, Dark Mailer was pricey, selling for around $500. But the program gave spammers unprecedented power to manipulate their email message headers, even though doing so was illegal under CAN-SPAM. Through trial-and-error testing, Hawke quickly discovered ways to tweak his spam and penetrate most ISP filters, including AOL's, pretty much at will.

Meanwhile, Bournival was trying to comply with CAN-SPAM just enough to stay out of legal trouble. He began using valid "From" addresses in all of his spams and always included instructions on how recipients could opt out of future mailings. But Bournival was reluctant to list his mailing address in the spams, as required by the new law. And he still relied on Super Mailer, which illegally used proxies, to send his messages. In order to further differentiate his mailings from Hawke's—who was paying no attention to CAN-SPAM—Bournival arranged with Certified Natural to provide him a new, private-label brand of penis pills. Soon, he was spamming emails for Sizer XXX.

Bournival did pretty well without Hawke or his merchant account, although he certainly was at no risk of maxing out his $25,000 processing limit. Nor was he making enough to consider an offer he got from Alan "Dr. Fatburn" Moore to take over his order processing. Fatburn had been repeatedly pestering Bournival by phone and instant message to outsource the function to him for a flat fee per order. Bournival figured Fatburn was just hungry for cash now that he had been sued out of the spamming business. But something about the offer made him suspicious. Bournival wondered whether Fatburn was simply trying to lure him into a trap, as part of the settlement agreement he had signed with AOL in December.[6]

Come February, the Phoenix Company's profitable spamming run temporarily hit the skids. As was its habit, AOL had fine-tuned its spam filters, and suddenly RaveX spams were not getting through. Ruiz and Clark went back to the drawing board, in hope of tweaking the messages so they would slip by. But Hawke decided it was a perfect time for him and Brown to dust off the abandoned cell-phone spamming project.

The first task was to create mailing lists. The two men scoured the Internet to find information about the various six-digit area code and prefix combinations in use by cell phone carriers. They could find nothing comprehensive, so they began manually compiling lists based on cell phone numbers of friends and relatives. Then they moved on to extrapolating from cell phone numbers they found published on the Web.

Next, Hawke and Brown sent test spams to Brown's Verizon Wireless cell phone and Hawke's Sprint PCS phone. They were surprised to discover the carriers apparently had rudimentary filters in place. After some experimentation with the content and headers of the messages, they were able to get most of their spams through.

At that point, late February 2004, Hawke and Brown began pounding out millions of RaveX ads to Verizon Wireless and Sprint PCS addresses.

To stay under the SMS message limit, Hawke included just a subject line ("Banned in 30 days?") and a short message body ("Get EPHEDRINE now! Guaranteed to work or your money back!"). The messages also listed one of the several toll-free numbers Hawke had set up. Spam recipients who called the number heard a sixty-second advertisement recorded by one of Hawke's female employees. Listeners who lasted until the end of the recording were instructed to press 2 on their phone keypad to place an order, or press 1 to unsubscribe.

Cell phone customers, it turned out, were even more hostile toward spam than email users. Irate recipients phoned the Phoenix

Company's toll-free line and vented at the handful of people Hawke had hired to handle calls. Others jammed the voice mail system with angry messages. Hawke managed to take in only a couple dozen orders before the phone company shut down the toll-free line. In the first week of March 2004, local papers in Oklahoma and North Carolina ran articles about residents who had been roused from sleep by their beeping cell phones, only to find messages advertising ephedra.

The plan that had looked so good to Hawke on paper proved to be a disaster. But Hawke wasn't ready to give up on SMS spamming just yet.

AOL v. Davis Hawke et al.

Brad Bournival's ringing cell phone woke him on March 10. It was eight in the morning; he'd hit the hay at around five a.m., his usual bedtime. Bournival's half-brother, Erik Francoeur, was on the line. He told Bournival that someone had just been at the apartment on Montgomery Street and was trying to serve Bournival with a lawsuit. The man was waving a photo taken from Bournival's Yahoo! member profile, which showed him, unshaven, wearing a cowboy hat and sunglasses. The man wanted to know if anyone had seen Bournival.[7]

"What did you tell him?" asked a groggy Bournival.

"The usual drill," said Francoeur. Bournival had instructed his family members to play dumb with anyone who came looking for him.

Bournival thanked Francoeur and hung up. He assumed the visitor was just another schmuck trying to get settlement money out of him. Bournival went back to sleep.

Bournival awoke again early that evening. As he was checking his email and reading the headlines at *Yahoo! News*, Bournival spotted an article about spam lawsuits filed that day by AOL, Earthlink, Yahoo!, and Microsoft. Bournival leaned in.

According to the story, the lawsuits were the first by ISPs under the new CAN-SPAM law. AOL's lawsuit targeted Davis W. Hawke, Braden Bournival, and fifty unidentified "John Does." The article quoted AOL's general counsel, Randall Boe.

"If you're a spammer, this is not a great day for you," said Boe. "Ultimately, we're going to locate you and sue you."

Bournival stood up beside his desk, nearly overwhelmed with the fear that The Authorities were about to pound on his oversized front door. Then he forced himself to relax. He gazed back at the computer screen. Seeing his name among the top stories on Yahoo! was unreal. He had known for months—ever since Dr. Fatburn got sued—that this day might come. It was the risk he took every time he clicked the Send button. Yet he didn't think AOL would choose him, not with so many bigger, more egregious spammers in the business.

But according to AOL, he and Hawke had generated over 100,000 complaints from members since January 1, 2004. The company had sicced its superstar outside counsel on him—Jon Praed, the same lawyer who sued Moore and Ralsky. AOL claimed Hawke, Bournival, and their affiliates falsified headers so that messages appeared to come from Hotmail or other ISPs. It said they had sent spam using dictionary attacks and address harvesting, which were prohibited under CAN-SPAM.

The law gave AOL the authority to seek damages of $100 per violation. What was that, twelve million dollars? Bournival looked around his high-ceilinged study, in the home that looked like a fraternity house minus the frat boys. How could he possibly survive this lawsuit?

Bournival reached for his cell phone. He was about to call Hawke, but he stopped. Instead, he dialed Dr. Fatburn's number. He needed the name of Fatburn's lawyer.

That evening, Mauricio Ruiz was over at Hawke's house. He was surfing the Web on one computer while Hawke used another. Ruiz spotted the article first.[8]

"Yo, Johnny, you are not fucking going to believe this!"

"Yo yo, what up," Hawke replied. He pushed off from his desk and rolled his chair across the floor toward Ruiz.

"Look," said Ruiz, jabbing his finger at the computer monitor.

The two of them stared at the screen, nearly cheek to cheek. Hawke impatiently scrolled through the article, waiting for the punch line. He was disappointed that the story buried his name in the tenth paragraph. But he began to laugh, a big, natural laugh.

"What is so funny?" Ruiz asked.

"How are they going to sue me?" Hawke said, his eyes flashing. "I have no assets."

Then Hawke pointed to the bottom of the screen. The last paragraph of the article stated, "Hawke did not return a telephone call from The Associated Press to his home in Massachusetts."

"Hell, they don't even know where I fucking live!" he shouted.

Later that evening, when Bournival phoned him, Hawke was still laughing about the lawsuit.[9]

"Congratulations," Hawke told him.

Bournival wasn't able to make light of the matter. He told Hawke that he was going to call a lawyer in the morning.

"Why? What can he possibly do for you?"

"I don't know. I'll find out my options," said Bournival.

Hawke told Bournival to lighten up. He reminded Bournival that it was just a lawsuit, not a criminal case. It was nothing more than a huge corporation complaining that someone had unfairly taken its money. The police were not involved. It wasn't about doing jail time.

But after he hung up, Hawke gave some thought to hiring his own lawyer. He knew just the guy to battle AOL. The previous December, spammers cheered when an attorney from Albo & Oblon convinced a federal court in Virginia to throw out an AOL lawsuit. AOL lost on a technicality; the judge said the court didn't have jurisdiction over the case, which involved alleged spammers in Florida.

And AOL later re-filed the lawsuit in a Florida court. But the attorney from Albo & Oblon vowed he'd get that case dismissed as well. That was the kind of chutzpa Hawke wanted in a lawyer.

There was no doubt that AOL had the advantage. Not even the best defense lawyer could dispute the evidence: Hawke, Bournival, and their affiliates had obviously sent the spams. The only thing open to debate was the damage they caused to AOL. As Hawke saw it, the case would probably end up the way spammer lawsuits always did. There'd be a settlement between his lawyer and AOL's lawyers, whose goal was to take all his money, to "disgorge" his illegal profits, as they called it. AOL would also get a court injunction, saying he could never spam AOL again. AOL was just trying to make an example of him, to show the world that spamming AOL did not pay.

No way was Hawke going to give AOL that satisfaction. They could get Amazing Internet's bank records from Bournival to calculate how much Hawke had made. But they'd have to bulldoze five states to put their hands on any of the money. He'd say he lost it all gambling at Foxwoods. He'd plead poverty, and they couldn't prove otherwise.

In a way, being sued by AOL was liberating to Hawke. Now that the deterrent of a lawsuit was gone, he could spam with impunity. What was AOL going to do, sue him again? Hawke went to his computer and composed a brief ad:

Highly desirable list for sale or trade. Only the BEST addresses. Will trade for other high-quality list or AOL internal mailer.

In the "from" line of the spam, he listed his name as "Doctor Bulker." He also provided a Yahoo! email address and one of the toll-free numbers he had set up for the Phoenix Company. Then Hawke blasted the spam out to a list of 80,000 addresses he had harvested from spam sites and other "bulk-friendly" sources.

The next day, Hawke kicked his spamming into high gear. He registered a couple of new domains, including ephedrazone.com,

listing ImtheGingerbreadMan2003@yahoo.com as his email
address. In hopes of recruiting new RaveX affiliates, he sprayed the
Internet with want-ad spams:

> Sell the HOTTEST RX supplement in the country! It's called
> RaveX and contains 100% pure ephedra...the FDA is banning the sale of
> ephedra on April 12th, so people are buying it like CRAZY right now!

Hawke's spamming frenzy was short-lived, however. As word of the
AOL lawsuit spread—the story made the front page of the *New
York Times*—Spamhaus posted an entry about Hawke on the Rokso
list, and his various Internet addresses were added to the Spamhaus
Block List. Suddenly, many would-be customers couldn't reach his
web sites. To head off further problems, Hawke and his crew emptied the 150 Main Street office in the middle of the night. But
Hawke's troubles got worse a few days later when he received a call
from his merchant-account contact. The deal was off. Hawke tried
to negotiate, but the man just hung up and told Hawke never to call
him again. Stuck without the ability to process credit card orders,
Hawke scrambled to find a new merchant account. In the meantime, the Phoenix Company was relegated to accepting orders by
check.

   After retaining Dr. Fatburn's lawyer from Whiteford, Preston
& Taylor, Bournival decided not to play any games with AOL. He
just wanted the legal process to run its course as quickly as possible.
AOL's attorneys served Bournival's lawyer on March 17, and soon
thereafter Bournival began a series of long telephone conversations
with Jennifer Archie, the Latham & Watkins lawyer who teamed
with Praed on AOL's spam litigations. On his attorney's advice,
Bournival cooperated fully. He didn't volunteer information, but he
told Archie pretty much anything she wanted to know about
Amazing Internet Products. To his surprise, instead of treating him
like a criminal, she acted as if the lawsuit was just a business deal. It
gave him hope that he might emerge from it all with his future intact.

Maybe, if he played his hand right, he'd get to keep the Hummer and a couple hundred thousand dollars. He'd use the money to launch a new Internet business that was legal, or even become an anti-spam consultant.[10]

Archie warned Bournival that he'd be in limbo until the lawsuit was wrapped up. That could take six months, she said, or even longer if Hawke continued to be difficult.

Over ten days had passed since AOL filed the lawsuit, but the private investigator AOL hired to serve Hawke still hadn't managed to track him down. The PI knew Hawke maintained a post office box in Pawtucket, and AOL had received information that he was living in nearby North Smithfield. But without an address to go on, the PI was stuck. He hung around vegetarian restaurants in Pawtucket and Providence with a photo he had printed out from a 1999 newspaper article about Hawke. He staked out the former Phoenix Company office on Main Street. He parked on the street outside Hawke's old Crescent Road apartment, hoping to spot his black Crown Vic. He waited at the tennis courts in Slater Park on the chance that Hawke would show up for a chilly game of spring tennis.[11]

Then AOL got a tip that Hawke was renting a single-family home at an address on North Smithfield's Black Plain Road. The PI checked the deed for the property and contacted the owner. She confirmed that the man in the photo was her tenant but had signed the lease using a different name. The PI staked out the tidy colonial for two days, hoping to catch a glimpse of Hawke through the bay window. Upon returning the third day, March 23, he saw the Crown Vic in the driveway. He banged on the breezeway door and called Hawke's name but got no answer. He tried the front entrance, but still no response.

The PI pulled out his cell phone and dialed the number he had for Hawke. He heard a phone inside the house spring to life. After the phone rang three times, the PI hung up, and the ringing stopped.

At that point, the PI realized it was going to be a "nail and mail" case. The PI tacked the envelope to the front door and departed.

Inside, Hawke held his breath until he saw the car drive off. Then he retrieved the documents from the front door and locked it again. He was furious that AOL had been able to serve him so quickly. Now the clock was ticking. By law, if he didn't respond within twenty days, AOL could ask the court for a default judgment.

Obviously, someone had squealed. Only Hawke's closest associates knew his home address, so that eliminated Dr. Fatburn, despite the man's obvious wish to take him down. Hawke's former partner Bournival potentially had the motivation. To keep in AOL's good graces, he was probably singing like a canary about his side of the business. But Hawke didn't think Bournival would give up Hawke's address. Brad's innocent mistakes were the cause of their legal problems, but the guy was not a total snitch. The other possibility was Margie, the girl he'd brought up from Columbia whose services he'd stopped using several weeks before out of boredom. (He was still trying to line up a new girl from South America.) But Margie didn't have the language skills to report him. Besides, she was a best friend of Liliana, and no way would they want to jeopardize Mauricio.

Then it dawned on Hawke—his mother knew his address, although she'd never been to the house. The lawsuit probably brought back for her the shame she had felt in 1999, when her hometown paper, the *Boston Globe*, reported that Hawke was running a neo-Nazi group. After all, she was the one who had told the *Washington Post* that Hawke was a "chicken," and that's why he didn't show up at the rally in Washington, D.C. She was the one who, that same year, sobbed into the phone to a reporter from *Rolling Stone* that she wished someone would *kill* him, her only son. That's the kind of mother she was, thought Hawke. If AOL's lawyers leaned on her, she'd willingly give him up.

Hawke picked up his cell phone from the table. On the screen was a message that he had missed the call from AOL's private investigator.

According to the caller ID, it was from area code 617 in Massachusetts. But the prefix—the three numbers after the area code—was new to him.

"Hello," Hawke said to the empty house. He jotted the number down on the envelope of legal papers. Later, he would use it to turn the tables and begin investigating the PI. But first, he'd use the number's area code and prefix combination to create a new mailing list for cell phone spam.[12]

The Gingerbread Man

Under the rules of chess, a player can claim a draw if fifty consecutive moves occur in the match without a piece being captured or a pawn moved. Throughout the spring and early summer of 2004, Davis Hawke seemed to hope the "Fifty Moves Rule" would end his legal problems with America Online.

As AOL made a succession of maneuvers against him in Virginia's Eastern District federal court, Hawke retreated to the back streets of Pawtucket.[13] He phoned AOL's attorneys Archie and Praed a few times to ask questions about the case. But then he'd go silent and flagrantly ignore court dates. From time to time, Hawke would pop up on the Internet to send out a run of cell phone spam. After that, he'd vanish for days, apparently having generated enough cash to keep going.

Hawke had been living in a succession of motels ever since an incident the week after he received AOL's summons. Hawke had spotted AOL's private investigator in his driveway, trying to attach something to the underside of the Crown Vic. Hawke assumed it was a global-positioning-system (GPS) device for tracking him. The next day, he moved out of the Black Plain Road house and abandoned the car.[14]

The cell phone spams, especially the ones advertising mortgage refinancing, were beginning to bring in some decent cash. Hawke decided he didn't need to spam AOL, and it was a good time for a fire sale with the AOL member database. Using the alias Mark, he boldly sent his bulk-friendly mailing list a message bearing the subject line, "Super Secret Email List for Sale." The spam offered an eight-million-address list for $8,000, or sets of one million addresses for $1,500:

> I'm not going to bore you with hype or games. This is simply the best email list you will ever, ever buy. This is a database of over 8 million users of THE BIGGEST online provider. You know which one! This list contains FULL MYSQL DUMPS .. which means you get not only the emails, but the address info, names, etc. That makes it easy to send personalized emails that appear to be opt-in. You will experience an unbelievable response rate from this list.

To throw AOL and other anti-spammers off his tracks, Hawke had begun registering domains under the name "Bubba Catts" and a bogus Louisiana mailing address. Later, his domain registrations included the name and address of the bank in Spartanburg, South Carolina, to which Hawke owed money. For the name of the domain's registrant, Hawke listed Thomas P. Barnum. Hawke also sprayed out tens of thousands of spams selling pirated copies of the Dark Mailer program. Hawke signed the spamware ads using the name of south-Florida spam king Eddy Marin.[15]

Hawke temporarily stopped advertising the AOL list in June 2004, after federal agents arrested two men on charges that they had stolen AOL's entire customer database in 2003 for use in spamming. Jason Smathers, a former AOL technician, and Sean Dunaway, an alleged spammer, each faced up to five years in prison and a $250,000 fine for their part in the conspiracy to misappropriate the database. Prosecutors said they cracked the case with the help of an unidentified informant. The source (Bournival) was said to be a spammer who was the subject of a 2004 AOL lawsuit. The informant had purchased a copy of the list from Dunaway and used it to sell herbal penile-enlargement pills, authorities said.

Suddenly, Hawke's endgame with AOL wasn't the only case that required his attention. Now he was potentially facing criminal charges over his brazen attempts to sell the AOL member database. Concerned that FBI agents might be following him, Hawke cut off his shoulder-length hair and shaved his head. But soon he was back on SpecialHam.com, under the username MrLucky, offering to sell an AOL address list for $6,000.

Then, at the end of June, fresh legal problems arrived. A private investigator hired by Verizon Wireless left a summons on the windshield of Jacob Brown's blue Oldsmobile while it was parked outside 40 Crescent Road in Pawtucket. (Brown had taken over Hawke's old apartment when he moved out.) The summons informed Brown that Verizon Wireless was suing him and fifty unidentified "John Does" in a New Jersey federal court. The cell phone provider accused Brown and the others of inundating its subscribers with over four million cell phone spams since March 2004.

Hawke was undaunted by the fact that he might soon be dragged into the litigation.[16] In July 2004, he spammed his bulk-friendly list with an ad that began, "Become an cellphone spammer." The spam advertised a $1,000 kit with "everything you need to start mass mailing text messages instantly." The ad, which was signed "Eddy M," included an unusual revelation as proof the offer was legitimate:

> I am not a ripoff. Upon request, I can fax you a copy of the 74-page lawsuit against me by Verizon. I have been a bulker since 1996 and focused entirely on text messaging for the past six months.

A few days later, Hawke decided it was time for a breather. He drove north to his favorite spot in New Hampshire—Tuckerman's Ravine, on the southeast shoulder of Mount Washington—for a hike with Dreighton.

The summer of 2004 was shaping up as one of the coolest and rainiest on record in New England. As Hawke picked his way in a drizzle along the Lion Head trail, he contemplated leaving the country altogether for someplace warm and dry—Algiers, perhaps. Loay Samhoun, his former number-one Pinacle affiliate, had already fled to Lebanon to avoid litigation from AOL.[17]

But with almost all of his money in greenbacks, Hawke knew he had serious portability problems. Somehow, he'd need to get the cash into bank accounts, but he worried that those deposits might trigger investigations and put him at risk. Hawke figured he could disappear somewhere else in the U.S. and start over under a new identity. He could use his cash to buy and sell real estate. Or he could earn a living playing poker.

But Hawke decided to remain in Rhode Island a while longer. His only friends—Mauricio, Mike Clark, and the others—were there, and Patricia was serious about her grad school program. But something else made him want to stay put.

Hawke had tried running from failure in the past, and it got him branded a coward and a loser. This time, he wasn't going to slink out a window in the middle of the night. He was going to go down with guns blazing. He might not be the biggest spammer in history, but Hawke was going to make sure he was the most outrageous one of all time.

The mist lifted suddenly, allowing Hawke a glimpse of the Mount Washington valley below the grey ceiling of clouds. He vowed he would retire from spamming after he made a little more money. Until then, he'd stick to his credo: *I'm going to be dead for a very long time. Every moment counts.*

epilogue

A special subcommittee of the United Nations called an urgent meeting in July 2004. The team of international experts convened in Geneva, Switzerland, to formulate battle plans against what one leader called "a disease which has spread around the world. We have an epidemic on our hands which we need to control."

The UN committee was not charged with fighting AIDS or SARS or hepatitis. The experts, all part of a working group of the UN's International Telecommunications Union (ITU), were there to defeat spam. According to the ITU, spam costs nations worldwide $25 billion each year.

Yet the international team was confident that, with the right technology and international cooperation, spam could be brought under control by 2006.

As of this writing (September, 2004), the global spam problem appears to be getting little help from CAN-SPAM. The volume of junk email hitting in-boxes has risen since the new U.S. law took effect on January 1, 2004. (Spam-filtering firm Brightmail says spam now composes 65 percent of email traffic, up from 60 percent in January.)

Meanwhile, few junk emailers are complying with the new regulations. One study declared that less than 3 percent of all spam is fully in compliance with CAN-SPAM. Another analysis found that even legitimate marketers are slow to adhere to the law. Only 36 percent of the email offers from mainstream companies meets CAN-SPAM's requirements.

Yet in Australia, a tougher, opt-in spam law seems to be making a difference. Just months after the enactment of Australia's Spam Act of 2003, several of the country's larger spam outfits appear to have closed up shop. (Failure to comply with the law, which prohibits spamming consumers without their consent, can result in penalties of up to AU$1.1 million per day for repeat offenders.) Admittedly, Australia isn't a significant source of junk email; the nation isn't even on Spamhaus's list of the top ten spam countries. But Spamhaus director Steve Linford and other spam opponents are taking heart.

"Governments looking to get it right and implement effective legislation need look in one direction only—follow Australia!" wrote Linford in a July 2004 statement at Spamhaus.org.

The first half of 2004 also saw a number of promising developments in defeating spam through technology. More consumers recognize that equipping their computers with spam-filtering programs is just as important to online hygiene as using anti-virus software. At the same time, several major ISPs and software manufacturers are looking to new technology in the fight against email forgery at the server level. Many have already taken steps to adopt systems designed to verify a message's true source. One solution, based on technology known as Sender Policy Framework (SPF), has the backing of Microsoft and AOL, among others. Another option, the Trusted Email Open Standard (TEOS), adds encoded data to message headers to help email users sort out incoming spam from legitimate email.

But the pernicious root of the spam crisis does not appear to be legislative or technological. It is human—in particular, the humans who buy from spammers.

The ability to move relatively incognito online may have created a perfect medium for surreptitious e-marketers such as Davis Hawke and the rest of the two-hundred-plus spammers listed on the Spam-haus Rokso list. But the Internet has also engendered a corresponding segment of consumers. Call them *furtive shoppers.*

Why does so much spam tout penis pills, pornography, black-market software, multilevel marketing schemes, and other illicit products and services not generally available in offline stores? It's not just because legitimate, ethical marketers have mostly eschewed email advertising or are having their messages drowned out by pitches from the likes of Amazing Internet Products. Blame it on junk email's customer base. After all, as Hawke's evolving product portfolio shows, spammers sell whatever people will buy from them.

The Internet didn't invent plain, brown-wrapper deliveries. But spam provides Internet users with new levels of anonymous access to the dodgiest of items. By double-clicking a hyperlink in a spam message, consumers can order cable descramblers, "free" government grants, and fake diplomas. Thanks to junk email, any consumer with an Internet connection and a credit card now has access to raunchy, and in some cases illegal, porn without the inconvenience of having to drive to the nearest adult bookstore. From the privacy of their homes or offices, spam recipients can get nonprescription access to controlled drugs via the web sites of fly-by-night apothecaries on servers in South America.

If email were around during the Prohibition, you can bet that spammers would have been selling moonshine.

In an effort to cut off junk emailers from their customers, an international trade group known as the Internet Industry Association (IIA) unveiled an unusual initiative in late 2003. Known as the "Hit Delete" campaign, the IIA's effort was essentially a boycott. According to the group, which included AOL, Yahoo!, Microsoft, and other major Internet firms, the best way to discourage spammers is not to buy from them.

"If enough users started hitting the delete key on questionable, unsolicited offers, the commercial case for spamming will soon erode," said an IIA press release. But less than a year later, the Hit Delete campaign's web site has been dismantled, its user education program apparently a bust.

Such efforts seem doomed to failure, as long as junk email successfully taps into consumers' private hopes and dreams for themselves. According to Latham & Watkins cyber lawyer Jennifer Archie, who has studied more than her share of junk email, spam reveals something profound about the American consumer psyche.

"People say, 'I can have a university degree overnight. The government is going to give me money, not take it away. I can be thinner and more virile. I can have better sex.' Something about email gives them hope it's all possible," said Archie.

Maybe Davis Hawke was right about one thing: some people *are* stupid.

♛

As this book was going to press, **Davis Hawke** was still living somewhere in Rhode Island. He continues to frequent online spammer forums using a variety of aliases. He also persists in sending spam and selling mailing lists. A federal court has ruled Hawke in default on AOL's lawsuit against him. The ISP has asked the court to order Hawke to pay AOL in excess of $10 million in damages resulting from his spams.

Brad Bournival, also awaiting the resolution of the AOL litigation, is believed to be close to an out-of-court settlement. Currently unemployed, he is living off his savings and devoting more time to chess. He intends to move out of his 5,300-square-foot rented home into a smaller, less expensive place.

The whereabouts of **Jacob Brown** and **Mauricio Ruiz** are unknown. Both are in default on the spam lawsuits pending against them. In August 2004, a judge permanently enjoined Brown from spamming Verizon Wireless customers.

Susan "Shiksaa" Gunn remains a volunteer for the Spamhaus Project. She continues to be an infrequent contributor to the Nanae newsgroup.

Director **Steve Linford** announced in June 2004 that Spamhaus would begin charging its biggest customers a subscription fee for the previously free spam-blocking service. Earlier in 2004, Linford was honored by the British Internet Service Providers Association, which named him its "Internet Hero" of 2004.

In July 2004, the office of the New York Attorney General announced a settlement with **Scott Richter**. Under the deal, Richter agreed to pay the state $50,000 in fines and legal expenses and to allow state officials to regularly audit aspects of his business. Richter's suit from Microsoft is still pending. In April 2004, Richter sued the SpamCop spam-reporting service for $1 million, alleging trade libel and tortious interference. In September 2004, SpamCop announced it had settled the lawsuit, with neither party making any changes to its practices. In June, Richter announced he was abandoning plans to market a line of "Spam King" apparel after receiving warnings from Hormel, owners of the SPAM trademark.

George Alan "Dr. Fatburn" Moore settled litigation with AOL and Symantec in December 2003. He is currently buying and selling real estate, as well as running a multilevel marketing program for diet pills and other health products from his web site, UltimateDiets. com.

Jason Vale was sentenced to sixty-three months in federal prison in June 2004 for criminal contempt. Vale is currently serving his sentence in the Brooklyn Metropolitan Detention Center but has reportedly asked for a transfer to a penitentiary in Florida. Vale has said he will not accept traditional medical treatment, including surgery, for the tumor in his back.

Karen Hoffmann continues to serve as an email marketing and abuse desk consultant to several clients.

Thomas Cowles is awaiting a September 2004 retrial in Florida's Broward County Court. In June 2004, a hung jury was unable to come up with a verdict on the third-degree grand theft charges against him. Cowles and his firm, Empire Towers, remain on the Spamhaus Rokso list, a position they have held since October 2000.

David P. D'Amato (a.k.a. Terri Tickle) was released from prison in February 2002. He is believed to be living somewhere in New York State, where he holds a permanent teaching certificate, according to officials with the New York School Education Department.

Rob Mitchell is a full-time public school teacher in Texas. He no longer frequents Nanae or fights spam.

Rodona Garst was sued for stock fraud by the Securities and Exchange Commission in July 2002. In December of that year, she settled the lawsuit by agreeing to pay $15,673 to the U.S. Treasury, an amount representing her profits from the pump-and-dump scheme.

Ronnie Scelson claims he is sending out up to 40 million CAN-SPAM-compliant junk emails per day. He told members of the U.S. Congress in May 2004 that he was recently forced to move his office into a former nuclear fallout shelter due to threats and harassment from anti-spammers.

Andrew Brunner was removed from the Spamhaus Rokso list in late 2001. Brunner continues to sell Avalanche bulk email software from his site, CyberCreek.com.

For the past two years, **Sanford Wallace** has been operating Club Plum Crazy, a popular nightclub in Rochester, New Hampshire. In 2004, Wallace moved to Las Vegas, where he hopes to open the area's first chemical-free nightclub for people aged eighteen to twenty.

glossary

Affiliate
A spammer who sends junk email on behalf of a sponsor, usually on a commission basis.

AIM (AOL Instant Messenger)
A free computer program published by AOL that allows users to communicate instantly through text messages to other AIM users.

Anti
Short for anti-spammer. A term used by spammers to refer to people who fight junk email.

AUP (acceptable use policy)
A collection of rules set by an Internet service provider that restrict how customers may use the service. For example, many AUPs expressly prohibit users from sending spam.

Blackhole list
A list used to filter spam or cut off traffic to spam sites. Typically, such lists contain a collection of Internet protocol (IP) addresses or domains used by spammers.

Blacklist
See *Blackhole list*.

Blog
An online journal of short web postings, usually posted in reverse chronological order (most recent item first).

Brute-force attack
In spamming, a computerized attempt to deliver an email ad that involves randomly constructing possible valid addresses. For example, a brute-force attack might begin by sending spam to *001@aol.com* and then try

---

For more online definitions of spam-related terminology, refer to "The Spam Glossary," by Ed Falk (*http://www.rahul.net/falk/glossary.html*), and "The Net Abuse Jargon File," by Andrew Nellis (*http://www.ncf.carleton.ca/ip/freenet/subs/complaints/spam/jargon.txt*).

002@aol.com, etc. (See also *Dictionary attack.*)

Bulker
Used by spammers to refer to people who send spam.

Bulletproof hosting
A web server that stays accessible for long periods of time and is relatively immune to complaints from anti-spammers.

Caller ID
A telephone feature that displays the name and/or number of the calling party when an incoming call is received.

CAN-SPAM (*The Controlling the Assault of Non-Solicited Pornography and Marketing Act of 2003*)
The first U.S. law governing junk email, which went into effect January 1, 2004.

CAUCE (*Coalition Against Unsolicited Commercial Email*)
A volunteer organization created in 1997 to advocate for a legislative solution to the spam problem (*http://www.cauce.org/*).

Chickenboner
A label given to small-time spammers. Anti-spammers stereotype chickenboners as living in mobile homes with a personal computer on the kitchen table, surrounded by empty beer cans and empty buckets of fried chicken.

Convert (*v.*)
Used by spammers to describe the act of a spam recipient responding positively to an email ad. A "high-converting list" contains email addresses likely to generate sales.

De-duped
Used by spammers to refer to mailing lists that have had duplicate email addresses removed.

Denial-of-service attack
Also known as a DOS attack. An incident in which a malicious Internet user attempts to prevent other users from using online resources such as the Web or email. In a *distributed* denial-of-service (DDOS) attack, a group of Internet users flood another computer on the network with so much data that it may crash or be unable to handle real network traffic.

Dictionary attack
In spamming, a computerized attempt to deliver an email ad that involves constructing possible valid addresses using common words or names. For example, a dictionary attack might begin by sending spam to *amy@aol.com* and then *bob@aol.com*, etc. (See also *Brute-force attack.*)

DNS (*domain name server*)
A system used to route Internet traffic by translating alphanumeric domain names into numeric Internet protocol addresses. (See also *Domain* and *IP address.*)

Domain
A name, such as oreilly.com, that identifies one or more IP addresses. Domain names are

used to identify particular web pages as well as email servers.

Drop box

A temporary email account, usually at a free, Web-based email provider such as Hotmail, used by a spammer to receive mailing-list removal requests, orders, or other communications. Drop boxes are used by spammers to protect their permanent email accounts.

DS3

A very high-speed, dedicated phone connection used mainly by Internet service providers to connect to the Internet backbone. DS3 lines are capable of sending data at rates up to forty-three megabits per second. (Also known as a T3 line.)

DSL *(digital subscriber line)*

A fast phone line used to connect a home or office to the telephone company's central switching station. Most residential DSL lines send data at rates around 128 kilobits per second, with download speeds of around one and a half megabits per second.

Extractor

A spam-related program designed to locate and compile email addresses from web pages, online discussion forums, and other Internet databases. (See also *Harvesting*.)

FBI *(Federal Bureau of Investigation)*

The United States law enforcement agency that is the principal investigative arm of the U.S.

Department of Justice (*http://www.fbi.gov/*).

FDA *(Food and Drug Administration)*

The U.S. government agency established to regulate the release of new foods and health-related products (*http://www.fda.gov/*).

Flame war

An argument or fight that takes place in newsgroup articles or over email.

Forged

Used to describe a fraudulent email address or email headers.

Fresh

Used to describe proxies or email addresses that have been recently collected.

FTC *(Federal Trade Commission)*

The U.S. government agency charged with enforcing antitrust laws and prohibitions against false, deceptive, or unfair trade or advertising practices (*http://www.ftc.gov/*).

FTP *(file transfer protocol)*

A system for transferring files over the Internet from one computer to another.

GI *(general Internet)*

A mailing list composed of email addresses from a wide variety of ISPs.

Golden Mallet

An award given to elite anti-spammers to recognize "outstanding lifetime achievement in the spamfighting arts."

Harvesting
The act of compiling email addresses from web pages, online discussion forums, and other Internet databases, usually with the use of a special computer program. (See also *Extractor*.)

Headers
The part of an email message that includes the path the message took en route to its destination: a sort of electronic passport.

Home page
A web site. The term is also used to refer to the front page of a site.

Honey pot
An email server or proxy set up to attract spammers seeking open relays or proxies. Anti-spammers create honey pots to track the activities of spammers.

Host
A service that provides online systems for storing information, images, video, or any content accessible via the Web. Web hosts are companies that provide space on a server they own for use by their clients.

HTML (Hypertext Markup Language)
The computer language used to create documents on the World Wide Web.

ICC (Internet Chess Club)
One of the first online chess clubs, at chessclub.com.

ICQ ("I seek you")
A free instant-messaging program, such as AIM, that allows users to chat and send/receive files with other ICQ users.

IRC (Internet relay chat)
A chat system that enables people connected anywhere on the Internet to join in live, group discussions.

ISP (Internet service provider)
A company that provides access to the Internet.

IP (Internet Protocol) address
A unique number that is assigned to every computer connected to the Internet.

Joe-job
Spam designed to tarnish the reputation of an innocent third party. First used to describe such an attack on Joe Doll, webmaster of joes.com.

LART (Loser Attitude Readjustment Tool)
An email notifying an ISP that one of its customers is spamming. Also referred to as a mallet, since it is metaphorically used to clobber delinquent ISPs into action against spammers.

Leads
Sales prospects generated by spam. Leads are often sold by spammers to mortgage companies and other marketers.

List washing
Removing the addresses of complainers from spam mailing lists.

LLC (Limited Liability Corporation)
A U.S. business entity that is a hybrid of a partnership and a corporation. The owners of an LLC

are somewhat shielded from personal liability.

Lumber Cartel
A fictitious group formed by anti-spammers in 1997 in response to assertions by some bulk emailers that wood-products companies were funding anti-spammers in an effort to preserve paper-based direct-mail promotions.

Mailer
A synonym for the term spammer, preferred by people who send spam. Also used to describe software designed to send junk email.

Mail bomb
A denial-of-service attack using a large volume of email, designed to overwhelm the victim's email program or server.

Mainsleaze
A mainstream, well-known company that resorts to spamming.

MAPS (Mail Abuse Prevention System)
An anti-spam service founded in 1997. MAPS operates the Real-time Blackhole List (RBL), one of the original spam blacklists (*http://www.mail-abuse.com/*).

Merchant account
An account established with a payment processor for the settlement of credit card transactions. Any spammer who wants to take credit card orders must establish a merchant account.

Munge
To modify a published email address so that address harvesters won't get a usable address, but humans can still figure it out.

Nanab (news.admin.net-abuse.blocklisting)
A relatively new Usenet newsgroup devoted to discussing spam blackhole lists such as Spews.

Nanae (news.admin.net-abuse.email)
A Usenet newsgroup devoted to the discussion of email abuse or spam.

Nanas (news.admin.net-abuse.sightings)
A Usenet newsgroup to which participants post copies of email or newsgroup spam they have received.

Newsgroup
An Internet discussion forum, such as news.admin.net-abuse.email or rec.pets.cats. All together, the thousands of newsgroups form a global bulletin board where people talk about every topic imaginable.

Nuke
To cancel an ISP user's account for spamming or for other policy violations.

Opt-in spam
Involves sending email ads to people who have requested to receive them.

Opt-out spam
Involves sending spam to recipients and giving them the option of being removed from future mailings.

Pink contract

A tacit deal between an ISP and a spammer under which the spammer is allowed to use the ISP's network to send spam or host a spamvertised site. Takes its name from the color of the Hormel luncheon meat.

Port 25

The computer port commonly used by Internet servers to send email.

Proxy server

A computer network service that allows users to make indirect connections to other network services. Proxies have been widely abused by spammers to cloak their identities.

RBL (Realtime Blackhole List)

One of the original spam blacklists, developed by the Mail Abuse Prevention System (MAPS) to filter spam and control access to spamvertised web sites (*http://www.mail-abuse.com/services/mds_rbl.html*).

Relay

An email server that allows an outside user to relay email messages to other Internet mail servers. Spammers often abuse open relays to obscure the source of their messages.

Rokso (Register of Known Spamming Operations)

A database launched by Spamhaus.org in 2000 to track the largest spammers on the Internet (*http://www.spamhaus.org/rokso/*).

SBL (Spamhaus Block List)

A spam blacklist created by Spamhaus.org in 2001, based in part on data from Rokso (*http://www.spamhaus.org/sbl/*).

Screen name

An America Online subscriber's username. Also used to refer to any alias used by an Internet user.

Seed

An email account created by a spammer and added to mailing lists to test whether a run of junk emails is successfully delivered and is not blocked by an ISP's filters.

Sender ID

A technical specification designed to address the problem of email forgery and domain spoofing. Sender ID is backed by Microsoft and other high-tech companies and is currently being considered for implementation as an Internet standard.

SMS (short message service)

A feature available on many mobile phones that allows text messages of up to 160 characters to be sent and received via the cell phone provider's message center to a subscriber's mobile phone, or from the Internet, using an SMS gateway web site.

Sock puppet

A secondary screen name secretly used by an individual during online discussions to support his position in an argument. Spammers are often accused of creating sock puppets to defend their actions on newsgroups such as Nanae.

Spamhaus

One of the leading anti-spam web sites launched in 1999 by Steve Linford. The term is also generically used to describe an ISP or other company responsible for spam (*http://www.spamhaus.org/*).

Spam trap

An email address set up by a spam fighter to capture unsolicited email ads for the purpose of tracking spammers.

Spamware

A software program designed to send junk email.

Spamvertise

To advertise something via spam.

Spews (Spam Prevention Early Warning System)

A mysterious spam blacklist launched in 2001 by a team of anonymous individuals (*http:// www.spews.org/*).

SPF (sender policy framework)

A technical specification designed to combat email forgery. SPF is designed to make spammers send mail from their real domains instead of hijacking the accounts of innocent users. The technology forms part of the basis of a proposed Internet standard called Sender ID.

Sponsor

A spammer who hires affiliates to send email ads on a commission basis.

Spoof

To alter the "From" line of an email message so that it appears to come from someone other than the actual sender.

T1

A digital telephone line capable of carrying data at one and a half megabits per second in both directions.

TOS (terms of service)

The rules governing use of an Internet service.

Trojaned

Refers to a computer that has been compromised by attackers and can be used, without the owner's authorization, to send spam or perform other actions.

Troll

Someone who creates newsgroup postings designed to spark a flame war or otherwise create controversy.

UCE

Unsolicited commercial email, or spam.

Unix

A computer operating system originally developed at Bell Labs in the 1970s. Today, a variant of Unix called Linux is preferred by many computer aficionados over Microsoft's Windows operating system. Unix-based software runs on the majority of Internet servers.

URL (uniform resource locator)

The address of documents and other resources on the World

Wide Web. *http://www.oreilly.com* is one example of a URL.

USCF *(United States Chess Federation)*
The official sanctioning body for over-the-board chess tournament play in the U.S., with over 90,000 members (*http://www.uschess.org/*).

Usenet
A worldwide bulletin board system that can be accessed through the Internet or through many online services. The Usenet contains thousands of forums, called newsgroups, which cover every imaginable interest group.

Username
The name subscribers use to sign on to the Internet. The username is also the name that appears to the left of the ampersand (@) in an email address.

Valid "From"
A return address on a spam message that represents an actual email account controlled by the spammer.

Verified
Refers to a list of email addresses or proxies that has been checked to ensure that its contents are valid.

WHOIS
An Internet service that enables users to query the ownership records of domains (*http://www.whois.org/*).

Whitelist
A list of email or IP addresses from which an individual or service wishes to receive email.

XBL *(Exploits Block List)*
An anti-spam blacklist launched by Spamhaus.org in 2003 to combat the increasing use by spammers of Trojaned computers and proxies (*http://www.spamhaus.org/xbl/*).

Zombie
A compromised computer controlled by a malicious attacker for the purpose of performing a denial-of-service attack on other systems.

notes

chapter one

1. As reported by Thomas Farragher in "Top Westwood Student, Now Suprema-
    cist, Denies His Past" (*Boston Globe*, 28 February 1999, page A1).

2. This detail first reported by Erik Hedegaard in "Rise and Fall of the Campus
    Nazi" (*Rolling Stone*, 14 October 1999, p 81).

3. In a May 2004 telephone interview, Hawke revealed that Jeff Krause, executive
    vice president of the American Nationalist Party, was the only member of the
    ANP who showed up at the march.

4. The first use of the term "spam" to refer to junk email and Usenet messages
    appeared in April 1993, after an incident involving a program called ARMM
    (Automated Retroactive Minimal Moderation). Created by Richard Depew, a sys-
    tem administrator in Ohio, ARMM accidentally posted 200 copies of the same
    message to the news.admin.policy newsgroup on March 31, 1993. In response, an
    Internet user in Australia compared the ARMM incident to a comedy routine
    from the British television series *Monty Python's Flying Circus*. First broadcast in
    1970, the sketch features two customers at a café who discover that every item on
    the menu includes Hormel's SPAM canned meat. At one point, a group of
    Vikings enters and loudly sings a song about "spam, lovely spam, wonderful spam,"
    drowning out the café customers' conversation.

chapter two

1. In a February 2004 telephone interview, Peggy Greenbaum told me Hawke signed
    up for the credit card as a seventeen-year-old freshman. She said the Greenbaums
    owe an outstanding balance to Wofford College for their son's final semester, but
    they refuse to pay it because they believe the college essentially forced Hawke to
    withdraw without a diploma.

2.   The outline of this conversation was recounted to me during a January 8, 2004, interview with an InnovaNet employee.

3.   June 23, 1999, posting to the Nanae newsgroup.

4.   Shiksaa published the log file of this conversation July 11, 1999, on the Nanae newsgroup.

chapter three

1.   From a transcript of the April 14, 2000, deposition on file with the U.S. District Court for New York's eastern district.

2.   From a March 12, 2004, interview with Reid Walker.

3.   The attacker's statement that he had "escalated my remote access to that of a full privileged local user" made it appear that he had broken into a system running the Unix operating system. Yet according to the screen-grab photograph he provided, showing the programs running on Garst's computer, the hacker appeared to have compromised a laptop computer running Microsoft's Windows 98, which gives all users the same access rights. Plus, there was the anonymous June 5 Nanae posting that announced the Behind Enemy Lines site—a message from "John Doe" posted from an Internet Protocol address registered to Premier Services. These inconsistencies made some anti-spammers suspicious that perhaps the whole incident was actually the work of a disgruntled insider with local access to the computer, or even a hoax.

4.   Payne posted a log file of his conversation with Garst at his web site, cluelessfucks.com, in June 2000. The site is no longer available, but a copy can be accessed via the Archive.org service.

5.   A few months before Behind Enemy Lines was published on the Web, Shiksaa assisted a new Nanae participant using the name Spam Hater, who complained that Garst had forged his company's domain name in her spam runs. In his April 6 posting to the newsgroup, Spam Hater listed Garst's phone number, ICQ number, and other contact details. (The same day, Garst's associate Shary Valentine warned spamming colleague Shannon Redmond, "We got hacked yesterday by an AOL user. Also got posted on an anti-spammer site today with ALL of Rodona's info." A log of the two women's online chat was among those posted at Behind Enemy Lines.) In his Nanae message about Garst, Spam Hater had included a sample of one of her spams, with the domain name of his company—the Joe-job victim—redacted. But a search on the message's subject line—"Need money?"—turned up a nearly identical spam sample posted by Leah Roberts, a Nanae regular, to Usenet a few days prior to Spam Hater's complaint. Roberts's sample, however, included the intact "From" line, which showed the domain of an Internet

provider in Michigan. It was possible that the ISP was the Man in the Wilderness's employer. But Shiksaa never brought up the matter on Nanae.

6. This transcript of the conversation between Catts and the crank callers was created from an audio recording of the conversation obtained from Chickenboner.com.

chapter five

1. An unidentified anti-spammer celebrated the turn of events by providing Shiksaa with a new graphic for Chickenboner.com. It was a parody of the DVD case for the movie *Gladiator*. The anti-spammer had replaced actor Russell Crowe's head with an image of Hawke's, taken from a newspaper article about his neo-Nazi days. The title of the movie had been changed to "Spaminator."

2. Author interview with "Rob Mitchell" (a pseudonym) on March 23, 2004.

chapter six

1. A transcript of the message was published at Spamhaus.org.

2. MAPS continued to provide free access to nearly anyone who asked, as long as the interested party agreed to sign a standard agreement shielding MAPS from legal action. Despite the change in its policies, MAPS retained many large customers and remains an influential force in the battle against spam.

3. During a May 10, 2004, interview, Brad Bournival first described Hawke's method of hiding his money. Hawke confirmed the technique in an interview later that day.

4. The following conversation was first described to me in the May 10, 2004, interview with Bournival. Ruiz confirmed the details in a May 28, 2004, interview over AOL Instant Messenger.

5. Bournival recalled this feeling to me in the May 10, 2004, interview.

6. Statement published at the CAUCE.org web site in March 2001.

7. Bournival recounted this conversation to me during a June 11, 2004, interview.

chapter seven

1. Shiksaa published a log file of this conversation with Richter at her site, Chickenboner.com.

2. Richter published the email from Thompson on Nanae in a March 16, 2002, posting to Nanae.

3. Richter posted this comment to Nanae on February 9, 2002.

4. On February 10, 2002, Shiksaa published an excerpt from this exchange with EZBulkMail4U on Nanae.

5. Richter's offer to Shiksaa appeared in a March 17, 2002, note on Nanae.

6.   Recipients of the spams posted copies to the news.admin.net-abuse.sightings newsgroup. In a May 2004 interview Hawke confirmed to me that he sent them. Bournival revealed to me in a June 2004 interview that Hawke kept money hidden in a book at his grandparents' house.

7.   Recipients of the spam posted copies to the news.admin.net-abuse.sightings newsgroup. During a June 2004 interview over AOL Instant Messenger, Hawke confirmed sending them as a Joe-job against the Internet Chess Club. In a May 2004 interview, Martin Grund, one of the operators of the ICC, recounted the site's problems with Hawke and the Joe-job.

8.   Hawke made this statement to me in a March 29, 2004, conversation over AOL Instant Messenger.

9.   Sledd, Andrew. "The Negro: Another View," *The Atlantic Monthly* 90 (July 1902): 65–73.

10.   Matthews, Terry. "The Emergence of a Prophet: Andrew Sledd and the 'Sledd Affair' of 1902." Ph.D. dissertation, Duke University, 1990.

11.   This exchange was described to me by Thomas Cowles during an April 2004 telephone interview.

12.   In describing the arrest of Thomas Cowles, I have had to reconcile discrepancies between Cowles's first-hand and Hoffmann's second-hand accounts of the event. Unfortunately, the Bureau of Criminal Investigations agent-in-charge at the raid was of little help clarifying the incident. In a March 2004 interview, the BCI agent said he was unable to recall whether Cowles was found hiding when agents stormed the office, or whether Cowles was simply in the process of getting dressed at the time. (Readers might wish to be mindful of Rule #1: Spammers Lie.)

13.   Hoffmann published the details of this courtroom confrontation at her web site about Thomas Cowles and Empire Towers.

14.   From Hoffmann's account of the extradition hearing, as published at her web site.

chapter eight

1.   Bournival shared this explanation during our May 10, 2004, interview.

2.   From a June 14, 2004, interview with Bournival.

3.   The conversation that follows is from a July 28, 2002, chat log published by Shiksaa on Nanae November 30, 2002.

4.   Shiksaa posted an excerpt of the December 4, 2002, exchange on Nanae the same day. It also became a signature line in her newsgroup postings for the following three months.

5.   Shikaa published a copy of her February 25, 2003, AIM log on Nanae.

6.   The details of these court proceedings were transcribed from an audio recording provided by the Clerk of the Circuit Court for Anne Arundel County.

chapter nine

1. Details of this phone conversation were provided by Bill Waggoner during a June 23, 2004, interview.

2. Shiksaa used this brief December 2002 exchange with Waggoner as her newsgroup signature line beginning in April 2003.

3. Shiksaa published the AIM log file of this conversation with Richter in the "Bulk Barn Diaries" section of her Chickenboner.com site.

4. Ibid.

5. Shiksaa explained her determination to fight back against The Gang That Can't Shoot Straight during an April 1, 2004, interview.

6. *South Florida Business Journal*; May 9, 2003. The newspaper also quoted Felstein as saying "I can't give out the names right now because of a history of threatening calls and e-mails to my office."

7. Bournival described Hawke's problems contacting Patricia during the May 10, 2004, interview.

8. During our May 10, 2004, interview, Hawke cited these things as reasons why he would never get married.

9. Copies of spams that were traceable to Hawke and advertising for such lists appeared in the news.admin.net-abuse.sightings newsgoup several times in early 2003.

10. Bournival first described Creampie Productions during a May 20, 2004, interview. Ruiz confirmed the general outline of the project in a May 28, 2004, interview over AIM.

11. Hawke detailed his utilitarian approach to eating, which he called "the only correct choice," during our May 10, 2004, interview. In the course of the discussion, he said, "I don't eat for pleasure. I only do one thing for pleasure."

12. During our May 10, 2004, interview, Bournival said Patricia had told him Hawke's having a prostitute didn't bother her because she knew Hawke didn't have any real affection for the prostitute. But Bournival said he could tell she was upset by Hawke's infidelity.

chapter ten

1. Copies of the recruiting ads from "Dave Bridger" were posted to the news.admin.net-abuse.sightings newsgroup by several recipients beginning June 9, 2003.

2. A note about Miss Daisy's bonus was published at the Pinacle Partnership site when I viewed it in August 2003. I had signed up as a Pinacle affiliate under a pseudonym as part of my research into Amazing Internet Products.

3. Hawke failed to notice that Pinacle Affiliate 164 was actually Alan "Dr. Fatburn" Moore. Dr. Fatburn had signed up without giving his name, but he had listed an

email address that could be traced back to him. Already sued out of the spamming business by AOL and Symantec, Dr. Fatburn was merely hoping to keep an eye on his former nemesis.

4. Amazing Internet stored a log file containing customer names, postal and email addressees, phone numbers, and credit card numbers at its Pinacle sites. I found one of the logs in July 2003 with the help of a former Amazing Internet Products employee. (I located him after a tip from Mad Pierre.) The employee told me about the company's habit of leaving its order logs in plain view at its web sites. The order data was stored there, he said, so sales affiliates could easily monitor how well their spam runs were working. Each day, Bournival would download the logs, submit the orders for processing by Amazing Internet's credit card processor, and delete the log files.

But for some reason Bournival hadn't been deleting the order logs. Some 6,000 orders, all of them placed in the month of July 2003, were viewable. Most of the orders were for two bottles (or one hundred dollars worth) of pills.

It was possible that some of the orders were the work of junk email opponents. Earlier in 2003, a self-proclaimed anti-spammer had released a software program named FormFucker (FF). Its purpose was to screw up spammers' web sites by automatically entering bogus order data. According to the tool's anonymous author, FF analyzes a spammer's order form and then pumps his database full of realistic-looking orders. As a result, the spammer can't tell which are real and which are bogus, so he ends up throwing away the entire batch.

Amazing's order log did include hundreds of lines of random characters and other bogus data that had been manually input by irate recipients of the company's spams. Other visitors crammed angry messages into the space on the form allocated for the customer's mailing address and other details. This message, from someone using an Internet service provider in Massachusetts, was typical: "YOU MADE A BIG MISTAKE WHEN YOU STOLE MY EMAIL. I AM GOING TO FIND YOU AND YOU WILL BE *SORRY*. YOU WILL ROT IN HELL."

One AOL user, apparently frustrated by the site's lack of contact information, used the order form to leave the following request: "I need to know if this product will be harmful to me. I had heart surgery and use Lanoxin, Zocor and Zestril and Dilantin. Please return my inquiry. I did not know how to contact you. Send return by email."

Another possible explanation for the voluminous orders at Goringly.biz was that credit card thieves, or "carders," had fraudulently placed them. Such online crooks have been known to sign up for online affiliate programs in order to "monetize" their stolen credit cards, according to Dan Clements, CEO of CardCops.

When I inquired why he didn't offer to buy the data from Bournival and Hawke, Dr. Fatburn said he didn't want to get involved with them.

"I would rather work with someone who is honest, like a reporter," he said.

"Selling a list like that is hardly honest," I replied.

Dr. Fatburn suggested I was being inconsistent.

"You were willing to take the list down and contact the people. Weren't you? Was that fair of you? I do not see where you should be drawing a line now when you did not draw the line in the beginning," he said.

Dr. Fatburn signed off before I could reply. But he approached me again a few hours later that day.

"You have a list that contains $500,000 in sales (so you say). I have offered you a partnership on all future sales generated using that list. You are a freelance reporter. Let's get together and partner up," he said.

"I can't give you the file, period," I replied.

Dr. Fatburn finally relented. The next day, while I was away from my computer, I received an instant message from him.

"Just so you know," he said, "I am going in a different direction for marketing my Thinkmeds.com website. I will not ask you for the file anymore. I will also not waste my time trying to find Amazing's files on the Net. I got better things to do with my time."

8. In November 2003, an anonymous person contacted me over AOL Instant Messenger and offered me a dozen photos he said an acquaintance had stolen from Hawke's PC. The photos included images of Hawke standing in his North Smithfield, Rhode Island, driveway, as well as "screen grabs" of Bournival's computer while it was sending spam. Also included was an image of a fake State of Indiana driver's license, which pictured Hawke's face above the name Michael Girdley.

9. A spammer named Richard Cunningham, who used the alias Dollar, published a warning about the Trojan horse program at SpecialHam.com on August 15, 2003.

10. As junk emailers increasingly banded together to do battle with spam opponents, membership to clubs such as SpecialHam.com surged in mid-2003. One such organization, a new, members-only site named TheBulkClub.com, caught my attention in the end of August 2003. A sign-up page stated that, for a twenty-dollar monthly fee, Bulk Club subscribers could get access to a variety of how-to articles, a members' message board area, and a system for uploading mailing lists for trade with other members.

I decided to contact Shiksaa over ICQ and ask whether she knew anything about the site. She told me she hadn't investigated the Bulk Club yet. But moments later, she messaged me again.

com, which tracks Internet credit card fraud. The technique, known as carding cash, enables the crooks to rack up sizable commission fees. The carders simply submit fake orders using purloined credit card numbers at sites where the crooks get bounties for orders. Such a scam often goes undetected, says Clements, because the cardholder is unlikely to open an investigation when a fifty-dollar charge for penis pills shows up on his account. Banks usually refund the charge to the cardholder and charge the amount back to the online merchant who took the order.

The exposed order log quietly disappeared after I sent email to Amazing Internet Products notifying it about the security problem. But the incident would send a ripple through the spam scene. As I reported in an August 2003 article for *Wired News*, the data provided the world with a depressing answer to the question, "Who in their right mind would buy something from a spammer?"

5. My article, "Meet the Spam Nazi," was published by Salon.com on July 29, 2003. Wired.com published "Swollen Orders Show Spam's Allure" on August 6, 2003.

6. The former Amazing Internet Products employee agreed to let me interview him on the condition that I wouldn't publish his name.

7. In the middle of August, I gave a copy of Bradorders.dat, Amazing Internet's order log file, to the New Hampshire Attorney General's office. Later that month, I got an instant message from Dr. Fatburn. We had chatted a few times about Hawke and Bournival earlier that summer, after I discovered his name in many of Amazing Internet's domain registrations. Now Dr. Fatburn said he wanted to buy my copy of Amazing's database. He said he wanted to send postcards to the addresses on the list. The cards would advertise his site, Thinkmeds.com, where he was selling Pfizer's Viagra.

"I would make it worth your while. We only use postcard mailings, so no one would know where the list came from," Dr. Fatburn said.

When I ignored his proposal, he continued. "If you want to sell that database outright or do a joint venture with me, you could easily make five to ten thousand dollars in the next few months," he said.

I told Dr. Fatburn I would think about it. But I had no intention of giving the list to anyone (aside from the New Hampshire Attorney General's office).

"With a list that's targeted at males, its a perfect match. I bet five to ten thousand dollars would come in handy for you at Christmas time," he said.

A week went by, and Dr. Fatburn contacted me again. He wanted to know if I had given any further thought to selling the customer database.

"Alan, I wish I could help you, but I can't give up the order log," I replied.

"Why? It was public domain and you were doing freelance work at the time. What's the conflict?" he asked.

"Hey Brian," she said. Then Shiksaa sent me a link to an internal file accidentally left exposed at TheBulkClub.com. The file contained a log of file transfers
made by the site's operators over the past month. It was the same type of file she
had previously dug up at web sites operated by Davis Hawke and other junk
emailers.

"Dumb spammers," she said.

I looked at the address of the file transfer protocol (FTP) log a moment and
then decided to try a trick I had seen Shiksaa use in the past. If the Bulk Club's
operators had misconfigured their site, truncating the address after the final back-
slash ("/") would enable me to view all the files in the directory containing the
FTP log. Sure enough, when I tried the shortened address in my web browser, it
displayed a list of dozens of other files at the site.

I sent a message to Shiksaa, telling her that the site's directories could be
"trolled."

"Yes, I know," came her immediate response. "Spammers are so much fun."

After she signed off, I spent a few moments examining the files left exposed at
the site. I found a document that contained a list of anti-spam organizations
including Spamhaus and Spews. There was also an article entitled "How To
Spoof," and there were summaries of various state spam regulations. Also available to members were seventeen articles on the topic of harvesting email addresses
from web pages and discussion groups.

But the most interesting document was a list of the Bulk Club's members.
Nearly 450 people had joined the spam club since it launched in February.
According to the list, some 150 were "active" members. Among them was Damon
Decrescenzo, one of the operators of Rockin Time Holdings, a Florida junk
emailer sued by Microsoft the previous June. Also a member was Jon Thau, the
head of Cyberworks, a longtime Rokso-listed spam operation. But one name especially caught my eye. John Milton, one of the aliases used by Davis Hawke, was
listed as a Bulk Club member.

A few days later, I published an article about the Bulk Club at *Wired News*.
The piece, "A Support Group for Spammers," quoted the site's operator, a man
from Akron, Ohio, named Drew Auman, who said the club was dedicated to promoting "responsible" business practices. According to Auman, the site had
recently been knocked offline by hackers. The impact to his business, he claimed,
was extreme. "Members who enjoy conversing with fellow members are unable to
get access, and potential members cannot learn about us," said Auman.

Within days, Auman was added to the Spamhaus Rokso list. But it hardly
mattered. Soon, the Bulk Club was back online, this time hosted on a new server
in India.

11. Based on a trial transcript obtained from the U.S. District Court, Eastern District of New York.

12. On the first day of the trial, as jurors were about to be brought into the courtroom, Assistant U.S. Attorney Charles Kleinberg spotted a Bible on the table in front of Vale. Kleinberg quickly brought it to the judge's attention.

    "I would ask that the jury not be allowed to see it," said Kleinberg, the government's lead prosecutor on the case.

    Judge Gleeson asked Vale if he had any response.

    "I heard what he said. I'm completely against that," said Vale.

    "You need the Bible, sir?" asked the judge.

    "I need the Bible," answered Vale.

    "You can have it, but I would like to strip the proceedings of any overt trappings of religion, and I'd like you to place it in a spot that is not visible to the jury," instructed the judge.

    Vale put his bible on a chair beside him, and the government began a nearly weeklong task of laying out its case against Vale.

13. Adapted from articles by the author that originally appeared at Wired.com in August and November 2003.

14. Shortly after my August article, "Turn Back The Spam of Time," appeared at Wired.com, I received an angry email from Todino. "I have had multiple threats against my life, including temporal incarceration. You cannot even begin to comprehend what danger you have put me in and what certain agencies and groups who do have the technology are capable of doing!" he wrote. His email went on to cite the various laws that these unnamed authorities would consider him to have broken, including the "Dimensional Displacement Diversion Act of section 44563b-232 Article 40498.442" and the "Chronographic Travel code, section 54.1, page 364." Todino concluded his message with a threat: "So help me God if my chance of life or life is harmed because of you I have already arranged to have you killed and am currently being guarded fully! It will not matter you see because if I die you die! That is a promise!"

15. From a memorandum recorded June 6, 2003, by the New York State Board of Law Examiners.

16. Ironically, Middlebrooks was also the judge who sentenced Eddy Marin in June 2000 to twelve months in jail for money laundering.

17. While others have also speculated about Shiksaa's connection to Spews, I have been unable to confirm any of these rumors. Shiksaa adamantly insists she is not involved with the mysterious block list.

18. Based on the December 11, 2003, affidavit of Scott Richter in *OptInRealBig.com LLC v. Jeff Perreault et al.*

19. Ibid.

20. Author interview with Susan Gunn, April 7, 2003.

21. Case docket on file with Denver County Court.

22. Shiksaa published the AOL Instant Messenger log of her December 17, 2003, conversation with Richter at her AOL Hometown web page.

23. While not illegal at the time, none of the messages contained instructions on how to opt out of future mailings. Recipients were forced to click a link labeled "Privacy Policy," which would take them to a web page that contained, among other things, information on how to unsubscribe.

chapter eleven

1. The new UK spam law was created in response to the European Commission's Directive on Privacy and Electronic Communications. That directive obliged EC member states to introduce anti-spam laws by October 31, 2003. In addition to the UK, Austria, Denmark, Ireland, Italy, and Spain had already adopted the European Union law. But the other nine member states of the EU, including France and Germany, had yet to adopt anti-spam regulation.

2. "Congress Set to Pass Bill That Restrains Unsolicited E-Mail," New York Times, November 22, 2003; Section A, Page 1.

3. Text from service description at AssetProtection.com.

4. Shiksaa recounted her conversation with Steve Richter during an April 7, 2004, interview.

5. Author telephone interview with Peggy Greenbaum, March 10, 2004.

6. In late August, 2003, Alan Moore told me that AOL would be interested in any information I had gleaned in my reporting about the company. "My attorneys could bring the idea to them this week when we speak next, if you have any interest at all," said Moore. The next day, he contacted me with questions about where Amazing Internet Products's offices were located. When I asked why, he said it was so they could "get served by anyone suing Hawke."

7. Bournival described the phone call during our May 10, 2004, interview.

8. Author online interview with Mauricio Ruiz, March 17, 2004.

9. Hawke recounted this phone call to me during our May 10, 2004, interview.

10. Bournival mentioned these post-litigation goals in the May 10, 2004, interview.

11. From an affidavit filed March 23, 2004, by David McLain in AOL v. Davis Hawke et al.

12. During our May 10, 2004, interview, Hawke boasted that he had obtained the PI's cell phone records. "I feel that's my right. If someone's trying to investigate me, I'll investigate them," he said.

13. In late March 2004, AOL amended its complaint to include Mauricio Ruiz and Jacob Brown and served the two men outside their homes. By late April, only Bournival had met the deadline for responding to AOL's summons. So the big ISP moved to have the court declare all the defendants, except for Bournival, in default. The judge accepted AOL's motion and scheduled a hearing to set damages for July 2004.

14. Author telephone interview with Davis Hawke, May 10, 2004.

15. Copies of the ads Hawke signed "Eddy Marin" were posted to the news.admin. net-abuse.email newsgroup by recipients beginning June 30, 2004.

16. Since the new CAN-SPAM law didn't specifically address cell-phone spam, attorneys for Verizon Wireless filed the lawsuit under the 1991 Telephone Consumer Protection Act. In addition, they accused Brown et al. of violating New Jersey's computer fraud statute. According to Verizon's complaint, the company was able to track down Brown after discovering that his cell phone number appeared in numerous spam runs. Investigators determined that Brown was using the phone as a "seed" to test whether messages were getting through Verizon's spam filters.

17. Hawke revealed that Samhoun had left the country during our May 10, 2004, interview.

acknowledgments

The genesis of this book was an unusual onslaught of junk email in May 2003. Over the course of two weeks, I received over one hundred spams for pills and other products that I traced to a company in nearby Manchester, New Hampshire. I discovered spammers practically in my backyard and decided to tell the world about it.

I am grateful to my editors at Salon.com, especially Andrew Leonard, as well as my editors at *Wired News*, including David Ian Miller, for encouraging me that summer to write about the company, Amazing Internet Products LLC, and its fascinating founders. Thanks also to Mark Beavis and Jon Greenberg of New Hampshire Public Radio for working with me to advance the story further for radio.

I am indebted to my agent, Martha Jewett, for recognizing that a book about some of the major figures behind the spam problem was long overdue. Martha's help in conceiving *Spam Kings* was immensely important to me.

My editor at O'Reilly, Allen Noren, guided this project with just the right mix of hard-boiled skepticism and patient handholding. Nothing motivates an author like knowing your editor is a better writer. Special thanks to Allen and to the rest of the team at O'Reilly for their dedication to this project.

I appreciate the help of John Levine, who provided a crucial technical review of the manuscript.

My initial research was greatly assisted by Piers Forrest and Gordon Shumway. Reporting on Davis Hawke's neo-Nazi years by Erik Hedegaard and Gary Henderson was a big inspiration. I am also grateful to the scores of people who provided important background but were not mentioned in the book, including Bill Cole, "Relic," Jeanne Kempthorne, Anne Mitchell, Dan Clements, Jeffrey Eilender, Brendan Battles, Stan McDonald, Bill Nelson, Tanya Bibeau, Ted Bernard, Andrew Broome, Blair Russell, and the numerous sources who've asked to remain anonymous.

I couldn't have written *Spam Kings* without the thousands of people who have sent their spam samples to the news.admin.net-abuse.sightings newsgroup. The Archive.org web site and Google Groups search engine were also essential to my research.

Finally, thanks to my family, especially my wife Diane, for accompanying me on this journey and for your feedback along the way.

Index

ABOUT THE AUTHOR

Brian McWilliams is a veteran investigative journalist who has covered business and technology for web magazines, including *Wired News* and *Salon*, as well as the *Washington Post, PC World, Computerworld,* and *Inc.* The author of hundreds of articles about spam, Internet security, and online consumer protection, McWilliams gained international attention in 2002 when he wrote about the contents of Saddam Hussein's email in-box for *Wired News.* He has appeared on *NBC Nightly News*, Fox News, BBC Radio, NPR's *Here and Now*, and PRI's *Marketplace* programs, and has been quoted by the *International Herald Tribune*, the *Boston Globe*, and the *New York Times.*

COLOPHON

Matt Hutchinson was the production editor and copyeditor for *Spam Kings*. Sanders Kleinfeld proofread the book. Sanders Kleinfeld, Jamie Peppard, and Claire Cloutier provided quality control. Reg Aubry wrote the index.

Ellie Volckhausen designed the cover and produced the cover layout with InDesign CS using Andale Mono and Helvetica. The cover image is derived from a photograph by James Day, licensed from Getty Images.

David Futato designed the interior layout. This book was converted to FrameMaker 5.5.6 by Julie Hawks. The photographs were prepared for print by Robert Romano using Photoshop CS. The text font is Adobe Jenson, and the heading font is Andale Mono.